PRAISE FOR

OPENING THE DOOR: MY JOURNEY THROUGH ANOREXIA TO FULL RECOVERY

"'Full recovery is possible.' These words, written by Meredith O'Brien, are not only powerful and hopeful but represent the culmination of many years of intense work that led her to a place of peace and appreciation for all that life offers. This memoir is a compelling and engaging journey from despair to triumph over her life-threatening and life-robbing eating disorder. Any reader who has personally suffered or who has watched a loved one suffer through the agony of an eating disorder will find a destination to land on in this book, where they will feel seen, understood, and be comforted by the knowledge that full recovery can be a dream that comes true."

—**Elyse Resch,** MS, RDN, CEDS-S, FAND, Co-author of
Intuitive Eating : A Revolutionary Anti-Diet Approach

"I can really connect to the younger version of Meredith. It feels like reading a story of my own childhood, which makes this book even more personal and intimate. The timeline Meredith takes you through really assists you with identifying where limiting beliefs and patterns can originate. It also calls attention to the difference between our conditioning and our natural makeup. Being able to witness the timeline of events and how the multitude of experiences led to her eating disorder really illuminates how little there is to blame for this disease. She gracefully highlights the benefit of embracing the lessons and personal power that comes from choosing your own happiness through recovery. I'm deeply touched and honored to read this manuscript and felt moved through the entire experience. Thank you so much for creating this palpable experience!"

—**Laura Mazzotta,** LCSW-R, Founder of Emerge Healing &
Wellness, Inc., and Co-author of *Sacred Medicine* and *The
Ultimate Guide to Self-Healing Techniques*

"Meredith O'Brien has always been my hero. She has helped so many people, including me, to recover from the ugly diseases of mental health and eating disorders. Now, Meredith is bravely sharing her amazing story with everyone in her memoir, *Opening the Door: My Journey through Anorexia to Full Recovery*. I immediately related to the little girl with the bowl cut and the loud voice. I again related to the teenager who lost that voice and who had a hard time even wanting to live. I hope to one day relate to the woman Meredith has fought to become. This book will open your eyes and reveal how Meredith has become the strong, healthy healer that she is today. In sharing her personal and sometimes painful story, she delivers hope and the promise that there is such a thing as a full recovery."

—MS

"From impact to recovery: A beautifully written and compelling journey through the complexities of a body and mind at war."

—Dr. Shannon Parks, DO, Founder of the Parks Center for
Women's Wellness and Medicine

"As a mother, sister, doctor, and friend, these written words have given me a much better understanding of trauma and its associated harmful coping strategies. The dangers of dissociation are real and unfortunately very common. Never before have I been given a window to help me understand the self-destructive nature of disordered eating and the way that it cuts off one's ability to feel love. This book helped me to understand some of the root causes and helped me to see how self-love, honest communication, and connection are imperative in healing trauma and ultimately in reaching full recovery."

—Dr. Deirdre Donovan, MD, Family Medicine Physician

"*Opening the Door* should be required reading in high schools. In it, Meredith O'Brien details her descent into the hell of anorexia and her against-all-odds journey back. Oddly, I met Meredith over two decades ago while she was in the midst of this living hell and had no idea what she was going through. On the outside, she was beautiful, smart, and upbeat. Thus, I was shocked to learn that at that very time, she was battling a very powerful inner demon. And I'm sure she's not alone. There are other young women grappling with the same foe for which this book could prove invaluable, as it offers a cold, frank view of what it's like to escape the wretchedness of hell."

—**Douglas Henderson Jr.,** Esq. Author of *Endeavor to Persevere: A Memoir on Jimmy Connors, Arthur Ashe, Tennis and Life*

"*Opening the Door* is an honest account of how a happy young girl with a good upbringing can develop an eating disorder and spiral out of control. This book not only demonstrates why this could happen to anyone but gives hope to a path of recovery to those who are struggling."

—**Sandi Vilacoba,** Owner of the Pilates Project, and fully recovered from anorexia

"Meredith's style of writing really puts me right there with her. Her journey is so difficult, and I'm so proud of her for bearing her truth—an extremely brave thing to do. She will help so many others who are walking along the same path as her."

—**Effie Drossman,** Owner of Clementine Spinning Studio

"Meredith's book takes the reader on a detailed journey from the depths of an eating disorder to full recovery. As I read her story, I felt like I was walking beside her, sharing in her struggle and her hope. She is a testament that full and lasting recovery is possible. As I have the pleasure to know Meredith, I know how the story ends and I'm grateful she's chosen to share her recovery story with the world."

—**Cathy L.,** NJ Behavioral Health Outreach Professional

Opening the Door:
My Journey through Anorexia to Full Recovery

by Meredith O'Brien

© Copyright 2022 Meredith O'Brien

ISBN 978-1-64663-715-7

Published by

 köehlerbooks™

3705 Shore Drive
Virginia Beach, VA 23455
800-435-4811
www.koehlerbooks.com

OPENING THE DOOR

MY JOURNEY THROUGH ANOREXIA TO FULL RECOVERY

MEREDITH O'BRIEN

VIRGINIA BEACH
CAPE CHARLES

"And I said to my body, softly, 'I want to be your friend.'
It took a long breath and replied, 'I've been waiting my whole
life for this.'"

—Nayyirah Waheed

I dedicate this book to my four nephews. You helped me to conquer my fears and to love with an open heart.

I dedicate this book to those who get up each day and move toward healing. I share my story to empower others, to inspire hope, and to share how my recovery journey allowed me to find my voice and open the door to my life.

TABLE OF CONTENTS

PART 1

HISTORY

HELLO, DOLLY

I n my baby book, my mother writes that I am her "little garbage pail." I am a healthy eater and enjoy food. I am the opposite of picky, thus the garbage pail comment. I also like being the center of attention. I usually have a wide toothy smile, puffy cheeks, and a look of pure joy on my face in old, faded photographs, curled at the corners. I cross my hands over my chest and stand confidently with a carefree attitude, like "Look at me, world." My neighbor calls me the happiest girl in the world. Maybe because she watches me twirling a baton for hours on our lawn with a huge grin on my face. I love spending time with other people so much that I even befriend the old man down the street, and we have outside picnics with lemonade and Ritz crackers in his backyard.

Every Sunday, we drive from New York to New Jersey to visit my mother's parents after church. My grandmother keeps a secret wooden box in the third drawer of the armoire in her bedroom. She calls it "the magic box." It looks like a long-lost treasure from *The Goonies*. Each week, I fill with anticipation while my two brothers, Conor and Aidan, and I open it, finding penny candy, stickers, and other small items. It is the highlight of my week. As "the adults" talk in the kitchen that my grandmother keeps at a toasty seventy-five degrees, Conor, Aidan, and I wrap ourselves in a blanket and sit side by side at the top of the short staircase leading to the front door. We then push off and gleefully slide down, arriving with a thud at the landing. As a child, it feels like we are on a ride at Six Flags Great Adventure. We scream and laugh unrestrained, only pausing to take soda breaks, sipping through our red licorice straws.

• • •

My cream-colored tights bunch up at the bottom of my ankles around my black, patent leather, Mary Jane shoes. I sashay down the drab brown elementary school auditorium aisle in my off-white dress with three small red roses on the front and a long strand of pearls that I borrowed from my mother. A large, droopy straw hat covers my flaxen, blonde bowl cut and one of my grayish light-blue eyes. An ivory fur cape adorns my shoulders. I assertively walk up to the stage and stand proudly as the rest of my classmates gather behind me.

I am the star of Mrs. Kaufman's first-grade class show of *Hello, Dolly.* Each day, my teacher sits at a large piano, and we sing along, following the lyrics in miniature blue booklets. When she announced we were having an end-of-year show, my heart skipped a beat. I love to sing and dance. I am chosen for the lead.

"Hello, Dolly, well, hello, Dolly. It's so nice to have you back where you belong. You're looking swell, Dolly, we can tell, Dolly," I bellow, a smile bigger than my cheeks forming. This is where I belong—in the spotlight. Singing. Dancing.

And I spend most of my childhood doing just that—well, before I start a war with my body.

• • •

"What do you think?" my mom asks, grabbing a Bachman pretzel stick from the small, yellow container encrusted with salt. She holds her chestnut-red, permed hair away from her face and says, "Whatever you want, sweetie."

The sun shines down brightly as I shuffle through the after-school activity pamphlet, sitting leg to leg with my mom on our ashen blue front steps in between two honeysuckle bushes.

"Irish step. Origami and pretzel-making," I decide, sure of myself.

A week later, we pull up to the local church three blocks away from our house in my mother's lime-green Chevy Impala. It is my first day of Irish step dancing. Class is held downstairs. I have only been to the church building and feel adventurous as I open the large, heavy wooden door leading to the basement. I bop down the stairs. I see a large empty room with some bleachers, random chairs, and a stage on one side. The floor is sparkly, like a bag full of glitter was thrown on top. After I take my shoes off, I notice it is slippery too and I glide in my socks from side to side. I lace up my brand-new, shiny black Irish step shoes. Within minutes, I see a girl slightly taller than me with a dark-brown bob, freckled skin, and a friendly smile. We stand next to each other in line. We become instant friends as our parents chat on the bleachers, watching us learn how to stand up with a straight posture, keep our arms rigid by our sides, and point our toes.

Darcy is my sidekick and quickly becomes a regular at my house. After my younger brother, Aidan, moves into my older brother's bedroom down the hall to share bunkbeds, I finally have my own space. A child's dream! My parents let me decorate. I pick out a baby-pink rug, a pink-and-purple-flowered bedspread, and curtains to match. I buy a white desk and vanity from Conran's that fall apart about once a week.

LYLAS
(LOVE YOU LIKE A SISTER)

Darcy and I spend hours in my pink bedroom making up dance routines to "Gloria" and "Flashdance." We listen endlessly to the forty-five records, singing into air microphones and swirling around wildly. We practice nonstop to perfect our turns, kicks, and lip-syncing abilities. When the movie *Grease* comes out, my mom buys me shimmery, tight black pants; high-heeled, open-toed magenta shoes; and a matching purse. I pretend that I am Sandy singing to Danny Zuko of the T-Birds. One of my happiest childhood memories is coming down our tan-carpeted stairs on Christmas morning to find *Grease* playing on our very new, exceptionally large, and very heavy VCR, set up in our cozy den. We watched it on repeat.

Darcy and I obsess over Barbie. I have the Barbie pool, townhouse, and car. My parents buy me multiple dolls, and I keep them in a red, white, and blue box that has a latch that I close tightly. On most days after school, Darcy and I idle home, making sure not to step on any cracks on the sidewalk or streets. This keeps our attention on the three-block walk. When we get to my house, we slide open the glass back door and throw our book bags on the ground next to a crowded row of shoes and sneakers. We hang up our coats in the closet that is bursting at the seams, and it is a small victory when we tuck the jacket in, sliding it into place. We both kiss my mom hello and then run down to my chilly basement with a cement floor to play. We spend all afternoon preparing for Barbie shows. We make up their names and careers. We have bathing suit and talent contests.

"Coming down the stage is Jasmine, who is twenty-five and an interior designer. Here she is wearing an off-the-shoulder one-piece. She plans to sing opera for her talent."

Aidan plays the judge.

Darcy's mom buys us Cabbage Patch dolls for Christmas the year that they are popular. I adopt Faith Lucinda, with blonde hair and blue eyes. My mom gets me a small gray suitcase with a silver front clasp down from the attic in which I store my own childhood clothes for her to wear. I carefully fold my pink eyelet dress and turtleneck with small colored hearts on it perfectly into the case. Even at a young age, I like order. Symmetry.

I love school and everything about it—the pencil cases, the notebooks, and the crisp, colorful Trapper Keeper folders. At every chance, we play "school." We make up writing assignments and real math questions on small pads of paper and grade them in red pen or with stickers that I am intrigued by, especially the scratch-and-sniff ones. Darcy and I take turns playing the teacher and the student. We play for hours until my mom shouts that dinner is ready from the basement door. Every Friday night, Mom makes homemade pizza. The dough, sauce, and shredded mozzarella cheese are fresh from our local Italian shop. She makes it rectangular shaped and cuts square pieces with scissors from our junk drawer. The best pieces are where the cheese browns on top.

Darcy, Aidan, Conor, and I snuggle on the couch that takes up most of our snug den. My parents have two small burgundy chairs behind us by the two back windows. We use TV tables to eat. We sit so close to one another that it is impossible to get up in the middle of dinner to go to the bathroom or get another slice. My mom serves us.

She also spoils us. For dessert, she puts out gallons of different flavors of ice cream and bowls of sprinkles and candy, jars of hot fudge and caramel sauce, and a can of Reddi-wip for us to make sundaes.

It is also common for Darcy to stay for dinner during the school week. She fills up the sixth seat. Our unfinished wooden kitchen table is usually pushed against the yellow-and-gold wallpaper to make extra room in the kitchen. It is not until mealtime that we drag the table out to create more space. We have wooden chairs with small circles on the seats and backs. When we wear shorts, our legs become plastered with tiny red indentations.

I sit under the mustard-yellow telephone, the spot nearest to the hallway. Conor sits catty-cornered from me. Aidan sits next to me against the wall. At meals, we try to shimmy into our seats without scratching the wall. We are rarely successful, and a faint line of faded wallpaper cuts the wall in half. My mom sits across from me, close to the stove and sink. My dad sits at the head of the table, inches away from the refrigerator. When Darcy joins us and takes up the sixth seat, he almost touches it.

Darcy's family has a vacation home in Maine, and each year, I go for a week's visit. We spend the time going to the beach, riding the duck boats, going to the arcade, and eating homemade ice cream at Goldenrods after we finish our tasty cheeseburgers and fries. On cloudy days, you can find us playing gin rummy 500 for literally hours at a time. My family rents a beach house on the Jersey Shore each summer, and Darcy visits each year too.

FAMILY TREE

My dad was a limo driver for my mother's sister Dana's wedding. My mom was a bridesmaid. They met. There was a story about an umbrella. The rest is history, and my parents married on a beautiful, sunny day in June 1969.

As my dad attended graduate school in Upstate New York, my mom worked full-time to support them. They sometimes had Oreos for dinner. Two years later, Conor arrived. By this time, my family had moved into a two-bedroom apartment in Westchester County, New York, near the local train station. My mom stayed home with Conor and my dad got his first job as a marketing executive in the city. Four years later, I joined them.

My mom is thoughtful, resilient, and unbendable. Some of her go-to phrases are "More hands make light work," "Wait until your father comes home," and "Can I get you a blanket?" She has this keen sense to notice when I am cold at exactly the right moment. I can be sitting on our green corduroy couch, and out of nowhere, my mom places a warm blanket on me the second a chill starts. Her eyes are emerald. Her hair is short with tight curls and red with shades of chestnut and mahogany. She puts notes and stickers in our brown paper lunch bags each day. Something sweet, like Nestle Tollhouse chocolate chip cookies or Betty Crocker brownies, is always cooling from the oven when we get home from school, the sugary smell wafting out the kitchen window and meeting me as I turn onto our back steps.

She is always on the phone with Dana, talking for hours at a clip; however, she never sits still, the phone cord wrapping around the walls as she heads to the dining room, den, and foyer. Her happy place is for her entire immediate family to be snuggled together in the attic, reading Little Golden Books. Inside is safe for her. She cannot control the outside. She tells us that she wants to be the perfect mother. At a young age, I do not know that perfection does not even exist, so what she is seeking is impossible.

My dad is a big teddy bear. While his parents were taking vacations, Nora, his nanny, took the bus up from the Jersey City projects each day to care for him in his childhood home. The first time I saw my dad cry was at her funeral. He is rational, analytical. He is ambitious and caring. He has a strong work ethic. Little do I know how lucky I am to have him eat dinner with us when I am in grade school. As my dad gets promoted and shifts to different companies, his dinner seat will often be empty. However, as a small child, we have barbeques on school nights, and he coaches my elementary basketball teams.

My dad has brown hair and light-blue eyes. He starts to lose his hair early and has a small, round bald spot that gets larger each year. He stands about six feet tall. He smokes a pipe and can often be found in "his chair" in the living room by the piano, puffing on it. When his doctor tells him that he will die young from smoking, he stops cold turkey, but the smell of the pipe still reminds me of him. And reminds me of simpler times. Doo-wop makes him happy. Taking our family on yearly vacations where we all can be together in a villa or hotel suite fills him with pride.

Conor has thick, dirty-blond hair a little darker than mine and indigo-blue eyes. His cheeks fill with freckles from the sun. I have a perfectly squared photograph of him opening the door of our tan station wagon back seat that sat parked on our steep diagonal driveway for me. He wore a suit. I wore a flowered dress. I imagine we were on our way to Mass, which we attended every Sunday morning. Conor represents stability to me. I feel safe with him. He is the problem-solver. He is witty and funny. Conor is tremendously intelligent. He is calm and even-keeled. I never realize the pressure that he may feel to take care of me as his younger sister. I am more of an attention-seeker, and I notice in elementary school that I have mood swings and shifts that I do not understand.

Aidan was born three years after we move into our lovely home with an L-shaped lawn. He came out breach and has lived to the beat of his own drum ever since. He has more energy than Conor and I have combined. He is creative, introspective, and clever. He has white-blond hair, lighter than us all, and pastel-blue eyes. He is both social and introverted. He loves to read for hours at a time and visit libraries and is self-assured. His spunk and confidence make him popular. He is outspoken and his assurance is captivating.

HOME

We live in an upper-middle-class town. Our house is a three-bedroom, one-and-a-half bath, colonial home. It is dark gray with snowy white shutters. We are on the corner and hold numerous hide-and-seek games and snowball fights in our side yard. There is a dead-end road next to our house, and all the kids from the neighborhood play there—kick the can, ghost in the graveyard, kickball. Each day after school and homework are finished, we play outside for hours on end until Mom shouts, "Dinnertime!" from our back door.

On the first floor, we have a small, narrow den; a large living room; a dining room; and a pocket-sized kitchen. Upstairs, we have three modest bedrooms and the singular, coveted full bathroom. Luckily, Mom showers at night, and Dad showers before the sun comes up. That leaves me and my brothers to duke it out each morning. The last one typically stands in the hallway saying, "You almost done?" "Almost." "C'mon. I am going to be late." And often, that person is me because I am late to most things. So, as I am waiting, I run downstairs to put my hand out of the sliding back door to identify the weather and influence my choice of outfit for the day.

My parents chose Westchester County as our primary location simply for the school system, one of the best on the East Coast. It is also a short train ride into the city. I am not aware of how competitive school will be—cutthroat, uncompromising, prestigious, wealthy. I am also not aware of our privilege. I am not aware of how fortunate we are to live in a safe neighborhood and to be financially secure. It is the only "normal" I know, and I think that every child grows up similarly.

Jefferson Park, our local playground, is one block away, and Aidan and I often sit on the big gray rock in the middle, making potions out of sticks, sand, and dirt. We sleigh down the small hill that feels enormous during snowstorms. We rock back and forth on the swings, eventually getting so high that we jump off, landing on the sand plot in front of us. We collect different-sized rocks and paint them brightly. We set up shop in our side yard, selling them from an orange-colored plastic table to our neighbors for a quarter. Every Friday night, Dad takes us to Video Ranger to rent movies to watch with our pizza. Our elementary school is only three blocks away, and each day, we walk there together without a parent. We come home for hot tomato soup and saltines with melted American cheese on top for lunch. After the final bell, we saunter home with Darcy by our side.

VEGETABLE TRUCK

"Neil is here," my mom says as she places a small brown comb to hold her hair back. I sit at the kitchen table doing my homework. It is the first thing I do after school. I follow her out the front door to the large fruit-and-vegetable truck parked in front of our house.

"Can we get apples? Grapes?"

"Of course, sweetie," my mom answers.

"Four peaches. Four plums. A bunch of grapes. Six gala apples," Mom orders as Ned, the owner, takes the fresh fruit from the large piles and puts them in small brown paper bags. His big belly spills over his work pants, and he wears a silly grin. I look up at my mom barely reaching midway up the blue truck as she reads off her list. We watch *The Magic Garden* each day after kindergarten and eat apple slices while we do. My mom eats an orange for dessert as we watch *Family Ties* or *The Cosby Show* at night. She peels the entire orange rind in one try as I snuggle by her side. The smell of citrus still makes me smile.

. . .

I run down the slippery foyer hallway and stumble into a small vestibule table that sits under a gold-trimmed mirror. On top sits a figurine of an old horse.

Smash! The small statue crashes to the floor.

"Meredith Eileen!" my mom yells, walking quickly into the hallway. She wrings a kitchen towel in her hands. Her words pierce through me. My small body freezes. Hot, stinging tears run down my face. Fear invades my body.

You are a bad person.

"Go to your room," she yells, looking at me with exasperation. "Wait until your father gets home."

She is a mom—moms get mad, but little do I know the impact her anger has on me. I am super sensitive—vulnerable to any perceived rejection or criticism. Each time she raises her voice, my fight-or-flight response goes into overdrive. When things are good and people are pleased with me, then I am happy as a clam. However, when things are not good or people are upset with me, I feel terrified. After the fury, she uses the silent treatment. While she is wordless, I learn to shut down too.

. . .

The doorbell rings. I closely follow behind my mom, walking down the foyer to the door. Standing there is an adult male about my mom's age. Maybe he is an Electrolux vacuum salesman? My mom chats with him while holding the screen door partly closed with her thin body. I stand to the side of my mom, wiping my blonde bangs out of my face as the rest of my bowl cut stays frozen in place.

"How old is your son?"

My face flushes bright red. My cheeks warm. My body freezes. A tingle of embarrassment washes over me, but I push it down.

Do I look like a boy?

My brown corduroy pants start to feel uncomfortable, and my tan wool sweater starts to itch at my neck. I slip behind my mom so that her legs and hips block me. I lower my head so that my bangs cover my eyes, brimming with tears.

THE POCONOS

The colorful brochure lies on the kitchen counter. Pictures of a woodsy and charming mountainside lodge, an Olympic-sized swimming pool, and generous, snowy ski slopes fill the pages. My family and I are going to the Poconos for a trip. We watched the commercials for Mount Airy Lodge in upstate Pennsylvania and, minus the heart-shaped hot tubs for newlyweds, we are excited about everything.

We climb into my father's station wagon, throw the bags into the back, and settle in for a three-hour drive. About halfway into our route, my ears start hurting. Due to the elevation, they clog up, and I spend most of the ride squeezing my nose obsessively with my fingers to unblock them. I am unsuccessful, and as we finally drive up to the lodge, I cry in pain.

After we check in at the dimly lit front desk, we walk down the long, dilapidated hallway to the last room along the corridor. The tight room is underwhelming, freezing, and smells like smoke. My father asks to change rooms, but to our dismay, there are no others available. We should take it as a sign that the trip would be overall disappointing, but we give it the benefit of the doubt. We crank up the heat, but it does not work. As we excitedly take a tour of the premises, we see that the Olympic-sized pool looks more like a barren pond and the large arcade room looks like it was recently robbed, with two video games and a pool table in the center. The hazy lights over the table leave the room dark and uninviting, and the slopes outside resemble bulky mounds of snow.

On the first evening, we head to the lobby before dinner. We notice a gregarious gathering in one of the banquet rooms with people mingling. We hear live music from four men in straw top hats and red-and-white-striped suits. The barber shop melodies are lively and fun, and we decide to stop by before our reservations, thinking, *Well, this is a nice welcoming party to start our vacation.* We enter as the barbershop quartet sings in the background. Conor, Aidan, and I grab small cubes of cheese and crackers from the waiters passing around appetizers. We each grab a soda, and my parents grab glasses of champagne. *The trip is looking up,* I think. It is not until a lot of the guests inquire how we personally know the quartet (one is named Bill) that we realize we have just crashed a private party. My dad comes up behind us, saying, "Drop the cheese, kiddos. Now" as we quickly scamper out in single file. I think it is hysterical and giggle all through dinner.

•   •   •

My family and I are new to skiing, so Aidan, Dad, and I sign up for a beginners' class on the bunny slope. Aidan and Dad immediately dislike our instructor, probably because she tells them what to do. We learn how to plow and ski slowly down the small hill. Whenever I fall, I bust out laughing. However, when Aidan and Dad fall, they get angry, mumbling under their breath, "You are so stupid" to the teacher. My dad, role-modeling stellar behavior, and Aidan gang up on her, so instead of learning to ski, they spend the day complaining about their common target.

I have a successful class, noticing that I am a quick-learner, and take the T-bar lift with Conor to the intermediary slope. Not knowing that the bar is supposed to drag you up the mountain, I sit on it and fall over. I chuckle. I try to get up, but with skis, a large winter jacket, and mittens, I continue to slip.

"Mer, get up," Conor says, in a kind tone initially. After I fall multiple times, I end up lying on the ground, laughing uncontrollably and losing all sense of strength to lift my body up. The other skiers wait for me to move to the side. As the line gets longer, he barks, "Mer, get up now!" embarrassed that I am bringing a lot of attention to us. I think it is hilarious and carry on with my snickering. I eventually stand up with Conor's help and we ski for a while. But as the temperature drops, my ears hurt again, and I go back to our freezing room to have Mom put warm compresses on them.

Looking back, this may be the trip that we decided to hang up our skis and plan yearly trips to warmer destinations, but it was also one of the best vacations I ever had. I laughed so hard I almost peed my pants (one of my favorite characteristics that I have to this day). None of our expectations were met, but I found it amusing and comical. My anxiety was quiet, and I had a ball. And as we continued to go on more glamorous vacation spots with high-end hotels and amenities, this trip and the memories created from it were etched into my heart. And as years went by, it became the trip we talked about most.

ADULT SWIM

My family and I spend our summers on the Jersey Shore, renting homes in a quaint six-by-six block beach town. Each year, after the final school bell rings on a late day in June, it is officially summer. I skip out of the school doors, thinking about lazy afternoons at the beach. I quickly see my mom and our packed camel-colored station wagon. She picks Conor and Aidan up and we head south. The car is filled with dishes, linens, towels, and sand toys. It is an earned vacation after a stressful school year. For a full two months, I can play all day, swim in the waves, build sandcastles, and relax. My dad meets us on Friday afternoons after sitting in bumper-to-bumper traffic from Manhattan, sometimes for four hours.

Each year, we rent a new house with unique nooks and crannies. One summer, we have a large home with a bright sunroom off the living room facing a vast lake. In one, a butler's pantry off the kitchen. In another, a secret staircase. And in another, a quaint lounge porch off the primary bedroom. And in all of them, we are just blocks away from the beach—my happy place.

My mom takes us to the beach every day. We stay there from nine to five like it is our job. (The best job in the world!) We eat sandy peanut butter and jelly sandwiches on an old, scratchy green army blanket and swim in the ocean for hours, our fingers and toes pruning. Each afternoon after lunch, I fall into a deep slumber under the shade of our large, lemonade-yellow umbrella. The crash of the waves, the low murmurs of families talking, and the feel of the soft sand under my body create a perfect combination. And when I wake, I notice the *Dukes of Hazard* beach towel Mom lightly dusted over me.

At the second house we rent, I meet Kelly, the landlord's granddaughter. My family rents the larger home on the property, and her family stays with her grandmother in the smaller brown cedar house. We become fast friends, instantaneous sidekicks, and within no time, inseparable. She is tall. I am short. I have short, sandy-blonde hair. She has long chestnut hair. But we just fit. We both have a witty sense of humor and spend most days laughing and making each other crack up. We search for shark teeth under the boardwalk, buy French fries at the pavilion, and spend hours upon hours in the ocean and the local pool. We have annual variety shows for our families where we sing, dance, and roller skate. We even make crafts using pipe cleaners and clothespins and sell them from a card table in the grassy yard. We spend our money at the candy store on the boardwalk. I have Darcy at home during the school year and Kelly in the summer. I am all set, recognizing that large groups of friends and crowds overwhelm me.

• • •

Aidan and I join the town swim team. Each morning, we wake up at dawn and walk to the pool a few blocks away. I love the team. Or I think I love it. Productivity makes me feel worthy, and I feel accomplished after we swim an hour of laps and use it as permission to then relax at the beach all day. Aidan hates it and stops after one season. Aidan is surer of himself. Lately, I notice that I wait for signs from others about what I should or should not like.

After practice, Aidan and I watch game shows like *Press Your Luck* and *Card Sharks* while eating Raisin Bran or Cheerios or moist crumb cake from the bakery up the street. Game shows make me nervous. They still do. As I watch, I make up stories about the contestants. This girl is lonely and the only happy thing in her life is to go on this show. Or this guy just lost his job and needs the money to buy food. When they press the whammy, my heart hurts. "Womp womp." And even though it also makes me crack up, I feel a dull ache. When a player leaves with zero dollars, I feel sad. From an early age, I feel my emotions quite strongly. I am not sure if this is normal, so I pretend they don't exist. Instead, I smile or crack a joke.

• • •

I hoist myself up onto the kitchen counter. I balance myself by holding the white cabinet with my left hand, peer into the shelves piled with food, grab the sugar cereal variety pack with my right hand, and hop back down. I go back and forth on what cereal to choose but decide on Apple Jacks. I'll have Corn Pops tomorrow. On the weekend, we are allowed to have sugar cereal. On the weekdays we eat "non-sugar" cereal.

I head into the small den at the back of the house that we are renting for the summer and turn on the TV. My uncle John, who slept on the pull-out couch the night before, lazily rolls his sheets into a ball and pushes the couch back into place. I hop onto it, balancing my bowl as I prop myself upright with the back pillow. *The Brady Bunch* plays in the background as our yellow phone rings loudly from the side table. Mom runs in and picks it up, but instead of saying hello—or anything, for that matter—she freezes as her mouth opens wide with a gasp. Her shoulders drop, and I think she is going to fall backward onto the floor. My body buzzes with worry, and I place my breakfast on the cocktail table that Uncle John moved back to its original place.

"Oh my God," my mother whispers and drops the phone receiver down sharply. It rattles until it eventually balances. "Aidan was hit by a car," she gulps. I feel like the room is closing in on me as Mom grabs her keys and drives to the local hospital a few blocks away. My uncle stays home with me.

Remarkably, Aidan is okay, even though he was hit head-on while he crossed the main street by foot and flew thirty yards in the air before dropping onto the sandy street. The doctors at the hospital tell my parents that if he were any bigger, there may have been another outcome. So, Aidan has a few scratches on his back but is overall unscathed. We stay home from the beach that day. The ring of a phone still makes me jump.

• • •

At age ten, I become aware that I have a body. I mean, I always knew I had one, but it in no way affected my life. I washed it, clothed it, and moved it, but I had no emotional connection to it. Lately, though, I start to feel the waistband on my shorts tug against my skin. I notice the lean bodies of some girls and compare them to my short, muscular legs and my roundish belly. My thighs rub together and get irritated as I walk to the beach. I detect the dimple in my cheek, the rolls in my stomach, the curve of my thighs, and the width of my wrists.

I stare at the oversized wall clock at the pool. *Seven minutes.* I swim in the deep end. I breathe heavily. *Five minutes.* My bloodshot eyes sting, and I feel the hot sun pulsing on my cheeks. *Four minutes.* My legs feel tired from paddling. *Two minutes.* My heart beats more quickly. *One minute . . .*

Tweet! the lifeguards blow their whistles.

"Adult swim. All kids out," they yell. The other children finish up their games of Marco Polo and doing underwater handstands for scores like they are performing at the Olympics.

I freeze. My body is submerged. I'm safe.

I have to get out.

Tweet! "All kids out."

I hang back briefly as the rest of the kids paddle to the wall. My bright-orange one-piece sticks to my skin. My goggles make deep indentations in my face. A wave of self-consciousness crashes over me and my face flushes. I slowly near the edge of the pool, my breath shallow.

Everyone is going to stare at me.

I lift my chubby body with both hands, leaning onto my right knee for support on the side of the pool. I pause, crouching, hoping everyone is too busy to look at me. To judge. The world stops momentarily as the water drips off me. I spring up and walk really fast to my beach towel, strategically placed for easy access. The moment I wrap myself in my towel, I realize I'm holding my breath enough to pass out. It is as if I am at the bottom of my beloved Atlantic Ocean—in that moment, my body dives in. Hidden. Invisible.

MY INNER CRITIC

As I reach third grade, I notice that I am hard on myself. It is like I cannot breathe until my homework assignments are completed, something I do immediately when I get home. My ability to rest is more challenging. Playing Barbies becomes a thing of the past. I am your classic type A personality. I either reach my image of perfection or I am a failure. I spend hours making color-coded flash cards. I obsessively rewrite my notes. I practice my times tables so I know them by heart, forward and backward in record time. Instead of enjoying the act of learning, I memorize facts to regurgitate them back onto a quiz or test.

• • •

Dad is my elementary school basketball coach. My dad loved the game when he was younger, and his passion for the sport is passed on to me seamlessly. If I had a time machine, I would fly back to this time. My dad in his matching sweatpants and zip-up jacket, an old Knicks cap on his head, a clipboard in his hands, and a pen behind his ear. His enthusiasm is hypnotizing.

For a while, basketball suspends time for me. It is a healthy outlet and a place I excel. Hands down, it is when I feel the most adrenaline, excitement, and spirit. I feel magical when my high-top sneakers hit the court. I am completely present. Other responsibilities, including school, Irish step, and social pressures, melt away. The crisp bounce of the ball. The swish of a basket. The high-pitched squeal of a whistle. As the point guard, I am the leader of the team. I memorize all the plays. Competitiveness fires in my body. I am quick. Aggressive. Passionate.

One time, Dad is booted out of a game after a player kicks me intentionally and he yells loudly at the ref from the sidelines. "Did you see that? She kicked my daughter in the chest. Are you blind?" he screams, moving onto the court. As soon as the whistle blows, I know the ref does not approve of his behavior, but I stand proud, knowing that he will protect me. The love of basketball connects my dad and me. I love watching college basketball games, practicing my foul shots at the playground, and having Dad as my coach.

I really am a natural-born leader until my body gets in the way.

I am acutely aware of my body and how it compares to others, especially other girls. I start to engage in weird eating rituals, like only eating sliced cucumbers or mini unsalted pretzels. Skipping dessert makes me feel powerful, dominating the nervousness that I push down. Food and morality clash in my world. If I eat dessert, I am "bad." If I skip dessert, I am "good." If I eat "less," I am better. If I eat "more," I am worse. It is exhausting, but it helps me to feel in control, even if it is a false sense of it.

• • •

Our town's stationary store is packed. It is the first day of third grade, and I excitedly look down the aisles for new notebooks, crayons, pencil cases, protractors, and rulers. The store has more supplies than can fit comfortably in its small space. Binders lie on the floor next to brown boxes filled to the brim with staplers and glue. There are two entrances to the store and people funnel in as the checkout line grows. The aisles are narrow, and I slip in between mothers and children loading their plastic baskets with school supplies.

I see the hot-pink, wide-ruled notebook in between the blue and gray ones. I love the color pink—the color of my bedroom walls. The color of my bedroom rug. The color I dress my Cabbage Patch doll and Barbies in. I shimmy it out by the silver binding.

"Mom. Can I get this too?" I ask as Mom stands patiently in the long line.

"Sure, sweetie," my mom answers, rarely saying no.

I imagine she has no idea that she is buying me something that will entangle the size of my body with my self-worth. That from now on, numbers and calories and food labels are the first things I think about when I wake and what I ruminate about at night as I struggle to sleep.

Each day, I write in pencil what I eat and how much I exercise. I quickly come up with a rating system. I use stars from one to five to grade myself. On days when I eat less food and exercise more, I draw more yellow stars next to my entry. On days when I eat more food and exercise less, I draw fewer stars. Sometimes I don't get any stars. And on those days, my inner critic gets loud. I write, "YOU ARE A FAT PIG!" or "YOU SUCK!" in capital letters with several exclamation points.

● ● ●

"I ran three miles today," I say to Mom, sitting in our white Buick Century. Earlier that day, I decided to stay after school to run with Mr. Davis, one of my gym teachers. There were about six of us, and we ran the hilly streets through town. I felt invigorated and had a desire to run more than the allotted mileage, noticing that pushing myself to the limit was in my DNA.

"Good for you, Mer," Mom answers.

It was the first time I had ever run that far on purpose unless it was on the basketball court. The next day, Mom and I buy new running sneakers for my new activity.

"Brooks has the best shoe," the salesman says. "It's our top running sneaker."

I try them on. They are black and white. All the other girls have colorful shoes.

Will they make fun of me?

My mind whizzes back and forth like a pinball machine. I can get the Nike ones—they are blue and yellow. Like the popular girls.

But Brooks' are the best.

I get the Brooks; however, I have this gnawing pit at the bottom of my stomach as the salesman rings them up and places them in a plastic shopping bag.

I made the wrong decision. I should get the Nikes.

The next day, I wait for the girls to put on their sneakers and head out to the front entrance of our middle school where we meet to run before I grab my sneakers from my locker. So, each day for cross-country, I lag, but I dodge the threat of sticking out. Being different is my nightmare. Uneasiness wafts around me.

I quickly discover that the anxiety I feel is too scary. It is too big. It feels like ping-pong-ball-sized hail beating repeatedly on a windowpane, so my body learns to protect itself. I shelter myself by disconnecting. I push the fear way down so much that it evaporates. Now, I do not feel a thing. Numbing becomes my armor. It is like I am watching myself through a movie camera, but I am severed—cut off from reality.

THE SECRET

After my dad gets a big promotion when I am in middle school, we buy a white beach house with pale-yellow shutters in the heart of town. It is two blocks away from the beach. No more renting. We start to buy two of everything—one for each house.

It is a sunny July day, and I spring down our back porch stairs and stop at the garage to grab my beach chair, which is propped up first among the ten or so chairs we have leaning against the side. Next to them lies my magenta boogie board that I used as a child, beach umbrellas, sand toys, and the wire shopping cart that Mom uses to bring all the necessary beach stuff when family is in town. At first, I was embarrassed that we used a shopping cart, but I eventually realized it is ingenious.

I head down the lane and meet Kelly at the corner, and we walk one more block to the beach. We get prime real estate at the back of the beach near the boardwalk. It is where the cool kids congregate. We sit in direct line of lifeguard stand number five. Our summer goal is to sun our bodies and reach a tan of perfect bronze and gold. To be honest, getting tan trumps most things, even precious sleep, and we never dare miss a beach day. Six hours later, we part ways on the same corner, knowing that after dinner with our families, we will reconvene at my house. We have a double date at the boardwalk later.

In the outside shower, I notice the dark hue that covers my body. My bikini lines are prominent, a contrast to the pure-white parts of my skin that never see the sun. Even though I am Irish, I have just the right amount of melanin in my skin to tan. My mousy-brown hair bursts with blonde highlights from the Sun-in Kelly and I use. I put on a navy-blue T-shirt and blue-and-white-striped shorts. My stomach is flat as a board, and it eases the anxiety that I have been feeling more often lately. One of my male friends gets to my house early. Kelly and our other friend are on their way.

He and I awkwardly talk for a few minutes, my knee up against the kitchen island to seem like I am doing something. His black hair falls over his brown eyes and he pushes it back with his hand. He wears a green Billabong T-shirt that shows off his deep tan. We kissed at a party a few weeks ago that Kelly and I arrived at by bike. Kelly biked me on my ten-speed's handlebars, navigating the large bridge into the next town, and I am still surprised we arrived in one piece unscathed. He kissed me after we drank several Coors Lights in the backyard.

He moves so close to me that I can feel the hot air of his breath. He kisses me. I feel nervous, unsure if I am doing it right. At the age of thirteen, I do not have much practice with kissing. I also have a major crush on him, so I want to be impressive. As soon as he pushes me down onto the cold wood kitchen floor, I sense that something is wrong. I feel strange. His body hovers over mine until he drops his weight on top of me. His breathing gets heavy. He kisses me intensely. I feel the hard pulse of his penis through his shorts. My brain feels like mush. I cannot think straight.

This is wrong.

He pulls my shorts down and pushes my cotton underwear to the side. Swiftly, he grabs his zipper down. I rustle, trying to push him off me.

"No. Stop!" I say, trying to get leverage and shove his body off me. I push my feet against the wine refrigerator to get more traction and shimmy out of his grip. He enters me and pain sears through my body. It feels like something has ripped.

I hear the loud thump of my heartbeat vibrate in my ears, and in an instant, time stops. I stare at the flowered orange overhead light. My body leaves me and floats next to the light, looking down. I hover there, watching myself underneath. The back porch door opens with a thud, and he jumps up quickly. Kelly and my other friend are here. I pull up my shorts with one hand and rush into the bathroom. I shut the door frantically and see blood in my underwear. Hot tears sting my eyes. I grab a glob of tissue paper and shove it into my underwear; however, my hands shake so violently that I drop it. As I pick it up, I hear the porch door open again.

"Well, hello," my parents say.

"Hello," my friends say in unison.

"I'll be right out," I yell in the cheeriest tone I can muster.

I stand up straight. I wipe the tears from my eyes. I take a deep breath and stare into the wall mirror. No one will ever know.

Nothing actually happened.

I stand up straight and smile as I exit the bathroom.

"Hey, Mom. Hey, Dad."

Nothing happened.

I dig and bury the secret down so deep that it does not exist. I submerge the trauma so low that it disappears from my memory. Eventually, the thought of *This is wrong* changes to *I am bad, something terrible is going to happen,* and *I am doing something that is wrong.* The thoughts nestle deep into my cells. Festering. Burning. A core belief is born.

BINGE AND PURGE

Our beach house has a substantial back porch that we spend most of our time on. One side holds our outside table where we have barbecues, and the other side is a sitting area where we play board games and relax on lazy summer afternoons. We have a pool table and ping-pong table in the basement where Kelly and I play for hours. We both get decent at ping-pong, engaging in tournaments with just the two of us.

The living room is one large room that stretches the length of the house. The house is newly built, and we are not used to the open concept. Mom spends years trying to furnish it appropriately, eventually dividing it into a family room and a more formal sitting area. Our kitchen table sits in the center by the double glass door, looking out over the porch into our grassy yard. We have a big kitchen and a formal dining room that we rarely use, eating most of our meals on the eight-person table on the porch. There are four generously sized bedrooms on the second floor. On the third floor is a bonus room. Since we spend most of our days at the beach, biking around the neighborhood, and playing Cornhole in the backyard, it stays unused, but eventually, we decorate it into a bedroom suite.

• • •

I skip up the stairs two by two to my parents' primary bathroom, which is tucked in the back of their bedroom. Today is my maternal grandfather's eightieth birthday party, and we are hosting a celebration. I hear clamoring groups of people talking underneath the white tent we put up in the backyard. It is an abnormally hot day in June and the shade is a godsend.

I wear white Benetton shorts, a white tee, and a pink-and-orange-striped sleeveless vest. Fifteen minutes earlier, I eat a turkey sub sliced up into wedges with Aidan on our porch steps, each of us balancing our straw meal trays on our knees. I also eat coleslaw, potato salad, and a sour pickle.

Most of my family and friends are on the back porch and under the tent, so my house is empty. It is eerily quiet. I listen to the buzz of the central air and the ceiling fans circling in each bedroom. I then take a deep breath, kneel by the toilet, and stare absently at the porcelain seat. I slowly lift it up with my left hand and shove three fingers of my right hand down my throat. Initially, I gag, but after the second try, the food comes up easily. The oil and vinegar from the sandwich burn my throat. My face gets red and splotchy, and my eyes and nose water. My hand is bright, flaming red, but not cut. I flush the toilet twice, splash cold water on my face, and slip back to the party.

After the rape, the purging started. I am always in my head—chaotically racing without reprieve. I spew self-judgments and disparaging comments, and I notice quickly that restricting and purging helps to stop the noise. They temporarily help me to detach from reality. I have no idea that I am disassociating—that I am numbing myself and desperately running away from my feelings. According to Jennifer L. Gaudiani in *Sick Enough: A Guide to Medical Complications of Eating Disorders*, "Dissociation is a psychological reaction in which an individual may feel absent, out-of-body, and unaware of what they are doing, with little or no memory of what happened while dissociated." One disconnects from one's thoughts, feelings, memories, or any real sense of identity. These self-destructive behaviors become my safeguard.

Is my stomach flat enough?

Everyone is looking at me.

I cannot eat for the rest of the day.

You suck, you fat piece of shit.

To the outside world, I can keep up the façade. My friendly, wide smile tricks people. Progressively, though, my eating disorder takes over until I am a fragile shell that can be easily crushed. Broken. Swept away by the ocean wind.

MY DIARY

"Meredith, please come upstairs."

I know something is wrong as soon as I hear the tone of my mom's voice. My heart drops like a weight in my chest. My limbs tighten. I feel heavy. My throat closes. I walk up the stairs slowly. With each step, I feel more and more detached. The walls close in on me. By the time I reach the end of the short hallway and see my white diary with pink hearts on it faceup and open wide on her gray-striped bedspread, my disassociation has enveloped me.

"Would you like to tell me about what you wrote in your diary?" my mom says brusquely. "I mean, I already read it."

My thirteen-year-old body is frozen. The world stops. A heaviness weighs my shoulders down. I cannot talk.

"I ate so much today. Pancakes and two mini donuts for breakfast. Popcorn, Sprite, two Twizzlers, and some Raisinets at the movies. For dinner, I had coconut chicken, peas, carrots, and rice. This week, I will go on a diet. I want to get to xx lbs. I have to look good in a bathing suit. I need to be skinny. I am talking major diet. No cookies, candy, cake, chips, donuts, or pies."

Isn't a diary supposed to be top secret? The diary has a shoddy, silver lock, but I imagine it was not secure. I want to yell at my mom that reading my diary is an invasion of my privacy; however, I stay silent. Voiceless. The room closes in more tightly, and I blank out. Even if I try to speak, my mom will cut me off immediately, making it clear that she is in charge. I am the child. She is the parent. My needs do not count.

It is not until many, many years later that I am able to have compassion for my mother. She had just read that her teenage daughter was starving herself and hated her body. Maybe she was scared, sad, or shocked. But, at that moment, my shame just tripled in size.

• • •

Three days later, I sit on a tan couch opposite this tiny woman, Nicole, who sits cross-legged on an oversized wingback chair. A legal pad sits in her arms, and as she talks, she waves her ballpoint pen around in the air. She annoys me immediately. The way she crosses her legs like she is hunkering down to hear my story pisses me off.

"So, your mom shared with me that you are struggling with food."

"Not really," I say.

"Well, what brings you here today?"

"I don't know," I whisper, looking down into my lap. My mouth feels dry and pasty.

"What grade are you in?

"I'm a freshman."

"Do you ever skip meals?"

"Not really," I say.

I can't stand to be in my own skin. If I am not skinny, I am nothing. My mind is like a skipping record on volume ten.

The session feels like it is two hours, but fifty minutes later, I sit in the passenger seat of Mom's car.

"I am not going back. I promise I will eat. I don't like her."

My mom does not say much. I imagine she does not want to take me back to therapy either. "Other" people go to therapy—not my family or me.

A week later we try an eating disorder support group at a local counseling center one town away. Mom and I walk up three flights of stairs to the meeting room. My legs feel like lead. We sit in a circle with other families. Neither my mom nor I share too much. My mind buzzes through the entire thing. We leave as soon as the group ends.

"That is not for us, sweetie," my mom voices. A part of me feels relieved. Another part dismissed.

See, I don't have a problem.

MOST IMPROVED DANCER

I have my one and only growth spurt. My body turns lean and
svelte, and the baby fat melts off. I stand over five feet tall. The
weight loss is intoxicating, and I start to restrict daily. I stay up late
when my family is sleeping, doing sit-ups and leg lifts on the floor
of my beach house bedroom. I compulsively count my ribs as I lie
in bed. I try on different pairs of shorts, praying that there will be a
gap between my stomach and the top button. I use the Thighmaster
by Suzanne Somers religiously. I lie down on my beach chair in my
bikini and the thoughts spiral.

Your stomach is sticking out. Everyone is looking at you.

I slow my breathing to prevent my stomach from rising and
falling. I hide my hideous bunions in the sand. They are wide on each
foot, jutting out with pointy bones. My body stiffens and the angst
grows inside me like a tidal wave. I know deep in my soul that when
I open my eyes and tilt my head, my large, fat, disgusting stomach
will be sitting there. However, each time I have the nerve to look, my
stomach is flat as a board. Taut like a string.

It won't last. You cannot eat today. You are not thin enough.

. . .

In the fall of my sophomore year, fellow Irish step dancers and my dance teacher comment about my weight loss. They comment on how different I look, alluding to the fact that I look better in this body. *Smaller is better.*

I start to feel special, something I have not felt in a while, since my elementary basketball days. I am good at something. I can starve.

While the dancers take their hair down in ringlets, I stand nervously in my celery-green Irish step costume. Pink, yellow, and light blue Celtic designs are embroidered down the chest and arms of my costume. The sketch was created by a seamstress in Ireland. My shoulder-length dirty-blonde hair sits flat on my head. I have one wave on the left side where my bangs are growing out, and I anxiously flip them behind my ears. It is my dance academy's spring festival. Darcy and I are partners for the group dance even though she stands much taller. Our best-friend status keeps us linked as a pair.

The loud, boisterous slip jig music starts from inside the hall. Darcy and I lightly grab hands, smile at one another, and get in line behind the row of dancers. This is our entrance. The doors open and we dance locked together through the small aisle, past the tables thronged with families, making our way to the vast space up front. The applause is loud. The air is dark with dust. I plaster a large smile onto my face and dance a ceílí, something that I can do with my eyes closed. Darcy and I separate, skipping in a huge semicircle, and reconvene in the middle.

. . .

"And this year's most improved dancer is . . . Meredith O'Brien!"

I hear the announcement as I sit with Darcy in the school hallway against the cold concrete wall. I pause, momentarily thinking I heard the wrong name.

"Mer, Go get your trophy," Darcy says, pushing me up from my seated position. I hurriedly creep backstage to the front. I clutch the award with both hands.

"Thank you," I articulate into the microphone, slowly but steadily. "I want to thank my family, my teacher, and my dance studio. This is a wonderful honor."

If I change the structure of my body, people will notice me. If I lose weight, I will get awards and accolades. I will be seen.

I'M NOT GOOD ENOUGH

The self-consciousness continues through high school, and most of my mental energy focuses on my appearance, my weight, and getting good grades. My body starts to change yet again. My hips fill out. My breasts develop. Even with restricting and bingeing and purging secretly at night, I feel like an alien in my body. I desperately want to hide in the locker, have someone click the lock shut, and throw away the key.

My acid-washed Guess jeans rip in between my legs as my friend Charles and I hang out by the lockers after school, waiting for my basketball game to start. I quickly cross my legs and straighten my back. I pull my pastel, striped J.Crew rugby shirt down past my waist (looking back, I guess I really liked stripes) and continue talking like nothing happened, even though shame strikes like lightning bolts.

Maybe I should become an actress because I am getting a hell of a lot of practice.

Charles and I met in middle school and the connection was instant. He is tall. His brown hair is so soft that it flops up and down like a toupee. He is kind and thoughtful. We spend eighth grade passing notes back and forth to each other during study hall. With each note, I feel joy, and it is a welcome break from my critical mind. He eventually becomes my best male friend and, in addition to Darcy, brings wonder and delight into my world. And even though he is so easy to talk to, and I slowly open up, I keep the eating disorder to myself for now.

You are useless. You are too fat to live.

I think everyone focuses on me, picks at my flaws, and judges me. I walk down the halls like I have a sign hanging over my head that reads "Not good enough." I hate the feeling of clothes on my skin, especially my waist. If leggings were in style when I was a teenager, maybe my life would have taken another path (Benetton did have a short run with their green and blue stirrups). Each day, I feel the jeans on my pale white skin like a noose. The self-hate talk loudens. It oozes from my lips.

You are the fattest person in the world.

• • •

My mom knocks lightly on the adjoining wall of our bedrooms. After ten minutes, she knocks a little louder. My dad left the house before the sun rose. Aidan is downstairs eating breakfast—a Pillsbury cinnamon roll with the pre-made icing melting off the sides. I smelled the delicious aroma whirling through my bedroom earlier but chose to roll over and place a pillow over my head. I never eat breakfast anyway.

"Rise and shine and give God some glory, glory. Rise and shine and give God some glory, glory. Rise and shine and give God some glory, glory, glory to the world," Mom sings, entering my room at 7:40 a.m., desperately trying to get me up for the 8:05 bell. My alarm dinged at seven, but I am still sound asleep. Her singing does not work. Her second line of defense is the lights and the blinds. She turns on the light. I pull the covers over my face to block out the glow. Light is my kryptonite. Then she pulls up the vinyl cream blinds to let even more sunshine in.

"Hey, Mer, it's time to get up. You have to drive Aidan to school. You are going to be late. Hey, Mer, get up."

"Ugh," I moan.

I unfreeze myself from the sheets, hit the floor with a thump, rip the shades down, and angrily flip off the light. I crawl back into bed. My comforter is my armor, my shield from the world. In my bed, I am concealed. But each morning, my used, slate-blue Ford Tempo screeches quickly out of our slanted driveway as I drive Aidan to school.

MONONUCLEOSIS

One of the roles I choose early on is that of an athlete. I grow up watching the Jets, the Knicks, and the Yankees. We spend countless nights watching college basketball, jumping up and down like crazy people. Sports, competition, and winning make me feel something. It gives me some semblance of an identity. I am naturally athletic, infatuated with running in the off-season, and I have this nervous energy that blows off on the court or field.

In high school, I play field hockey, basketball, and lacrosse. While basketball has my heart and still does, I am the most gifted at lacrosse. My years of obsessive running help. My competitive edge helps. My work ethic helps. My coach sees my talent, and I start to practice with the junior varsity team as a freshman. By sophomore year, I am on varsity.

Even though I purge almost daily, I still finish the timed mile with the best runners. Even though I skip lunch, I score two goals. Even though I am screaming inside for someone to notice my pain, I show up each day at practice, to work, and to each game to win.

In high school, behaviors become harder and harder to hide. I try purging in the sink, but the disposal wakes my mom up from a deep sleep, which she rarely experiences.

"Meredith," my mom grates under her breath. She checks the disposal and sees the ice cream sitting under the drain. Immediately, my body freezes. My mother's frenzy paralyzes me.

I don't want to do it. I must get the food out.

I do not want to purge, but I am compelled to. I cannot let the chocolate chip mint ice cream sit in my stomach for one more second. It is like I am playing a game of Perfection, and if I do not finish it in time, all the small yellow pieces will fly up into my face with a loud bang. Why in the hell did someone invent that game? It should be destroyed. It was definitely a reason why, to this day, I scare so easily even to the point of tears. It traumatized me!

I will get fat.

Everyone will laugh at me.

I will be excluded.

To reduce the risk of being caught, I bring the largest plastic cup I can find in our cupboard downstairs into the basement, tiptoeing slowly to diminish the earsplitting creaks. I bring multiple paper towels too. I go all the way to the farthest point in our basement and stand in the corner, pausing for any noise coming from upstairs. I slow my heartbeat way down and calm down my agitated hands by putting them in a prayer position and take a deep breath. Then I curl in half and purge into the cup. I purge all the way to the top and then carefully and slowly walk up the stairs, praying that I will not trip as my parents sleep upstairs. I pour the full cup into the first-floor toilet and flush. Usually, food particles remain, so I wait nervously until I can flush again. It is an exhausting process, but the calm afterward is addictive.

· · ·

My junior year, I get mononucleosis. I sleep all the time. Getting me out of bed, which is already awful for my mom, becomes her full-time job. She even pours cold water on me, and it does not work! I miss tons of school even though I know it is the most important year. I know colleges will look at my grades and SAT scores, but I can barely keep my eyes open. I sleep standing up. I sleep in the car on the way to and from Irish step class. The fatigue impacts my quickness on the field. I fall behind on timed mile runs. I feel uncomfortable not being among the best. Other classmates excel. I fizzle out. The praise from my coach shrinks. My identity slips away.

If I am an average lacrosse player, then I am nobody.

• • •

It is senior year. Pre-season starts. The field is too wet and muddy from a recent rainstorm to play on, so instead, we practice in the parking lot. The cement is slippery, and my rain jacket covers my face so much that I can barely see the lacrosse ball. As my coach works with the attack players, I warm up with the defense. As I bend down aggressively to snatch a ground ball, I wipe out on the sandy, damp ground. Before I even hit the pavement, I know it is not good as my leg flails out in front of me and my ankle rotates to the side. I tear ligaments in my right ankle.

I obsessively attend physical therapy. I do range-of-motion exercises, balance on a wobble board, sit in the hot tub, and perpetually place a bag of ice on it. I duct tape a five-pound barbell weight to an old Adidas sneaker and fanatically complete the prescribed drills morning, noon, and night, unable to think about anything else.

Despite my determination, I am out for the beginning of the season. Sitting on the bench infuriates me. I feel out of control, and after I finish physical therapy, I circle back to what I can control—my body. I eventually play again midway through the season, but it is different. My edge has wavered. My slowness irritates me. I still have passion on the field and for the sport, but the drive to win feels weary. Other players get by me. My legs feel tired more quickly. I know I have raw talent, but my dream to play Division I college lacrosse slips away as I grip onto my eating disorder even more.

BAGELS WITH CREAM CHEESE AND JELLY

Aidan has the most "normal" relationship with food. He eats when he is hungry and, from what I see, eats whatever he wants when he wants. I pick at a fresh plain bagel that Mom bought at a tiny bagel place on Norwood Road. The bagel is soft, airy, and still hot to the touch. I fixate that the bagel is "bad" and that I will need to do extra exercise today. I eat slowly to extend my eating time, picking minute bites at a time. This is the only "reward" I will get today, and in addition to running, I will also skip lunch.

Aidan stomps down the stairs and sits at the kitchen table in my spot under the phone because I rarely make it to breakfast, and if I do, like today, I eat standing up.

Maybe the calories will not count if I stand up.

Mom cuts the fresh cinnamon raisin bagel in half and plops it side by side in the toaster oven. As it reaches the toast level that Aidan prefers—slightly burned—Mom takes it out and smears Philadelphia whipped cream cheese from a pink-and-white container onto each side. Next, she puts an abundant amount of Welch's grape jelly on top. I stare at the bagel as Aidan vigorously bites into it. He gets cream cheese on the corners of his mouth and keeps eating. Jelly slides onto the plate after his second bite. I keep staring. Hypervigilant. Fixated.

You are not allowed to eat that. Just nibble on your bagel pieces and do an extra Jane Fonda workout video after field hockey practice.

• • •

Dad and I become consumed with the diet culture. I guess it is impractically impossible not to. He drinks Tab. So do I. He starts to put water on his Raisin Bran. I just stop eating cereal altogether. We have a scoop of Light n' Lively Ice Milk while my brothers make Breyer's vanilla ice cream sundaes for dessert. Dad goes on diets. So do I. Mom fixes him low-fat Alpine Lace cheese on pumpernickel toast for breakfast. My brothers eat french fries. Dad and I skip them. I feel a special connection to Dad and a sense of distinctiveness from my siblings. I play the roles of the "workout fanatic," the "no-dessert girl," and the "health nut." The roles give me purpose even though I truly have no idea of who I am.

For some of my dad's life, he lived in a higher-weight body. By middle school, I learned that he emotionally eats at night. After we all go to bed, he slips downstairs to eat cookies, muffins, and leftovers. Sometimes, he eats quickly and gags. Most nights, I stay up until Dad's binges are over. I am scared that he is going to choke and die. When I hear the squeak of Dad returning to bed, it is my cue to sleep.

Mom's relationship with food swings the other way. My mom, always svelte, does all the food shopping, prepping, cooking, and baking. She cooks three hot meals a day. It is normal for her to finally sit down to dinner after she serves all of us and say, "I am too exhausted to eat." She does eat a variety of foods, but not much of it. Food does not seem to bring her joy. She can go either way. Eat. Not eat. At a restaurant, Dad orders a salad, and Mom orders the cheeseburger with fries. After four bites, Mom is satisfied. Dad, tossing his salad around, usually slides her plate over and finishes her meal.

One of my mom's famous lines is "I wish I could just take a pill instead of eating. It is just so tiring to chew. That is why I like pasta. It just slides down my throat." She, in a way, role models normative eating, but I am too sick to notice. She eats a range of nutrients and eats until she is comfortably full, whether it be a few bites of a candy bar or her entire chicken francese dish. After my eating disorder hijacks my brain, though, I think she is taunting me when she sits down to a fresh piece of bread spread with salted butter or a box of juicy fruits.

You can eat that because you are thin. I cannot because I am fat.

To be honest, I have no idea about Conor's relationship with food. Him being four years older, we just miss that window of knowing those intimate details about each other's lives. When I start middle school, he is prepping for his SATs. When I start high school, he is over 250 miles away at college. I guess it takes a proper place in his life. However, it baffles me that I never talked to him about it. Eating disorders do that—my world becomes so small that I can only pay attention to my pain.

In my family, I start to wear a mask. I pretend I am fine even as my behaviors worsen. I do still have my laughing attacks from time to time, but they are fewer. There is little research about eating disorders, and my family and I think that if we do not talk about it, it will go away on its own. I will outgrow it. I will move on to another fixation. I tell them that I will eat, and they believe me. I think I do too. I am not aware of the insidiousness of the disorders. I have no idea they are dangerous, even lethal. There is some part of me that understands that my brain is off-kilter. Even after I am healed from mono, getting out of bed is simply too hard. My emotions fluctuate drastically. I feel sad even when something positive happens. I feel lonely in a room full of people. I shove the anxiety and depression down and hyperfocus on my body. My eating disorder becomes my best friend—my protector.

WAITLISTED

The screeching sound of the mail slot reverberates as the large stack of letters makes a thud. I crouch down into the foyer and pick up the envelopes and endless L.L. Bean and J.Crew catalogs. I neatly stack them in my arms and quickly scan if there is anything for me. I see my father and grandfather's alma mater college emblem under bills addressed to Dad. I grab the slim envelope and place it in front, dropping the rest onto the kitchen counter. I applied early. Mom is downstairs, ironing my father's shirts. Dad is at work. Aidan is at basketball practice. Conor is enrolled in the prestigious college the envelope was sent from.

My hands shake as I tear it open. Waitlisted. My body gets hot as I hold back tears.

See, you are not good enough. You are a dumb piece of shit.

Four years earlier, Conor opened a similar letter; however, his was an acceptance welcoming him to the class of 1992. Three years later, Aidan will also be accepted. And then both of my brothers marry graduates from the school. Conor marries Grace and Aidan marries Beth—two of the sweetest people I will ever know. But it is everyone on one side and me on the other. I am the one that does not belong.

I attend Loyola College in Baltimore, Maryland. In retrospect, Loyola is an ideal school for me—it enrolls about 4,000 students. I think it is big enough to challenge me, yet small enough to be personal. It has an esteemed lacrosse program, and I join club lacrosse. It also has a communications program, and I major in public relations.

The school is filled with party culture, but my eating disorder makes it nearly impossible to connect with other people. I go out often, probably too often, drinking large amounts of alcohol to keep my relationships superficial—right above the surface. I love my education, though, and I attend class religiously, am stimulated by learning (or should I say, getting straight As), and stay focused and organized. But when it comes to friendships, I make close to none.

And when I say I attend class religiously, I really do. I never like to rely on anyone but myself for notes. The only time I remember missing class—unless I was deathly ill—was during the winter of my freshman year.

Carla, a girl in the dorm room next to me, and I go out for quarter beers at a local bar that accepts our fake IDs. I must say, we have a blast. We laugh. We dance. We play pool. By 10 p.m., white snow flurries down from the sky. It feels magical. Going out on a school night feels liberating. It is the opposite of the rigid rules my eating disorder tells me to follow. And it is an amazing night until I decide to run from the cab into our dormitory building, slipping and landing face-first against the brick wall. The ambulance ride is fuzzy, and after getting ten stitches in my lower chin, I feel like I have been hit by a bus the next morning when my alarm rings. I miss class that day.

• • •

Getting close to people scares me. I stay hollow with my peers, keeping most things to myself. I allow them to see the parts of myself that are acceptable—the student, the partygoer—but I meticulously plan to be alone in my dorm often. Thankfully, most of my roommates go to the library to study, so I have the room to myself. Knowing from a young age that I am an introvert, it is during those times that I can breathe, re-energize, and let down the moat that I feverishly build with wet sand even as the waves crash over it. When I am alone, the waves pause. I can take off the mask that cuts up my face.

Also, the Towson Town Center, a large mall, is ten minutes away, and I spend most weekend days walking aimlessly around it. I shop excessively, obsessively. My father's credit card is a saving grace—it gives me the freedom to fill the cavernous hole inside. Buying a new dress at Banana Republic is an automatic dopamine hit. Purchasing cranberry-scented potpourri and votives at Yankee Candle distracts me. The shopping center is a safe place.

So is the on-campus post office. Mom sends me packages regularly, and as I walk back to my dorm with a large cardboard box filled with small gifts and snacks, I feel loved. Even though I keep my distance from other students, the twenty-four packets of Valentine's candy heart boxes, a freshly made Irish soda bread, and Christmas lights that I put up in our dorm corridor connect me with them, even if it is insincere. Each week, I also receive a handwritten letter from my grandmother enclosed with a crisp five-dollar bill.

Each year, I find the best way to purge in secret. I spend my days restricting and my nights eating and purging or sometimes bingeing and purging. It is not the amount of food that creates the urge; it is any volume or quantity. I wear workout clothes to class and exercise in between them at the school gym or at the John Hopkins track one mile away. While classmates walk into class dressed nicely in jeans and J.Crew sweaters, I arrive still sweating from my run, hair pulled back in a ponytail. I am completely malnourished in college; however, I sit in the front row and use every bit of my concentration on school. My legs feel like they will fall out from under me as I walk up the short hills to class, but I make it. I also make dean's list every semester.

Junior year is the best living situation since I only share a bathroom with one roommate. There is an extra door between the shower and the vanity. That year, I purge right into the shower drain, and no one ever hears me. Or so I think. And even if they did, I would not stop. Seeing all the food guzzled by the drain is so cleansing. The water rushing down. The food out of my body. Finally, peace in the midst of my chaotic world.

Senior year is more difficult since I share a bathroom with three other girls. I wait for them all to go out, and then I start my ritual, purging into a large cup and pouring it into the toilet. There is less splatter that way.

I hate being in my body. I want to cut it off. Just sever my stomach or the extra fat, only visible to me, around my thighs. I am still in a suitable weight range, so no one expects a thing. I play club lacrosse. I am an editor of the yearbook. I go out with friends and drink and attend parties. I smile a lot. I do not look emaciated, so I cannot be anorexic.

My parents and I have a verbal contract. They tell me I can only return to college sophomore year if I attend weekly therapy. Sheppard Pratt hospital is located five minutes away, and each week I see my therapist, Monica, there on Wednesdays at three. She specializes in eating disorder treatment. There is no part of me who wants to get rid of my eating disorder. None. It is self-protective. It is the way I numb my feelings. Purging gives me an opiate-like high that soothes my uncontrollable anxiety. Restriction gives me control. So, each week, my dad's Amex gets charged, but I stay the same—depressed, scared, and miserable.

GALWAY, IRELAND

"**H**i, I'm Mary," she says, smiling brightly, turning to shake my hand as she places her headphones in the front pocket of her airplane seat.

"I'm Meredith," I say, positioning my backpack neatly in front of my legs for easy access to my book, CD player, tissues, gum, water, and travel journal.

"You go to Loyola too, right?" she asks. I am drawn to her immediately. Her blonde hair, cut into a bob, shines, and her smile is radiating.

"I do." I saw her on campus, but we never officially met. Now we are sitting next to each other on a flight to Ireland. We are both studying abroad at University College Galway (UCG) for the second semester of our junior year. It is totally out of character for me to apply for study abroad, but I do anyway. I like routine, but there is a piece of me that needs a change. I must get out of my own head, and leaving the United States may be a way I do it.

Mary and I chatter during most of the flight unless we are napping. She is easy to talk to and my anxiety stays at bay. Her large smile brightens up the room, and her distinctive, high-pitch laugh is contagious. I quickly come to know that she is smart and strong and interesting. Up until this point, I have made no close friends at Loyola, but my instinct is to open my heart a little. Maybe it is because we are out of our comfort zones in a new country, but we also just click. She is Irish as well, and the coffee-colored freckles over the bridge of her nose look like they have been painted on.

Our first stop is to the city of Dublin for one week. We stay in a hotel that night after visiting our first pub and trying a pint of Guinness. It tastes thick, like custard, but I see one in every adult's hand, so I follow along. Luckily, Mary and I room together, and Robin from Providence College joins us. Maybe it is the magic of the city, or even the Guinness, but we bond instantly, becoming the three musketeers for the next six months. Our sarcastic and witty personalities mesh and we are well suited.

After staying with different Irish families for a few days to immerse ourselves in the culture, we reconvene on the UCG campus. Our rooms are close together and we are soon inseparable. We walk to class, explore the town of Galway, eat brown bread and sip on tea, spend time with friends from around the world, and travel to different places throughout Ireland on the weekends. We go to Cork to kiss the Blarney Stone, to Belfast and see the barbed wire fences and uniformed men with guns, and to the Cliffs of Moher in County Clare. Walking across the rope bridge, the heavy mist drenching my face, is both exhilarating and downright terrifying.

I love the cobblestone streets, small shops, and pubs that fill the town. I make friends with the owner of a flower shop and buy fresh-cut flowers for my room each week. I run the hilly paths surrounded by the lush green grass. I take Irish poetry, history, and art classes that I love; however, my need for perfection withers away, and grades do not take center stage. The pubs have an enchanting feel to them—always filled with neighborhood regulars smiling, conversing, and drinking Guinness. Live music is a staple. I find myself dancing a lot without self-consciousness—dancing to the rhythms and the beats, feeling jovial. And even though my eating disorder comes with me to Ireland, something shifts. I feel free. I can be anyone I want to be—no one knows me. There are no expectations or roles that I need to fill.

I feel different. I feel included, part of something. I embrace people instead of shutting them out. I enjoy connecting. I start to crave it. I do not feel like an outcast. At every turn, there are bunches of people going into town, heading to the pubs, or traveling on the weekends. I say yes to most things, and my energy is electric. It is like I turned into an extrovert by crossing the United States border. Most nights, we walk to the bars, drink tons of cider and beer, and dance to live bands. On Sundays, we go to brunch. We sit by the homey fireplace and listen to live jazz. The large, protective wall around me starts to crumble.

Traveling through Europe for three weeks during our spring vacation via Eurail is the highlight of my life. We travel to Italy and see the Colosseum, Trevi Fountain, and the Vatican. We visit the Eiffel Tower, the Louvre Museum, the Cathédrale Notre-Dame, and the Arc de Triomphe in France. We even see *Legends of the Fall* at a movie theater, and Brad Pitt is just as cute with subtitles. In Austria, we take a *Sound of Music* tour, and as if that is not exciting enough, we get standing tickets to the Vienna State Opera House. In Amsterdam, we are welcomed with pot brownies at our hostel, and the next day, we visit the Anne Frank House and the red light district. In Germany, we see the Berlin Wall. We spend a few days in the city of Barcelona before finding an adorable bed-and-breakfast in southern Spain by an expansive beach. Each day, we sit lazily on the sand and walk around the cozy town. Each evening, we drink sangria and eat paella for dinner under the stars.

After the three weeks end, I meet Mom, Dad, and Aidan, who have been traveling through Ireland in Cashel Bay in County Galway. We also visit Oughterard, a small town on the banks of the Owenriff River close to the western shore in Connemara, County Galway too. Next, we head to Dromoland Castle, the ancestral home of the O'Briens of Dromoland in County Clare. The stately luxury hotel leaves us speechless, expanding over 450 acres with rolling hills, a golf course, and mesmerizing castle. It is magnificent! After backpacking through Europe, I desperately need my laundry done, but I think, looking back, I just wanted to be able to say that my clothes were washed at a castle!

As we return to the States after studying abroad, my relationship with Robin is hard to nurture because she is in Rhode Island. Back then, we did not have cell phones, texting, or Facebook. My relationship with Mary drifts away a few years after college graduation, but she still holds a dear place in my heart. My heart was closed, and she opened it.

MY FIRST TRUE LOVE

I see him walk through the elevator door as I stand next to my client on the elliptical machine. He has super short brown hair, tan eyes, and a large smile. Mark, my boss of about three weeks, is interviewing him for a personal trainer position. As he gets to the small office at the front of the gym, Matt laughs out loud about something, leaning so far back that I think he might fall, and then stands up straight and slaps the table with a friendly bang—infectious.

After college, I quit my first "adult job" as a production editor in New York City. I worked almost a full year at *Power & Motoryacht* magazine downtown in the Chelsea area. Even though the movies make working for magazines extremely glamorous—think Anne Hathaway in *The Devil Wears Prada*—it was not. It took me a bus, a train, a subway, and a three-block walk to get to my office. I usually arrived with black specks of dirt on my face from the city air. And since I did not have a boat or even like boats and would much rather be on the beach in the sand, it was short-lived. I got certified as an ACSM fitness trainer, and within a month, I was a personal trainer at the Fitness Image in Greenwich, CT. I love to work out, so I think it is a good idea to get paid for it.

"Would you like to get lunch?" Matt asks, exuding confidence with his slight grin and puppy eyes as I put my morning charts away.

"Sure," I say nervously.

We go to M's Deli on Greenwich Avenue. Matt says that he is getting a wrap, and I try to act calm when I order my turkey sandwich on whole wheat bread; however, my heart is beating out of my chest. My eating disorder hates sandwiches. Despises bread. Matt pays for both of our sandwiches so quickly that I do not have time to object.

"Ahh. Thank you," I say perplexed.

Wait, are we on a date?

He drives us to the beach in his red Jeep Cherokee. I feel like I am playing hooky on a school day, even though we are on our lunch break. There is enough sun pulsing through the clouds as we sit down at an old wooden picnic table overlooking the waves.

"I told Mark that you were cute during my interview. He got all flustered and was like 'Ahh, we are all professional here,'" Matt laughs, cocking his head back. "I was like 'Take it easy. It's all good.'" He snickers as my cheeks burn with embarrassment.

So, he thinks I am cute.

"Did you always want to be a personal trainer?" I ask.

"Nah. This is just until I pass my series seven exam," he replies and takes a bite of his grilled chicken and bacon wrap.

"Me too. I think I want to go to graduate school, but I am not sure what for yet," I say, shrugging as I nibble on my sandwich, making sure not to get anything in my teeth.

"I played soccer in college. I was pretty good, so I thought I could help people train."

"I played sports too. Club lacrosse in college. I love to run and work out. Mark is nice so far. So are the other trainers. One of them competes in the Ironman. Have you seen her work out? Hardcore."

"No. Not yet. But I think I know who you are talking about. We should work out together sometime. We can use the studio whenever we want," he says, finishing his Snapple and screwing the lid back on it.

"Sure," I say, even though I like to work out alone. Matt is not aware that I often work out two to three times per day. I hide one half of my sandwich and roll it up in the white wax paper, making it into a ball.

"I'll throw out the garbage," Matt voices, grabbing it from the table and smiling. "We need to get back," he says, glancing at his watch even though I have totally forgotten about work.

"Oh no. We have to get back for our sessions," I respond uneasily.

"I'll get you back in time. Don't worry," he says evenly.

When we get back to the gym, my cheeks are bright pink in the training studio mirror. They are pink from the sun, but I also think I am blushing as he looks up from his client's chart and beams in the mirror at me. Our connection is automatic. Within a week, we go out on our first official date.

• • •

Matt picks me up right on time. I spend an hour getting ready. I blow-dry my hair, which has grown slightly past my shoulders; put on my Clinique eye shadow and blush; and slip a rhinestone bracelet on my wrist. I slide into my favorite tight black suede pants and a ruby-red fitted short-sleeved shirt. It is the first time he will see me out of "workout clothes," and I want his opinion to be favorable. Lastly, I place my pink chocolate lipstick softly onto my lips and smack them together.

"Wow. You have a nice body. I did not know what was going to be underneath all of those T-shirts and warm-up pants you wear to work," he jokes.

"Thanks," I say shyly. I know my body looks good, but I do not want him to say anything because now I feel the pressure to be in this exact body. Always.

I won't eat at dinner tonight. He likes me for my body.

I place the dozen roses he brings me into a glass vase. He helps me with my black wool coat and opens the passenger side door as I take a big step into his Wrangler. We park at the local train station and take the train into New York City. We burst into Central Station, bustling with people on a Saturday night. The throngs of couples, families, and friend groups are loud; however, the noises fade as he grabs my hand while we're walking down the sidewalk to a restaurant nearby. Matt made reservations. He is super simple to talk to. There are no awkward lulls or silences. He looks directly into my eyes, listening intently, really interested in each word I say. He makes me feel like I am the only person in the room.

I order a house salad and grilled fish and move my food around on the plate to look like I am eating. I drink my glass of shiraz, which warms my body on this chilly night. Even though I feel totally at ease with Matt, the wine cancels out any insecurities in my head. Matt also purchased tickets for Carolines comedy club on Broadway. So after dinner, we gently lock hands and walk to the show. The room is dark and intimate. Matt grabs us drinks and leads me to a table in the middle of the room. I can already tell that he likes it front and center. I typically like sitting on the sides for easy getaways, but I roll with it. I do not want to seem difficult, and to be honest, I want to be next to him wherever he sits.

Listening to comedians is one of my favorite things to do. I truly need to laugh out loud each day. Aidan always tells me that if he ever did stand-up, he would want me in the front row because when I laugh it is loud, completely genuine, and I sometimes have a hard time stopping. And despite my anxiety, I do have the ability to find most things funny. I often got "the look" when I broke out in laughter at church as a child, but I also have the gift of laughing so hard that everyone around me laughs too. My brothers hated it because I was notorious for getting away with things. Like the time I sat on our hallway steps, staring at my mom through the cracks in the banister after I got grounded. My punishment was to not go on a trip to the Dominican Republic with Darcy's family, but by the end of the day, I was packing.

The show is hysterical, and I get my laugh fix in for the day. Small white flurries of snow fall lightly from the sky as we get off the train at midnight. Snow was not in the forecast, and it looks beautiful, like we are in a fairy tale.

We fall in love and start officially dating.

COURTING

He adores me. I adore him. He is intense and sweet. He puts me on a pedestal and treats me like a queen. It is the first time I have opened my heart in a romantic relationship, and even though it is scary, it also feels natural. I had multiple boyfriends in high school and college, but this time, I feel my guard dropping.

"It's okay. You don't need to grill," I say as I sit down on his parents' olive-green living room couch after work one evening. The rain is coming down in buckets, but Matt is determined to grill me chicken for my salad.

"Here you go," Matt insists as he presses the remote until *Beverly Hills, 90210* pops on the screen. He sets a TV dinner table comfortably in front of me. He sets down a large bowl of tossed salad with tomatoes and cucumbers, silverware, a napkin, and a water glass.

"Voila," he sings as he places the piping-hot chicken on top of my salad. His yellow windbreaker drips with rain, and he rushes to pull it over his head to hang it up. I watch Brenda and Dylan's love story unfold with each delicious bite.

We stay up late talking at his kitchen counter. We feel electric with energy, barely needing sleep. Near midnight, we each eat a bowl of Great Grains Cranberry Almond Crunch cereal with milk. The sweetness of the cranberries burst in my mouth. Little does Matt know that my eating disorder does not allow me to have this cereal, or any kind for that matter. I feel rebellious—giddy with excitement that I am breaking the rules and liking it. This is unknown territory for me, but with Matt, I feel safe. My smiles become authentic. I feel happy when I am with him.

He quickly becomes my best friend. We already work together, but then we start to do everything together. He quickly realizes that something is not right with me—maybe it is because I only drink protein shakes, protein bars, apples, and salads or that he can find me at our gym late at night sweating profusely on the StairMaster. Often, I go back to the club in the evening to burn more calories. I have the key, so it feels like my own personal gym—not the best-case scenario for someone with obsessive workout tendencies and an eating disorder. He also notices that I cannot get out of bed for my early personal training clients. He often substitutes for me. I click off my alarm and fall back to sleep in seconds. And when I drink, I start crying after the third glass of wine about how fat I am. Matt sees right through me.

Little by little, I let him in.

PROZAC NATION

Matt and I look at each other as we sit in the small waiting room at the Wilkins Center, an outpatient eating disorder treatment center in Greenwich, Connecticut. His eyes look tired, and I have noticed the circles under his eyes darken over the past few weeks. I slowly talked to Matt about my behaviors, which are hard to hide when you spend every waking second with someone. He persuades me to get help. I trust Matt, so I go.

I like Dr. Martin immediately. She speaks loud and clear. She is a blunt and straightforward, take-charge woman with a lot of experience. She is in a larger body, and that makes me feel secure. During the session, she listens attentively as she gnaws at the corner edge of her eyeglasses.

"So, tell me what is going on."

"I have anorexia, binge-purge type, since I was young. I want to get better, but I don't know how. I restrict and then binge and purge or even just purge, like, a snack. I work out like a crazy person. I always feel exhausted. I am super tired. Depressed. Constantly on edge," I utter, feeling Matt's warm hand wrap around mine.

"I went to therapy in college, but it did not help," I continue. "At all."

"Are you suicidal?"

"I have thoughts, but I won't do it."

"Any trauma history?"

"Nope," I answer honestly.

"I am putting you on Prozac," she asserts in a loud voice as she pushes her short, puffy brown hair out of her eyes. "It has had some success with patients with bulimia, not with anorexia. I think it will help. You may have very vivid dreams. Come back in two weeks."

I leave with the prescription in my hands and with a sense of hope.

Maybe I can get better.

Maybe this is not my fate.

Maybe I can be happy.

I fill the script and two days later tell Matt about the most colorful dreams I ever had. It felt like I was in a comic book and the images were bright with highlighter-pink and vibrant, neon-orange hues. And I feel happy. Exuberant. I do not think it is a placebo effect. Prozac makes me feel better. It quiets the chaos in my brain. It softens the symphony. My behaviors do not stop, but I start to feel better.

Matt and I are deeply in love. I love all parts of him. He loves all parts of me. We bring out the best in each other. We laugh so hard that I pee in my pants. We stay up late into the night talking endlessly about random topics. We go to fancy dinners and plays and concerts and parties. We can make any errand an adventure simply because we are together. And at times, the eating disorder is suspended temporarily, and during those times, I feel free. He even loves the parts of myself that I hate—my impulsiveness, my abrupt mood changes, my shutdown episodes, and my self-consciousness. In those moments, Matt is the punching bag.

• • •

"Meredith, c'mon, it's my sister's baby shower."

I know he is right, but at that moment, I can only think about his sister and her friends making fun of my fat, disgusting body. I try on three different dresses. I rip each one of them off with aversion and splay them out on the guest bed in my bedroom, tears streaming down my face.

I am too fat to leave this house.

I am still hot from the scalding shower that I just finished. I feel sweat rolling down my forehead, and my hands feel clammy. I lower the window air conditioner's temperature and stand in front of it naked. I sit down, defeated, my bath towel hanging loosely from my body.

"You can't miss it," he says into the phone. "I want you there."

And I know he does. Months before, Matt and I had attended Conor and Grace's wedding on the Jersey Shore. It was a three-day affair, and Matt was by my side through all of it. The entire weekend was amazing.

"I just can't do it. I cannot leave the house," I sob. "I am too fat to leave this house!"

And just like on so many missed dates, appointments, workdays, and social events, I throw on boxers and an oversized T-shirt and head into my bed. I need to sleep. The thoughts will stop. I sleep all afternoon. I hide from the world.

I keep seeing Dr. Martin religiously, but my restricting and purging remain out of control. Overall, I feel better, but stopping the behaviors feels impossible. Monumental. They are a part of me. Sticky like honey. Glue. Cement. Prison shackles.

FALLING IN LOVE

We have the type of love that if Matt told me he murdered someone, I would grab a shovel and help him bury the body in the backyard.

"Darcy, Kelly, Amelia, Maggie, Grace, and Beth," I say out loud as I count the bridesmaids that I plan to have at my wedding. I am three pinot grigios in and decide that it is especially important to tell my work staff that Matt and I are going to get married one day. One of our clients is having a garden party at her expansive Greenwich home. As Matt plays pool with our coworkers on the beautifully decorated patio, I talk to the woman in the lush garden filled with too many types of flowers to count. I wear a black-and-cream Benetton dress that only fits when I am at my lowest weight. It hangs to the floor and wraps tightly around my small body. My straight, bleach-blonde hair is cut right above my shoulders, and my skin is sun kissed from my time at the beach. I walk over to give Matt a hug.

"I love you, sweetie."

"And I love you." Matt hugs me back and holds me tight, his cue stick dangling in his hand. He wears a plaid, short-sleeved button-down shirt that is tight around his biceps due to his slight obsession with bicep curls. He wears perfectly pressed khakis.

"I cannot wait to marry you," he whispers in my ear.

My smile is bigger than my face. Bliss.

We sit down to a beautifully catered dinner. I pick at my salad. The wine bottles empty one by one. The summer breeze is delicate. Perfect. We hold hands during the dessert that I skip. The alcohol keeps the bad thoughts away.

• • •

School centers me. Roots me to the ground. I apply to an allied health studies master's program at the College of Mount Saint Vincent in New York, and I am accepted. I know school will help me to feel productive and, therefore, worthy. Even though I am sick, there is a part of me that knows I will come out the other side. I have this gnawing pull to help people.

I must recover, right? This cannot be my life.

Matt passes his series seven exam and starts to work for a large financial company. Matt's goal is to have a lucrative career and financially take care of us. We both want children, and we both want me to stay home to raise them. Our lives start to move forward, but my eating disorder has other ideas. My mood changes abruptly. I am content and then, seconds later, flooded with irritation. I am excited, happy, telling jokes, and out of nowhere, I feel completely numb, detached. I feel energetic and then completely depleted.

Matt is full of compassion, but over time, he wears down. He desperately wants to take care of me. I want that too, but my eating disorder pushes him away.

How can he love me?

I am unlovable.

I don't deserve to take space up in this world.

I want to die.

• • •

I examine my flat stomach in the mirror as I pinch together minuscule pieces of fat with my thumb and forefinger. I press so hard that bright-red welts form around my stomach and thighs. My hair is soaking wet from the hot shower I just took, bordering on scorching. It is Friday night, and despite us both being exhausted from school and work, Matt and I have dinner reservations.

I sit on the edge of my bed and take a deep breath. I have already purchased a new shirt to wear, which helps to lower my anxiety and reduce the possibility of trying on multiple outfits. My black pants from the Limited lie on my guest bed. I bought three pairs of them and put on the pair still hot from the dryer, so they are perfectly fitted on my hips—no wrinkles and impeccably straight across my midriff. I pull the purple shirt over my head, and it flawlessly stretches over my skin like sweat, glued in place. I slide the shimmering ruby-and-diamond ring Matt gave me for Christmas on my middle finger and give a final smile into my mirror.

"Beep. Beep."

I slip my black wool winter jacket over my body. I grab my pocketbook, open the front door, and see Matt standing at the passenger door, smiling. As I reach the car, he opens the door and holds my hand as I sit down. He gave away his Jeep and bought a Lexus.

"There you go, my lady."

"Why thank you, my love." I nod gently and slide into the leather seat.

Thirty minutes later, we sit at the small bar of the restaurant, waiting for our table to be ready. As soon as the cold white wine hits my lips, I let out a deep breath—my marker to let go of the perfectionism, the criticism, the despair. The elixir of relief. All my self-hate drains from my overexercised, exhausted, trying-to-be-perfect body.

"How's school, honey?" Matt asks.

"I really love it. My classes are so interesting. I think I will be good at helping people," I say, taking a large gulp.

"People will be lucky to get help from you. I am glad you like it."

"How is your new job?" I ask, knowing that Matt is stressed but hides it so I do not worry. He never wants me to worry.

"I am trying to get leads. I just cold-call people all day," Matt says. "My boss is okay. I'll get him to like me."

"Oh, I know you will, honey," I chuckle.

"Now, let's talk about the weekend. We are going to Conor and Grace's tomorrow, right? And what do we have on Sunday?"

The maître d interrupts our conversation and leads us to a back table of the small Italian restaurant. I order a salad with dressing on the side and the halibut, well done. Matt orders a Caesar salad and the steak. Matt orders a bottle of red wine for both of us.

• • •

"You cannot love me," I yell, intoxicated from the wine and multiple vodka drinks I had at the local bar after dinner.

"Mer, calm down."

"Don't touch me!" I scream as Matt lays his hand on my thigh, trying to shift me back to reality. I scowl and rip his hand away. I jump up, and in seconds, I am across his bedroom and against the wall, hands up, guarding me against his love.

How can he love me?

I am broken.

I am gross.

I am fat.

I fall asleep in my clothes. I wake up with Matt lying by my side. We have played the make-up and break-up game for months, even years. Our love is true, but my eating disorder drives him away, and this time, I lose him.

INTO THE RABBIT HOLE

E nding my relationship with Matt is like a death, but I do not properly grieve. I push the feelings down and throw myself into anything but feeling. I write my master's thesis on how dialectical behavior therapy (DBT), a new type of psychotherapy that helps people regulate their emotions more effectively, can help treat those with eating disorders. I continue training clients during the day and attend school at night.

One evening, I arrive home late from school. My parents sit in the den. Mom is wrapped in a white terry cloth robe, watching TV. Dad wears flannel pajama bottoms and a T-shirt as he sorts through his mail. My mom has the job of recording *Beverly Hills, 90210* and *Melrose Place* on our VCR each Wednesday night from 8 p.m. to 10 p.m. After school, I stay up late watching the shows back to back. My escape from reality.

"Hey, Mom. Hey, Dad," I yell as I open the front door. "I'm going to go upstairs to watch my shows," I say quickly as I place my heavy backpack in the foyer hallway. I smell fresh fish, tomatoes, and mushrooms floating from the kitchen. This is a safe meal that Mom fixes for me on school nights.

"Hey, Mer, I am so sorry, but I forgot to tape your shows," she says as she gets up from the couch and heads into the kitchen, opening the oven as the timer rings. She pulls out the large Pyrex dish with an oven mitt and places it on the stove. She grabs a lemon wedge and squeezes it over the fish.

"Haha. Funny, Ma," I say, giving her a quick kiss on the cheek.

"No, I really forgot, Mer," she exclaims, pushing her now dyed-blonde hair out of her eyes with the back of her hand.

"You must be kidding."

"I am not."

"You're not?" I ask loudly. Large, wet cartoon tears fill my eyes. *I cannot believe this is happening to me.*

"This cannot be happening," I say, crying.

"Mer, it is a TV show."

"I know, Ma." She is right. My mom made a simple mistake, but it sends me into a tailspin. My shows are my respite—liberation from the painful thoughts. It is solace throwing myself into the worlds of others—real or not.

• • •

After I graduate, I start working for a start-up health and wellness center at Stamford Hospital in Connecticut. The most exciting part is that I can move out! I rent a large one-bedroom apartment with a cute back deck and huge closets in the heart of town, blocks away from bars, restaurants, and stores. My parents buy me a cute wooden kitchen table with four decorative white spindle legs that I can expand or collapse. They also buy me a large walnut desk and bookcase, a queen-sized bed, and a blue-and-white-striped couch. I fill the rest of my apartment with stuff from Ikea. I meet people at work, form a friend group, and feel like I am finally paving my path forward. I get a small handle on behaviors and start seeing a therapist regularly. I detect a part of me that wants to change.

My school alarm goes off again. I loved my first master's program, but if I want to help people, then I need a clinical license. I get accepted into Fordham University Graduate School of Social Service, another Jesuit school. I quit my job after one year and start school with a vengeance. That September, my first nephew, Liam, is born, and holding him in my arms after waiting at the hospital for forty-eight hours is incredible. Something shifts in my body, and momentarily, my obsession with my weight fades. I have a nephew!

I will be the best aunt to you! I'll spoil you silly.

I start to waitress at a local family restaurant, Long Ridge Tavern. The family takes me in, and I feel a community grow around me much like when I was in Ireland. I attend classes full-time, attend my internships, and take on waitressing shifts to pay my rent. My parents and family visit me at the restaurant. My favorite nights are when Liam shows up. His smile immediately cuts my stress in half.

I notice that I am drinking too much. I start to burn the candle on both ends. I stay up all night to write a ten-page paper, and the next night, I go out with friends. It is like I do not want to miss out on anything, but as my sleep dwindles, the eating disorder behaviors percolate.

After two years, I graduate. I complete my social work hours, pass my exam, and receive my coveted license in the mail. Hallelujah! I am officially a licensed clinical social worker.

Noah, my second nephew, is born. I am so mesmerized by his adorability that I do not hear Conor asking me to be his godmother. I guess I said yes, but days later, when Conor makes a comment about me being his godmother, my eyes widen, and I feel completely honored and surprised.

I am going to be the best godmother to you.

• • •

Liam and I have our first official sleepover. He is three and cannot wait to get to Aunt Mer-Mer's, the nickname he invented when he started to talk. It is a crisp autumn day in October. The leaves have changed to bright gold and ginger colors. There is an exuberant energy in the air. As Liam walks through my apartment door, rolling his child-sized suitcase and his favorite blanket on his left arm, time stops. It is in these moments I know that my life will get better. It is in these moments that I know happiness exists. His cheeks, his voice, his hands, his eyelashes. He is precious and I can connect with the joy. My tangled brain temporarily unwinds. My obsession with calories, weight, and exercise drift away.

"Okay. So, put this on," I say, handing him the new red smock as he sits at the head of the kitchen table, balancing on one knee. His cheeks are so full and adorable that it looks like he has marbles in his mouth. "I have a matching one for me too," I say, tying a knot in the back of mine. The table is covered with newspaper, paintbrushes, and paint.

"I can paint all of these?" Liam asks, pointing at the miniature pumpkins.

"Yes, bud. These are all for you," I say, wrapping my arm around his back and shuffling his thick blond hair with my fingers.

"This is the first activity of the weekend. We can also decorate cupcakes, go to the park, have milkshakes at the diner, and watch Star Wars," I list, going through the sleepover itinerary.

"This is so fun!" Liam exclaims, taking the white paint and smearing it over the largest one. "I am going to make one for Mom, Dad, and Noah."

"Perfect!" I bring over small bowls of water for him to wash his brushes. "Liam, do you know how precious you are?"

"I think so," he replies and smiles from cheek to cheek. He may never truly understand how important he is to me. That over the next twenty-four hours, my eating disorder takes a backseat because of him—because I want to be the best aunt I can be.

. . .

My drinking continues, and I decide that I need a new geographical location. A new start. New people. New job. Maybe a new me? I leave Connecticut and venture to New Jersey, a few towns away from my beach house. I get a job as a supervisor at the Children's Mobile Response program at CPC Behavioral Healthcare. I finally put my license to good use. I rent a cozy condo right on Shark River and desperately want a clean start. I think all the sadness will stay in Connecticut, but it follows me. In a short amount of time, my family has successive, unfortunate incidents, and the sorrow is a robust punch to my gut. The grief crashes down on me like an avalanche. It eats me up inside, and I can think of nothing else. The distress is too big. I feel out of control.

My restriction slips in like an old friend stopping by for coffee. And this time, I do not break up the cycle with binges and purges. Restriction is my escape. And I am damn good at it. The food rules I creatively develop give me a false sense of control. The list of foods that I allow myself to eat gets smaller and smaller. I bring a bag full of apples to a ten-hour work shift. For dinner, I eat frozen vegetables by the bagful, filling up my shopping cart so high that they barely all fit in my freezer. My treat each day is a Starbucks grande extra hot soy latte that I sip slowly and meticulously, savoring each drop.

I shop excessively. A trembling excitement engulfs me as my body size changes dramatically. My once size-C breasts shrink. I feel childlike, but also like the master of my own body. Ironically, I buy new clothes, but most of them sit in my closet with the tags still on, as I choose to wear baggy sweatshirts and sweatpants. The smaller my body gets, the bigger I feel. I stand on the toilet in my bathroom in front of a large mirror, looking for flaws. Obsessed. Hypercritical.

I am ravaged with fault-finding thoughts. I spend most of my time sleeping because it's the only time I can turn off my irrational brain and withdraw from the emotional pain temporarily. I am in my mid-thirties, single, and sad. There is no reason to live.

. . .

One morning, I wake up in a panic, late for work. I missed both of my alarms. The night before, I had gone out drinking and blacked out. I thought I had walked home from the bar, but I don't remember coming home. I call out sick from work and dial my mother's number.

Beep. Beep.

"Mom?"

"Yes, Mer?"

I stare at my face intently in my bathroom mirror. It is like I want to witness myself say the words out loud.

"I think I want to kill myself."

My mom clicks over abruptly to end her other phone call. Four hours later, my mother, father, and I meet with my current therapist. I was exploring my binge-drinking habits, but I conveniently kept most of the eating disorder stuff hidden.

Aidan flies in from California. I guess I have officially scared my family. Aidan and I sit closely on the couch. Mom sits on the love seat, and Dad sits on a brown leather chair. My voice is timid. Aidan takes more of a lead and shouts at my parents.

"If we don't do something, she is going to die. She has had this eating disorder for years. We have to freaking do something!" Aidan yells with a bite to his voice.

Sometimes Aidan's anger worries me, but at this moment, he feels like my knight in shining armor. He is using his voice because mine is too meek to speak. The words spin in my head with such velocity that I am unable to express anything. I feel my heartbeat thumping vociferously in my ears and detach. My body feels unreal, split off.

"Maybe Matt was right," my mom utters.

"What? Who? My Matt?" I ask, confused.

"Yes. Your Matt. After you broke up, he met with us."

"He met with you? Without me? Why?"

"Yes. He told us that if we did not get you help for your eating disorder, you would die."

FAMILY THERAPY

We pull up to an old Victorian house with a cranberry-red door at Reckless Place in Red Bank. A large, unkempt porch adorns the front, and two rocking chairs sway in the wind. The wood is splintered by the doorway. I feel suffocated going up the narrow spiral staircase to the second floor as I follow my parents.

I let out a deep breath as we reach the light and airy waiting room. The sun peeks through the blinds, and dust particles sit still in the air. There is a mini refrigerator filled with cold, pocket-sized waters. I grab one even though I can only drink them at room temperature. The cold ones make me shiver. Now I will have a chill for the rest of the day, but I need something in my hands to keep them from shaking.

"Water?" I ask.

"No thanks, Mer," my parents say in unison.

We are finally giving family therapy a try. I am desperate to convey my story, but when I try, my voice box fills with sludge. Nothingness. My thoughts become jumbled and disorganized. Maybe a therapist could be my voice and tell my parents that I did not choose to have an eating disorder, but I also need a lot of support to get better.

"Hello. Welcome," the therapist says.

We each introduce ourselves. My mom eyes her up and down, and I feel the judgments secrete from her skin. My mom does not like my individual therapist, and she has her reservations about this one too. My individual therapist is loud. My mom does not do loud. My therapist tends to sigh and brush her hand through her curly brown hair during sessions. My mom does not do the whole flustered thing.

I sit on a large maroon leather couch, the kind you sort of fall into and feel clumsy as you try to balance on it without success. My mom sits next to me and grabs the arm to stabilize herself. Dad sits to my right in the floral, light-blue club chair. The therapist sits to the left of my mother in a brown leather chair. The office has three large windows, and the sunlight creeps in.

"So, welcome."

My dad takes the lead.

"We are here to help our daughter, who has an eating disorder," my dad says flatly. "And she is losing weight and not getting better." He articulates each word slowly. "Something has to happen."

Gone is the teddy bear. "Work" Dad appears. This is all business. I place my untouched water bottle on the coffee table.

Words muddle in my head. I try to speak. I have so much to say. The words come up through my throat and sit in my mouth. Stifled. The room closes in on me, and my brain feels like mush. Everything slows down. I watch the words coming out of my dad's mouth and I am unable to register them. I disconnect. I am thrust into a haze. Frozen. I cry, tears falling from my eyes onto my cheeks. I do not have the words, but I hope my behavior is enough to show my anguish and the trauma of having an eating disorder for so many years.

"Those pants look too big on you," my therapist chimes as we get up to leave. My Express gray-and-white-pinstriped pants sag in the back.

I smirk, hopping back to reality.

Weight is my sole identifier.

And we never go back.

CHARITY GALA

"**Y**ou have such a cute figure," the boutique associate says in an envious voice as I try on dresses. "You can wear anything and look good."

My hands jitter, probably from the two large coffees I had for breakfast. My focus is blurry. I skipped lunch, of course. I am out shopping for a dress for a charity event that Grace is hosting for breast cancer awareness.

Eighteen months prior, Grace was diagnosed with breast cancer. It was a shock to her and the rest of our family. She had a double mastectomy, chemotherapy, radiation, and reconstructive surgery. Supporting the cancer community helps her to continue her healing journey. Years before, mom was diagnosed with colon cancer, but I denied her illness. Looking back, I completely rejected reality. The thought of losing her was too painful, so I pretended that it did not exist. I grabbed on to my eating disorder like a life preserver and pushed the feelings down.

See, all your willpower is paying off. Now you can go into a small boutique and put on anything and it will fit!

"Gorgeous," another associate says as I try on a Kelly-green knee-length dress that hits my shoulders in just a way that my collarbone pops.

You can never eat again. You need to stay skinny.

"Oh yes. It's perfect."

I stare in the mirror. It drapes over my body. There are no curves to pull at the fabric. My breasts are slight. My hips narrow. My stomach is hollow. Empty.

"I have just the dress for you. We just got it in. We did not even put it out yet," she says.

After two minutes, she shimmies the plastic wrap over the short, fitted, dark-green dress. The bodice resembles a tuxedo with silver sparkles and buttons. Spaghetti straps hold the dress together.

That is not going to fit me.

I slide the dress on. The zipper closes with room to spare.

"It was made for you," the saleswoman boasts.

Despite the $500 price tag and the fact that it is way too fancy for the event, I purchase it, along with the other green dress that is more appropriate for the gala.

One week later, I drive up to Conor and Grace's home for the event in New York. It is a blistering-cold night. The frigid air goes right through my wool jacket, black cashmere scarf, gloves, green dress, and emaciated body. The best part of the night is hugging my two adorable nephews. They light up my life. Their smiles lift me out of my depression. Having nephews gives me proof that my heart can literally expand with love and beauty and innocence. In my darkest hour, they are my beacons of light.

"Hey, cutie patooties," I say and snuggle their small, precious bodies into mine.

• • •

Multiple small tables adorned with pink covers fill the cocktail hour. A large white table sits with hour d'oeuvres. Staff in black-and-white suits pass around finger foods as people mingle. I stare at the different platters, knowing that none of it will pass my lips.

If I have one, maybe I will lose all control, and if that happens, I'll gain weight and my whole life will fall apart.

The host of the night is a woman in remission from cancer. Her message is to fight cancer with humor. She entertains us with a few good jokes as she starts off her bit. Some of her jokes miss the mark as the evening continues. My father looks down at his watch and shakes his head, like *Is this for real?* I smile intently at her with my full attention, feeling uncomfortable to my core. *You can do this,* I think as the audience laughs uncomfortably. I feel like I am watching a guest on *Card Sharks,* and I want her to get the ace.

"Chain . . . chain . . . chain . . . chain of fools. Chain . . . chain . . . chain . . . chains of fools," the three-girl a cappella group sings with utmost gusto. They are so into the moment that it comes across as a joke, but no, they are serious. The deep bravado of their voices scares me a little, and I sit up straighter in my chair. I laugh out loud. I am not good at hiding my laughter, and tonight is no exception. I try to stifle my giggles. Conor's face fills with a large grin as he tilts his head, saying without words *What is going on here?*—which makes me laugh louder. I have a flashback to church.

At dinner, I ask for the lemon sauce to be on the side. I take two bites of the halibut and gnaw on the string beans. I order hot tea to help warm up the chill in my body. Lately, I am cold to my core. I have the black pashmina scarf covering my shoulders, and I use my white cloth napkin as an extra layer on my lap.

As soon as I walk through the back door of Conor's house, a wave of relief washes over me. I quickly change into my flannel pajamas and put on two pairs of socks. I notice the daybed in the guest room is covered with a sheet, blanket, and two comforters—one red, one blue-and-green plaid—in preparation of my staying over. It is a running joke in my family that I am always cold, but at this moment, I know it is because of malnutrition. Not funny.

I congratulate Grace on a wonderful gala and give her a kiss and a hug goodnight. I give Conor a kiss and a hug too, knowing they have had a trying period where their lives turned upside down. By this time, my toes and fingers are numb. I jump into bed, desperate for warmth. I wrap my legs around each other, determined to add more body heat. I clench my hands and shove them in between my legs. I tense my feet, praying that it will slightly thaw the frozen feeling.

"Conor," I whisper. I hear shuffling from the den.

"Conor," I say more forcefully. Minutes go by; however, it feels like hours. My veins feel like they are filled with ice.

"Conor!" I yell. Nothing. Still nothing.

I hear a low knock on the door.

"Mer, do you need something?" Conor asks as he opens the door slowly and peeks in. Conor is always respectful of my privacy, probably because we did not have much growing up.

"I'm so cold," I say. My lips tremble.

Within minutes, Conor brings in two extra pairs of socks and two more comforters from the TV room. I grab the socks and strategically put them on over my pajama bottoms to trap in the heat. Conor places the comforters on top of my fragile body. I bury my head way under the covers and hopelessly wait for relief. My body tightens. Desperate. Hold on. Hold on.

RAGE

"**Y**ou are such an easy client," my current therapist says
midway through our session. "I have all of these tough
clients, and you just know what to do. It is such a relief."

"Yep. I guess so," I say, confused. I am not sure what to say for the
second half of our session. I do not want to seem difficult. Despite
going to therapy twice a week, seeing my nutritionist, trying family
therapy, and going to an eating disorder support group, nothing is
getting better. Things are actually getting worse.

I smile during the rest of our session and use humor to deflect
any real attempt to heal. My people-pleaser button goes off. I play the
part of the "good" client. I will be accommodating. But at the same
time, this feeling keeps coming up. And like always, I shove it down.
The feeling, however, keeps brewing in my body.

What the hell am I feeling?

Oh my gosh, I think it is rage.

PART 2

TREATMENT

COLUMBIA DAY TREAT-MENT PROGRAM

I sit despondently in the tiny waiting room at the Columbia Day Program for eating disorder treatment in New York City. I suppressed the rage that I felt in my last therapy session immediately, but I reluctantly agreed to attend an intake for a higher level of care. I guess I can fool my therapist, but not my parents.

It is a chilly day in November 2009, and midtown is bustling. I wear dark skinny jeans and a pale-gray sweater with red trim. I cannot feel the jean material on my waist as I sit, so today is going to be a good day—and by good, I mean holding on desperately to a breakable thread, my weight my only valuable identifier. My ashy blonde hair is thrown back into a ponytail. My straight, blunt bangs barely touch my naturally extra-long black eyelashes.

"Marilyn?"

A woman with a dark-brown bob reaches out to shake my hand. It looks like she just came from a meeting and is overworked. Unfocused.

Marilyn? I think. *How does she not know my name?*

Every cell in my body was against coming today, and she can't even get my name right? I would become fixated on this detail, but I am too numb to care.

"Meredith," I say, smiling, my people-pleaser persona jumping up to the plate. I don't want to be here, but I certainly want people to like me. We go into a small corner office with no windows. Long vertical filing cabinets line the pasty white back wall. The scale sits next to a small wooden desk covered with manilla folders, like an intruder ready to attack. I will not let her weigh me until I take off my gray suede boots. And my socks.

Can I take off my clothes? My socks? My hair tie? Am I even sick enough to be here? I should just leave.

"What brings you here today?"

"Um . . . I have anorexia and I am not getting better."

"I see."

"I rarely eat. When I eat, I purge. I only leave the house to go to the gym and Starbucks."

"Go on."

"I see a therapist, nutritionist, and psychiatrist in Red Bank, New Jersey, where I live. I keep losing weight. And my parents think I need more care. I think they are being dramatic."

I answer as my lithe body shifts uncomfortably in the wooden chair. My depression anchors my body down. My mind drifts to the scale that stands out like a unicorn.

You are a fat piece of shit.

"The PHP meets four to five days per week. This includes a primary therapist, therapy groups, and meal support. We offer lunch four days a week and dinner two days a week."

Hell no. I'm not fucking eating!

She's jealous.

She wishes she had my superpower.

I continue to half smile, but it is hard to fake. Alarms burst in my body.

I am not safe. This is a trap.

"I need to weigh you."

I take off my boots and socks. I breathe deeply as I stand and cautiously walk the few steps across the office.

Please be low. Please be low.

The tension in my body drops as she shimmies the dial to the left and then to the left even more.

Lower is better. Lower is better.

"Your weight is low."

No shit, Sherlock.

I grin. Just like I want it.

The intake is brief. I am not sure what I expect. Maybe more of a reaction? A concerned sigh? An intense plea? I told her that I qualify for inpatient treatment at Princeton Hospital and am waiting for a bed to become available. She seems disinterested.

I nod to my parents as I reenter the waiting room. They have driven from Westchester to be with me. My dad immediately stands up, taking charge. My mom remains seated, anxiety stricken.

"So, what is it going to be?" my dad inquires, wanting to know my exact start date.

"Meredith has all of the information and plans to call me back if she is interested in starting."

I imagine my parents are surprised that I did not invite them into the intake. Even at the age of thirty-five, I freeze at the thought of disappointing them. My mind starts to get loud. A wave of sadness crashes over me.

Did I let my father down? Was I being mean? Cruel? Did I do something wrong? I am a terrible child.

A heavy discomfort weighs me down. I want to be in my bed, under my sheets, my comforter protecting me. I do not know how to navigate this world.

Can everything please stop?!

"I'll think about it," I tell them, knowing my answer is no.

I hug them both tightly. I drive for ten minutes and let out a full exhale. Now I am alone with my anorexia for the whole weekend. No person or program is going to take it away from me. I escaped the threat. My eating disorder is safe. So why do I feel so alone?

FIRST DAY OF TREATMENT

My dad's passenger car door feels like a thousand pounds. I push it open. It goes almost halfway and then thrusts back. Now the door feels even heavier. I'm surprised that I get out. Hell, I am surprised that I even agreed to this. I stare up at the building in front of me—51 West 51st Street, Suite 340, Columbia Day Program. I am running a few minutes late because I insisted that we stop at Starbucks for a morning coffee. Every piece of my body is against treatment, but the coffee is my security blanket. There is also holiday traffic since Christmas is one-week away.

I knock lightly on the treatment room door. The leader lets me in; however, I learn quickly that lateness is frowned upon. I guess they are teaching responsibility—after five minutes, the door locks. I grab an empty chair. I wear black velvet sweatpants with a matching hoodie from Old Navy. I purchased one in black, navy blue, and eighties-eyeshadow blue—all the colors that were available. The pants have a drawstring and I tie it loosely around my waist. Over that, I wear a puffy black winter jacket that, when zipped, covers my entire face. A black wool scarf hides my neck. Black wool gloves warm my fingers. I keep my jacket on.

I am not planning to stay long.

I wrap my arms tightly around my waist to serve as protection from the other clients sitting in clunky metal chairs formed into a perfect square. Two wooden side tables sit in the corners, each with a green plant (I am not sure if they are real or fake) and a box of tissues. There are no windows. A man fiddles with his fingers and his leg hops up and down, making a soft pitter-patter sound. A woman stares absently. One older woman blots the tears rolling down her face with a tissue. Some clients are more animated, perhaps feeling elevated from their medication or finally feeling comfortable after a few weeks of the program. I sit paralyzed. My depression glues me to my seat. My body is rigid, my face like stone.

"Uh . . . my name is Meredith. I have anorexia. Today is my first day," I say, poker-faced.

I am quiet for the rest of the group. It is two and a half hours long, and we take a ten-minute break halfway through.

A woman with curly red shoulder-length hair starts the second half.

"I am depressed. My boyfriend thought he could fly during a manic episode and jumped out of our fifth-floor walk-up apartment. He died."

My stomach flips inside.

My body stays still.

● ● ●

So, I start the partial hospitalization program (PHP) with a devout unwillingness to recover. My weight is the lowest it has been. I take a leave of absence from my job. I go on disability, but I know my parents can financially help me—a safety net most people do not have. My grand plan is to go to the program during the week and then undo the program on the weekends. *Genius strategy*, I think. I often think my ideas are brilliant.

Like the time I got a postcard in the mail announcing that the Saucony sneaker I wore to workouts was being discontinued. I immediately panicked. I quickly did the math—I needed four pairs of sneakers per year since I bought a new pair every three months. I settled on six years for the time frame. By year seven, I would be well enough to tolerate the distress of wearing a different sneaker. I ordered twenty-five pairs online (one extra, just in case).

• • •

Lunch is next. I walk slowly up the staircase to the third floor. I pause at the door and, for a split second, think about making a run for it. This is voluntary treatment. I can leave at any time. But then I think of my nephews and place my sneaker tenuously into the room and grab a seat. Four of us sit around a square white Formica table. Minutes later, the clinician, Susan, walks in holding a large brown paper bag in her arms. Her long, straight brown hair is tucked behind her ears.

"Hey, girls," she says.

"Hey," some of the girls reply. Others stare down at the table, perhaps terrified that it is mealtime. She removes plastic containers from the bag and places one in front of each of us. She does this casually, removing plastic silverware and paper napkins too. My anxiety swells, and I hear my heart beating out of my chest. I imagine the other girls can hear it thumping. Again, my instinct is to run from the room, but I stay motionless. Her quick movements and slight head nod signal that it is time to eat. Inside the container sits a burrito filled with chicken, brown rice, and vegetables. A glob of sour cream lies on top.

"I'm not eating the sour cream," Dara, a girl with a porcelain face and long, curly blonde hair quivers, holding back tears. Her skin and hair are so perfect that she looks like a model. I see the food sitting there.

Isn't there some introduction class I need to attend before I just start eating?

My eating disorder is in charge, and all it sees is a heaping pile of calories.

"It is time to eat. You have thirty minutes. The goal is 80 to 100 percent of your meal."

The girls and I stare at each other, waiting to see who will be the bravest and take the first bite.

Is she fucking serious?

I want to cry and scream. I want to run back to my condominium in New Jersey. I want to be anywhere but here. But I am also one hell of a rule follower. It goes back to me always sitting in the front row of class and getting my homework done as soon as I got home. Teacher's pet. I need people to like me.

One girl starts to unwrap the white paper from her burrito, giving us permission to do the same. Soon, all of us have the burritos out. One girl takes a bite. Then another.

"I cannot eat this," Dara crackles, tears streaming down her dewy face. She grabs a brown napkin and blows her nose.

There is no way I am going to eat the burrito either, but I do not trust anyone to actually say it out loud. I keep my head down and hover into myself, expanding the space between me and the other girls. It is in that moment that I decide to just keep everything inside. Do what I must do and then get the hell out of this place. I am completely cut off. Expressionless. Blank. Utterly confused.

Where am I again?

How did I get here?

I feel like a robot being programmed by a computer.

After I push the sour cream to the side with a fork, I take a bite. The morsel feels dry in my mouth, and it is excruciating to swallow. I feel it sit in my stomach like a rock.

I am going to gain weight.

The girls and I eat in silence. From time to time, we look up with nervous glances, looking for some solidarity. I take one bite at a time and, after the thirty minutes, I finish about half the burrito. I have no idea how I get it down my throat. I would like to say that part of me is scared to continue to live a life that is so meaningless and hollow. But at that moment, I do it for my nephews. In the beginning, I solely choose to live for them.

• • •

After lunch, I sprint out of the building, frantically looking for a Starbucks, which I am surprised is not on every street corner. My legs pick up the pace down the long city sidewalks, my head bouncing from side to side. My breath sighs loudly as soon as I see the green sign from a distance. I am uncomfortably full, but I need to follow my daily ritual of drinking my grande soy latte, extra hot. Typically, I go to Starbucks completely empty of food, and coffee is my reward. I sip it very slowly and try to read, extending my daily outing since it is my only one besides therapy and the gym. Today, my thoughts are too chaotic to read.

I ate half of a freaking burrito!

This Starbucks is smaller than the one in Red Bank and I feel claustrophobic. But ritual is control, and I need order to distract me from my fullness. My breaths are heavy and quick, but I take sip after sip. I want to shriek. I want to cry and huddle up in the fetal position on the dirty floor. Maybe then someone would carry me to safety. Maybe then they would find me a good hiding space behind a dumpster, and I could stay there forever, alone with my eating disorder.

I reluctantly go back to the program and finish the last group session with the nutritionist. The people pleaser in me wins. As I sit through the group, I feel foggy and try to contemplate how my life got to this point. At 5:45 p.m., Mom and Dad pick me up.

"How did it go?" my mom asks.

"I had to eat a burrito with sour cream," I say, annoyed as I shimmy onto the tan leather seats of my dad's Volvo, bursting with exhaustion.

Can everyone stop caring?!

CHRISTMAS

The holly-red placemats and napkins with gold angel napkin holders line each table setting in our dining room. The stained glass nativity scene that I made from a kit as a young girl sits in the center. The artificial tree glistens in the living room with balls, decorations, and multicolored lights. Underneath is my maternal grandmother's Christmas village that consists of an ice-skating rink; a ski mountain made of thick cotton with tiny skiers; and small colorful homes that shine bright due to the bulbs in the back. It is Christmas Eve, and my family and cousins are here in Westchester to celebrate the holiday.

Christmas Eve is one of my favorite holidays, but this year is different. I completed a few days at my program, but my hope is low, almost depleted. Instead, I fixate on obsessive thoughts about my body. I purchased a new maroon dress for the occasion and am preoccupied with my collarbone—continually looking in the mirror to make sure it pops out prominently. I think it represents my suffering, my anguish. Maybe my family will finally see that I am hurting and put me out of my misery. Just take me out back and shoot me.

I eat string beans for dinner. Yes, string beans. While my family passes around dishes of lemon chicken, grilled salmon, buttered carrots, and twice-baked potatoes, I stick to my "safe foods." When two Christmas platters filled with multiple types of homemade cookies are brought out for dessert, I look around, distracted.

You are not allowed to eat a cookie.

When Mom places a tray of cream puffs with confectionary sugar on top on the table and the sweetness glides in the air, my eating disorder taps me on the shoulder aggressively.

No cream puffs either.

At the end of the night, we start the ritual of putting out the gifts in each person's personal spot. My space is the yellow club chair by the fireplace. Liam and Noah take above, below, and around the piano bench. Conor and Grace use the space against the dining room entrance wall. Aidan and Beth's gifts go on the other club chair, closest to the tree, and my parents use my dad's brown leather chair as their gift spot. I start to feel some joy as I head to the basement, grabbing shopping bags stuffed with presents. I carefully place the gifts in the correct spots. I notice a large rectangular box laced up with a shiny bow in my area, and I wonder what it is. I smile, placing the gifts that I bought for my family in their designated locations.

I sleep soundly, and I do feel a jolt of excitement waking up on Christmas day. I have flashbacks of me, Conor, and Aidan sitting on the top step, anxiously awaiting our cue from our parents to come downstairs to see if Santa came. And like clockwork, Dad shouts, "Oh no. Santa did not come this year. No gifts this year. Too bad!" as we dash down the stairs to our living room that resembles a department store, overflowing with stockings and presents. I will never forget the year Santa got me a yellow kitchen play set and a Betty Crocker oven.

On Christmas day, I eat an apple. I bring it with me in a holiday napkin in my black pocketbook to my aunt Dana and uncle Pete's house in the next town. No part of me thinks it is odd to stash apples in my purse. Sometimes I notice that my purse is unusually heavy, and I find an apple or two at the bottom of it. I try and connect to my family members, but my brain feels like a muddled mess.

Months later, I go on to my mother's Shutterfly account to look at pictures. There is only one picture of me. I am in the background, sitting in an oversized chair next to my mom. The picture is blurry. My face is ashen, haggard. I wear an oversized black cotton sweater wrapped around my body and black leggings. My eyes are dead.

That year, there are no family pictures, a yearly tradition. No pictures of me and my siblings near the Christmas tree or by the fireplace adorned with our stockings that my grandmother sewed by hand. No extended family picture of us saying "Cheese!" or "Merry Christmas!" as one of us tries our best to get everyone in the photo. Maybe my family wanted to pretend this version of me did not exist—that without photos, we could skip Christmas this year.

CONTROL

I think I am in complete control. No part of me thinks I am out of control. None. Zip. Zilch. I think that if I can just get to that "magical number," I will be happy. I will be completely satisfied. I will finally find some peace. I will then eat. I promise.

But anorexia is insidious. There is always more to lose. There is always one more rule. It is never content. It is never placated. There is always something to change, to dwell on, or to obsess about. The more weight I lose, the more isolated I become. I often imagine that in my thinness, I will have this booming social life, my confidence will surge, and I will feel indestructible. The reality is that I spend most nights home in baggy sweats, sequestered and alone, bodychecking and feeling dejected and glum.

I guess this is a good time to tell you that I am late for everything. I am late for class. School. Work. Surprise parties. Dates. You name it, I am late. And yes, I am late for my first day at the program. "You are going to be late to your own funeral, Mer," my mom says constantly. My type A personality thinks I can always fit one more thing in. I will be leaving for an appointment and see a package at the door and think, *I have time. Let me grab it.* And before you know it,

I am decorating my dining room table with candles from Amazon.

I move in with Conor, Grace, Liam, and Noah in New York. My plan is to stay with them during the week and then drive to my condo on the weekends. They live thirty minutes from the city, so my commute to the program is shorter, and it may increase my chances of being on time. I also imagine no one in my family wants me to be alone.

That's all I want.

Grace is like a sister to me. Conor met Grace in college, and they have now been married for ten years. She is tall and slender with light-blue eyes and blonde hair. She seamlessly fits into the O'Brien clan. She is kind and nurturing. She is my crisis buddy and is often the first person I go to when I am struggling. Her soft voice centers me.

Liam and Noah are the absolute joys of my life. I was at the hospital when Liam was born after a forty-eight-hour labor and awoke to a phone call after Noah prematurely entered the world.

They make my heart sing. I would take a bullet for them. I would give them my last breath. I would withstand any pain for them to go through life unscathed. I take my job as an aunt seriously. My eating disorder has an opponent. I need to be alive to be an aunt. In the beginning, I solely fight for them and our relationship.

I have a funny feeling that I am invading their lives, but Conor and Grace welcome me with open arms. I am at the program for most of the day, and I pray that I am not being a burden. I also pray that being around them will strengthen my recovery.

Two months ago, prior to the PHP, I was at Conor's house for the day. I wore Gap jeans, bootcut style; a long white crew tee; and a cornflower-blue fleece that I bought at the outlets a week before. When I saw the fleece at the Gap, I doubted it would fit. It looked child-sized—it slipped right onto my small frame. My eating disorder lit up like a Christmas tree.

Today, there is room between my jeans waistband and my stomach. That inch of space holds such power—it represents my willpower, my unrelenting dedication, and my dark but exhilarating deprivation.

"Do you want anything to eat?" Conor asks my family and then turns to me and whispers, "Obviously not anything for you."

"I'll have a tea." I am so cold. A chill pierces my hands and feet.

"Mer-Mer, you are so skinny," Liam says as he wraps his arms around my waist.

I pause. I halt like I am playing freeze tag. I do not want any attention directed at me.

Then the sadness hits. *Oh my gosh. What am I doing?* And then, instantaneously, my eating disorder blasts in my head—it is the only way to make sense of this scary world.

THE PHP

There is a bleak lull after the holidays end—you know, the few weeks after New Year's when you are not sure if you should sleep all day or plan another party. I unwillingly continue the program, rarely missing a day. A part of me does yearn for structure. I thrive on order, and downtime scares me—too much time to think, to be, to sit still, to feel. If I am not doing something, I feel useless, unproductive, lazy—intimidating words for a person with anorexia. My personality centers around me accomplishing things, crossing off items on my forever to-do list and doing more, always more.

Princeton Hospital calls to tell me that they have an available bed in the inpatient program. I had been on the waiting list for over one month. My eating disorder feels incredibly special, but I turn it down. I need the momentum of the PHP to carry me through. I fear that any small change will swallow me whole. I have never failed at anything. God help me if I fail at this.

Slowly, a part of me realizes that my eating disorder is running the show—that my journal entries are written by my anorexia and that it orders me to starve and self-destruct. It is my armor. It is the clunky, impenetrable tin buffer that I wear each day to numb out. A huge part of treatment is to acknowledge that I have two selves. One part is my eating disorder self and the other part is my healthy self. I was born with a healthy core self. I mean, we all are, but over time, another part of me takes over—my eating disorder self. That part of me has been so reinforced for so long that it will take tremendous patience to deprogram it and strengthen my healthy self.

• • •

I fall into a routine. Each morning, I wake up at 6:30 a.m. to go on the elliptical machine, which is conveniently located in the guest room where I sleep. I quickly take over the room with Laura Ashley bags filled with comfy clothes, toiletries, and books. I am an avid reader, and I hope that my weight restoration will help me read again. The malnutrition makes it nearly impossible for me to concentrate. By the time my nephews come in to get their jackets and book bags from the guest room closet for school, I am dripping with sweat. I jump off the elliptical to give them both sweaty hugs and kisses. They give me strength and a fragile sense of hope. They are my guardian angels.

After I shower, dress in comfortable clothes, and call the cab company, I wait for the beep outside, lock the front door with an extra key, and place my backpack onto my shoulders. The cab drops me off at the train station, which is a few blocks away. Then I hop onto the Metro-North train to Grand Central Station. On the train, I eat an apple. Each day, as my sneakers hit the platform, I am still not prepared for the hustle and bustle of New York City.

As a family, we went into the city for events, dinners, and plays. We saw a Broadway play each year and went to Madison Square Garden for basketball games, but it is not the same. I walk with a large swarm of people off the train track, all looking at their phones and almost running. I stop at Starbucks for an extra hot, grande coffee with soy milk. If it cools off, they have an old microwave in one of the therapy rooms to heat it up. I only drink it if it is burning hot.

Ironically, at the same exact time as I am in New York City to recover from anorexia, restaurant chains decide that it is a great idea to reveal the amounts of calories in big black numbers next to each food or item. As I wait for my coffee, I nervously glance at the bagels and muffins and freeze with fear. I start to calculate the numbers in my head. As I do, mobs of people scurrying to work buy egg sandwiches, scones, and other baked goods. My anorexia shuts down any craving. The big, bold calories are always "too much." And then I burst out into the cold weather and walk five blocks east down Madison Avenue to the program.

Each morning, I sit through the exceptionally long group process. As the weeks go by, I start to share a little bit. Not much. Just a little. I attend daily lunch meal support groups, and two nights a week, dinner group is available. Oh, joy! The program consists of various groups like body image, cognitive behavioral therapy, nutrition, and interpersonal group. I check in with my individual counselor sporadically. My anorexic shield is impenetrable, and we have a superficial relationship. I don't let her in. I keep her at bay. My personality is sucked out of me anyway, so she really has no one to get to know.

I am only stopping by.

The eating disorders track is small, typically ranging from three to nine girls. I am the oldest in the group, but I do not feel singled out. We are all here to get better. During the groups, I feel less alone. I feel like I am not the only one grappling with recovery.

DAVID—MY THERAPIST

In addition to my program, I see my outpatient therapist, David, at Mount Sinai Hospital. Two times each week, I leave the program, walk a block and a half to Madison Avenue, and make a left. His office is thirty blocks away, and often, my anorexia makes me walk it—head down, burning calories. Rain or snow. It is in charge. On other days, my anorexia allows me to get a cab. I feel relief as I reach 1468 Madison Avenue. The lofty building gives credence to my illness. I often think that I am overreacting or being dramatic—that I just need to eat and suck it up, but the massive hospital validates me.

Maybe I am sick.

David has soft blue eyes and light-brown hair that is cut short. He wears a shirt and tie, which I appreciate. His professionalism centers me. David is the director of the eating and weight disorders program and an assistant professor of psychiatry. He sounds important, so, in turn, my anorexia feels important. David is rational against my emotion-driven angst. He is stable against my chaos. He is my wise mind when my overwhelming emotions control my every move.

"Listen, I cannot take your eating disorder away from you. Only you can do that," David says evenly in our first session. "This is between you and you."

"Okay," I say softly as relief floods my body. My guard drops.

David has a calm demeanor, and I never seem to rile him up even when I walk into our sessions talking a mile a minute, often forgetting to breathe. I think that his evenness will rub off on me—that through osmosis, my anxiety-stricken personality will fade right here in his office.

"I know I can be the perfect anorexic. I think I can beat the disease and still maintain the perfect low-weight, thin body and my anorexia will not take over."

"If you could, don't you think you would have by now? You have had over twenty years of experience."

NO CARDIO

"**I** did not do cardio on Sunday," I broadcast to my cognitive behavior group two months into the program. "I did a yoga class instead."

The therapist nods in praise. The girls clap in unison. It is a Tuesday night, and the city skies are dark through the large horizontal windows of the therapy room. Over the weeks, I feel more comfortable at the program and share on most days.

"It was hard, but I did it," I say, pointing to my worksheet where I had written yoga before placing it neatly into my binder.

"Rest days are necessary," the therapist voices. "Self-care is a big part of the journey."

"I'm proud of you," Dara articulates, even though I can see she is struggling today. Dara wears her heart on her sleeve, and I notice that today is hard. I nod my head back with a half sneer, not believing that I stopped the obsessive workout count in my daily planner. My anorexia made me work out for hours, sometimes twice a day, sometimes three. There was a period in my life when my workouts consisted of me seeing my personal trainer, then completing extra cardio, then doing a step class, and finishing up with abdominal exercises and stretching.

One Christmas morning, Mom pleaded with me not to run after we finished looking through our stockings filled with gift cards, toothbrushes, and lip gloss. She was desperate for me to stay still. "Please, for me, Mer."

But right after her request, I popped in a movie, jumped on the treadmill in the basement, and got off only after the movie credits rolled on the screen. I could not give her that simple gift. To me, it felt like life or death.

When I was chosen for jury duty and then chosen for the actual criminal case, I panicked. *How am I going to fit in my workouts?* As the other eleven jurors went out to lunch (which I was learning that people actually do), I did walking lunges around the mahogany table in the center of the room. I lay on the twill carpet and did abdominal crunches and triceps dips off the cold, wooden chairs. I skipped lunch.

A "rest day," or taking a break from exercise, seemed impossible. My eating disorder would not allow it—see, the program is working! I identified the two parts of myself. I made a huge step on Sunday. I listened to my healthy self, and I did yoga and no extra cardiovascular exercise. Some of me feels proud, but at the same time, I feel like my lifeboat is slipping out of my hands.

THE WEEKENDS

On most weekends, I drive back to New Jersey on Friday afternoon, sitting in bumper-to-bumper traffic. On the two-hour ride, I can barely make it home before the binge and purge cycle consumes me. As I pass signs for rest stops, my mind fills with images of food—cinnamon rolls, muffins, pizza. I obsess about what I can binge on over the weekend.

There is a convenience store one block from my condo. One of the no-name ones that is just called Convenience Store, and you are not sure if they have a legal permit. The store has a sketchy vibe—dusty floors, no signs, empty shelves—and it looks like they may store dead bodies in the back.

I park erratically, barely breathing, and run into the store, grabbing two of everything. Pop-Tarts, Oreos, Fig Newtons, pastries, and small packages of sugar cereal. I zoom back to my place, open the door, and then fretfully close and lock it, expecting someone to pop out and catch me in my deception. I drop all the food onto the small wooden table my parents bought for me. One by one, I shove the food into my mouth without even tasting it. I eat ravenously until my stomach is large and extended. I drink large cups of water and let the food marinate. I hardly wait three minutes before purging the food up. It comes out of my nose. Sometimes I pee in my pants. I purge over and over, getting my ugly secrets and shame out. My eyes are red and watery. My face splotched. My knuckles bright red and bleeding. I hold my hair back with a hairband so tiny food particles don't attach to my hairline. I purge over and over until every piece is out of me.

Now I am empty. Now I am calm. I feel my stomach bounce back to its normal size, flat as a board. Completely exhausted. Completely soothed. Completely detached.

But despite my atrocious weekends, I show up at the program each week. I still have this irrational thought that if I can be impeccable with my anorexia, then I will finally be happy. My plan is not working. Each day, I become more depressed, mindless, and disconnected. Some days, I stand on the subway platform and contemplate jumping. I can just end the pain. Just take one more step. And then my mind gets fuzzy and confused and the thoughts zap from my brain. The subway stops with a loud, piercing noise like fingernails scratching down a blackboard. I get on shakily and go to my program like a good girl.

THE DREADED TRANSFER

Eight weeks into the program, I am not meeting the expected weight gain. The rules are clear—if you do not consistently eat your meals (80 to 100 percent) and gain weight, you will be transferred to a higher level of care. That means inpatient—the hospital. A place where I will sleep and be monitored by machines. Each weekly weigh-in is nerve-wracking—the dissonance. Desperately wanting to lose weight or at least stay the same but at the same time fearing the dreaded transfer. I lose weight.

The next morning, Dad and I drive to Columbia University Irving Medical Center. As we pass Westchester Medical Center, which is five minutes from Conor's house, Dad makes a joke.

"I wish it was this hospital," he laughs, even though I know he is dead tired.

I chuckle. "That would be convenient," I say ironically, knowing that my recovering from anorexia has shifted my entire family off balance, and not one part of it is convenient.

This is my dad for you—despite his distressing concern, he is trying to make me laugh. His corny jokes usually do the trick. They are just so endearing. My dad is a teddy bear—my number one fan. Each morning when I was younger, I heard the light drum of the shower that he took at dawn before heading into the city for work. It was my cue to go back to bed for another few hours. I then heard the front door open in the evening, Dad walking in with a smile plastered on his face, usually saying, "Where are the most beautiful women in the world?" in reference to Mom and me. Even after fifteen-hour days, he never complained. Ever. Usually, the dishwasher hummed as he heated up his dinner that Mom left for him, wrapped up in wax paper. It takes me a long time to have compassion for Dad and for the rest of my family—to slowly see life from their perspectives, and not from my small, sick, self-absorbed world.

We arrive at the hospital. White walls. White tables. White chairs. White hospital beds. The monitors beep loudly as the nurses shuffle quickly between patients hooked up to machines. I guess I was expecting inspirational quotes on the walls, pretty tables with mix-and-match chairs, fluffy comforters, and color, but it is sterile, bland, stark, and depressing.

Dad and I sit in the skinny hospital hallway, waiting. He checks his Blackberry, and I am reminded of the meeting he is missing to be with me. A male nurse comes to get me and leads me into a tiny office. The large scale takes up most of it.

"What brings you here today?"

"I am at the Columbia Day Program for my anorexia, and I am not gaining enough weight," I whisper as a wave of embarrassment that I am too fat to have anorexia passes.

"I see. Tell me what is going on."

"I'm eating my meals at the program, but then I restrict and binge and purge all weekend."

"Uh-huh. Please get on the scale," he utters.

I wear black leggings, a sports bra with no clasps, and a long-sleeved tee. I take my sneakers off and step up. I know I should not look, but I do.

Damn, I am the same. No weight loss. You suck. I cannot do anything right.

He writes down the number without an ounce of emotion. I imagine he has done this a million times. Maybe we have more in common than I think.

I probably don't even belong here. I am not skinny enough.

Part of me yearns to be a "better" anorexic—to be sick enough to be hospitalized, to eat through a feeding tube, and to prove that this pain inside is real. Maybe then my illness will feel validated. Then no one will think that I am making this whole thing up. Then, realistic glimpses that I am in a cold, sterile hospital surface.

Will I die here?

I am quiet after we leave. It is a lot for one day, and my body and brain shut down. The next day, I go back to the program and eat my meals. And yes, I finally start to gain some weight.

THE ELEPHANT IN
THE ROOM

So, let's talk about the elephant in the room. Weight gain is like those last thirty seconds when I am cycling in a spinning class, doing a sprint, desperately wanting the song to be over, and waiting for the teacher to say "Take your tension off" or "Go back to a flat road." The song is always longer than I think, my thighs are burning, and I might scream out loud. Weight gain is like that and then doing it over and over and over again. It is explained to me that initial weight gain during weight restoration may start in your stomach.

Are you fucking kidding me?

It feels like I am gaining weight while eating and sleeping and walking and talking—really, at every second of every day in initial recovery. And to boot, there is no way around it. I need to radically accept weight gain and see it as proof that I am nourishing and sustaining my body. It is mandatory. Radical acceptance is a DBT skill that helps me during this transition; according to the *DBT Skills Training Manual,* "Radical acceptance is complete and total acceptance, from deep within, of the facts of reality. It involves acknowledging facts that are true and letting go a fight with reality." Every few minutes, I turn my mind toward acceptance, but the rejection comes back to devour me.

You are nothing if you are not skinny.

Some days, I feel full and uncomfortable all day long. On others, my appetite is so ravenous that I wake up in the middle of the night to eat. I start to leave snacks by my bed. I wake up starving at 3 a.m. and shove Swedish Fish in my mouth. I then eat a protein bar. Next, I eat trail mix. I eat and eat and never feel full, waking up with peanuts and cranberries in my sheets. Gummy bears under my pillow. At times, I take one sip of juice and am immediately full. Other times, I eat a nutritious lunch and am still hungry. I eat a cracker and then consume the whole box.

I come to understand that each time I restricted or binged or purged, I undid my natural system to the point that my hunger and fullness indicators are nonexistent. I am not untouchable. I am not invincible. The trust within myself is broken, but I desperately hope that I will find my balance. In an individual session with David, I write on a pink index card that "feeling full does not mean I am fat." I keep it in my wallet, and it is still there to this day.

I have some mental breakdowns with my weight gain, which is minimal, but to me, it feels like the world is ending. I literally want to cut my stomach off with a knife. I stare at a knife set resting on my kitchen counter, and impulses jolt in my body. I dare myself to "just do it"—carve the fat off, destroy what is so terrifying.

My clothes fit differently. Pants that hung on my body now sit on my body. Rationally, I know that the weight gain is minuscule, but to my emotional mind, it is life-shattering. I connect my worthiness with weight. My body changes and my sense of control pulls out from beneath me. I clearly recognize that I am not like everyone else. I am a woman with anorexia. I need to respect my disease and eat. Each meal or snack I skip is like taking a piece out of a Jenga stack. At first, the tower stays built, but over time, it crashes.

MEAL SUPPORT

Eating meals at the program is grueling, especially in the beginning, but there is also a feeling of ecstasy. A constant dissonance between fear and desire. A clash between panic and longing. Eating a full-fat yogurt parfait with granola is daunting but also magical. While my eating disorder sees fat, my taste buds relish the sweetness of the creamy texture. I eat a real Caesar salad. Um . . . they are delicious. I never knew they were so good.

Recovery for me is strengthening my healthy self—my core self that is not brainwashed by diet culture, unattainable cultural beauty ideals, or what size I wear. I learn to distinguish between the two parts. My healthy self wants a strong relationship with my nephews. The eating disorder self gets in the way. It numbs me, and while yes, it has been protective, the consequences slap me dead in the face.

The program teaches me the prescription for "regular eating." They are similar to the "conscious eating guidelines" introduced by Carolyn Costin, a pioneer in the field. The main principles are to notice your hunger, eat regularly, not skip meals, never go more than four hours without eating, and allow yourself to eat all foods. Another guideline is not to engage in any compensatory behaviors such as vomiting, overexercising, or taking laxatives. I am taught to eat balanced, nutritious meals and that restricting food can lead to psychological problems and increase those behaviors. For most of my life, I have been trapped in the restrict, binge, purge cycle. To eventually balance out my relationship with food, all compensatory behaviors need to be eliminated, and I need to follow my meal plan even when I do not want to.

Recovering in New York City, while at times overwhelming, is a saving grace. Food is everywhere! I really cannot believe it. Walking the streets of New York is like living in a new world. And anything you want you can have in seconds—a bagel, a slice of pizza, a salad, a burger. Grand Central Station is a mecca of food of all varieties. If I want plain brown rice, I can get it. If I want a salad with edamame, sunflower seeds, and chickpeas, I can get it. If I want vegetable sushi with avocado, I can get it. Literally in minutes. In my hand. Boom.

I am amazed at the different meals they serve us. At each meal group, a paper or plastic bag appears with diverse foods and cuisines from different countries. At times, I feel like a kid in a candy store. My parents made it a mission to expose us to different types of food growing up (like escargot and octopus), but through the years, my eating disorder limited my meal choices so severely that I could fit the list on a Post-it note. So, when I am given Indian curry or fish tacos or simply an all-American grilled cheese on white bread, it is like I am eating it for the first time.

THE OLD-FASHIONED
CANDY STORE

One night during dinner group, I sit across from Dara. It is just the two of us. Patients come and go, but Dara and I are regulars and attend each day. We become close, running errands in between our groups, getting coffee, and simply connecting because we understand one another. We are attached by our pain, our torment. The small office is filled with oversized horizontal windows. It is dusk, and the city lights illuminate the room to a soft yellow hue. I am finally used to the muted traffic noises coming from below. It calms me now. We eat chicken and Swiss cheese paninis for dinner and a side salad with Thousand Island dressing.

"How's Jake?" I ask.

"He's good. He is almost done with graduate school, and he is also working while I am here all day trying to get better," she says with air quotes, shaking her head with uncertainty. They have been dating since college and live in a studio apartment in Chelsea.

The clinician slides a Dixie cup with monkeys on it filled with peanut M&M's to each of us. Dara and I pause, stare at each other, and then smile widely.

"We are allowed to eat those?" Dara asks, grinning.

I jingle the candy in the cup. The bright colors swish and rattle.

"This is all for us?" I inquire.

"Yes. This is dessert," the clinician voices.

Dara and I peer at each other, switching between puzzlement, fear, and eagerness. This is the first time we have been served candy at the program. I feel a soft, manic excitement come over me. I only eat candy during my binge and purge rituals. I have not had candy in so long. My body wakes. I feel the blood rush through my body as I sit straight up in my folding chair.

This is a trick. I am going to get fat. If I eat them, I will never be able to stop.

I stare at the candy as I scuffle between trepidation and desire. I place an M&M in my mouth and savor in the sweetness of the chocolate erupting on my tongue.

Oh my God, I am enjoying this.

"This is crazy," Dara says.

"This is totally crazy." I nod in agreement.

We eat the rest of the M&M's in silence as we continue to glance back at each other.

What is happening? I am voluntarily putting candy into my mouth. And liking it!

I boss back my anorexia. I feel terrified and exhilarated. I am flooded with fear but slowly walk toward it anyway.

"I cannot believe I just ate them," I say.

"Me neither," Dara laughs.

• • •

One of my favorite places as a child was the beach boardwalk candy store. The old-fashioned kind where red candy apples line the back shelf, small red-and-white containers are filled with buttery popcorn, and large mounds of blue and pink cotton candy sit in white cones. The bell chimes as I walk in the door, and I am welcomed by the smells of fudge, citrus, and sugar. Glass containers are filled with candy, like malted milk balls, Coke bottles, gummy bears, Sour Patch Kids, and Swedish Fish. Gummy bears are my favorite. Red Hot Cinnamon Dollars are a close second. There is something in the sweet and sticky consistency that I am a sucker for—the chewiness, the sugariness. When I was a little girl, my uncle Brian bribed me with gummy bears when we played long games of Monopoly as a family down at the shore.

"I'll give you a pound of gummy bears for Park Place."

"Go on . . ."

"A roll of quarters for Boardwalk?"

"Now you are talking . . ."

When they were selling the extra-large gummy bears at the candy store, I was a shoo-in. In those days, a roll of quarters would get you endless video games at the arcade, located right over the bridge in the next beach town. Rooftop miniature golf cost a dollar. One summer, I had my eye on this black radio decorated with a fluorescent palm tree. I saved every one of my ticket stubs from Ms. Pac-Man and Skee-Ball. Right before Labor Day, I traded them in for the radio. Reaching the proper number of tickets was a small victory when you were eleven.

There was an elderly woman with cropped silver hair who worked at the candy shop. And she was mean. She never smiled. I never understood why she worked at a candy store packed full of children on summer vacation, but as an adult, I can sense that maybe her life was filled with heartache or loss. Maybe she had lost her husband. Or wife. Usually, Kelly and I bought a quarter pound of candy each, and she filled the small white paper bags with a silver scooper. I paid with crumpled dollar bills or quarters (the bribe from my uncle). Back at the beach, we dug our damp, sandy fingers into the bag.

So, as I sit here and eat candy, listening to the soft beeps of the cars and trucks underneath us and the faded noises of the city, I smile. Maybe I can get back there. Maybe I can be happy. Maybe I can feel joy regularly, eat candy with total abandon, and experience life with a carefree attitude. I feel like I am breaking every rule in the book, and it feels amazing.

NUMBER 11

t is one of the first warm days after a long winter, and the sun on my face feels decadent as I walk to my appointment with David. I stop at a corner bookstore on the way. Lately, I've started reading again. I love bookstores—the act of browsing down the aisles, picking books up from the shelves and rifling through the pages, picturing the author poring over each word they choose. I always imagine Colin Firth in the movie *Love Actually*, writing on an old-fashioned typewriter in a European cottage. The silence soothes me. The shop is small and cozy, and only one person can stand comfortably in the aisle. I feel an urge to purchase something, but nothing grabs my attention, so I leave the store empty-handed. Very unusual. I typically buy something to superficially fill the gaping hole.

Due to the dimness of the store, my eyes have to readjust to the sunlight as I saunter back onto Madison Avenue. I pass a busy restaurant. And then another. I see the string of open windows in front. Loud and bubbly conversation passes through the screens, and for a quick second, I am intrigued but also cynical. I have tried so hard for so long to skip lunch, and here are people voluntarily socializing with others, eating food in the middle of the day. For fun!

There is no lunch group today, so I am expected to eat on my own. An idea pops into my head. I will eat lunch. By myself. In a restaurant. On a Wednesday. Instead of lingering in David's waiting room until our session, I will sit down to a meal.

Small tables are crammed in side by side. I shimmy sideways to avoid knocking into people's chairs or hanging pocketbooks as I follow the hostess to a two top all the way by the windows. It is warmer than expected, and I take off my coat. I order a salad with grilled chicken. Tap water, no ice. I feel relatively safe. A waiter drops a wicker basket of warm, deliciously soft bread on my table.

Oh, shit. What do I do now?

I got this. I have eaten rolls and toast and pizza at the program. My healthy self perks up. I grab a piece of the nutty, seeded whole wheat bread, and it melts in my mouth. See, I can do this—just like the swarm of strangers surrounding me.

My salad arrives. I cautiously pour the house dressing in a circular motion. As I pick up my fork, perspiration beads up on my skin. I take a few bites, breathing in between. Then, almost mindlessly, I finish the last two pieces of bread. My legs bounce up and down. The sweat builds, and small droplets slide down my chest.

Now you've done it. You have no willpower. You are going to get fat. You have no control. You are absolutely not normal.

Despite the heat, I wrap my winter jacket around my body. I pay my bill quickly, thinking the waitress can see fat budding from my stomach.

Everyone is looking at me.

I zigzag my way past the tables to the hostess station. I swiftly walk to the exit door but pause briefly and notice a large to-go counter with items like tuna fish, pasta salad, and cupcakes lining the glass shelves.

Just walk out. Do not stop. Don't you dare.

I stop. I stare. I hesitate. I snatch a number. My mind races. The world freezes like I have taken a painkiller. The hordes of people move at a snail's pace.

"Eleven! Number eleven!"

"That's me. Umm . . . I'll take a whole wheat bagel to go," I meekly say, barely getting the words out. I ferociously eat it as I walk intensely down the street toward therapy.

Well, now you've done it, you fat pig.

I notice another bagel store a few doors down. I walk in and stand inconspicuously by the checkout counter, pondering what to order. And then I leave quickly and sit on a bench outside. My left leg wobbles up and down frenziedly. I go back in.

"I'll have a whole wheat bagel, toasted with butter."

It will be easier to get up with the butter.

I snatch a large empty cup by the soda bar. I am spinning. My breath is quick and shallow. I slip into the next busy restaurant and rush into the bathroom in the back.

Everyone knows you are going to purge. Everyone is staring at you.

Luckily, it is a single stall, and the noise level is loud. It drowns out the sounds as I purge my lunch into the cup and then the toilet. I flush twice.

You are now back in control.

I cancel my therapy session—something I have never done. The guilt sits in my stomach, knowing that my dad will be charged. I hail a cab and take it to the New York Sports Club near Grand Central. I pay the daily fee. I frantically search for an open treadmill among the throngs of people. I find one, jump on, and run until my neck falls slightly away from my shoulders and I can breathe again.

PROS AND CONS

"**H**ey, girls," Danielle, our therapist, chimes as each of us enters the therapy room one by one. She has a stack of papers and hands them out as we each take a seat for cognitive-behavioral group. The room feels stuffy, and Dara opens a window.

"Hey," we voice in unison.

"Okay. Today we are going to review this 'daily choice monitoring' sheet. This is a skill for you to practice for next week. As you go through your day, start to observe your choices, then put the choice in the 'healthy' column or the 'eating disorder' column. What is an example of a healthy choice?" Danielle asks.

"Eating lunch," I voice as I neatly place the sheet in my blue binder under the color-coded tab that says "CBT."

"Pushing off an urge or not weighing yourself," Dara offers.

"Yes. So, consider each choice in terms of its promotion of a healthy lifestyle versus those that reinforce the eating disorder behaviors," she says, grabbing a sip of her water bottle. "Okay. So, last week, we reviewed relapse prevention and how to cope ahead with high-risk situations. I asked you each to identify a triggering situation and generate a list of explicit coping strategies. Umm . . . Meredith, would you like to share?"

"Sure," I answer as I redo my ponytail and wipe away pieces of hair from my face. "I wrote about eating meals by myself in New Jersey on the weekends. I put plan-specific meals; have set times for meals; mimic the program rules like eating at a table, using dishes, and possibly having tea after my meal or planning appointments for after meals so I get out of the house to not act on any of my urges."

"Well done," Danielle replies. "Very specific."

"Also, to remember that a thought is just a thought and I actually do not have to act on the thought, which still blows my mind," I chuckle. The other girls nod in agreement. They share their plans about visiting family, going out to restaurants, and dealing with boyfriends and girlfriends. The hour is up, and we have a forty-five-minute break. I find an empty chair on a quiet floor and pull out a book. My stomach is queasy, and I take a deep breath, relaxing my stomach muscles that feel like concrete.

Ugh, my stomach.

My stomach usually hurts, but I turn my mind toward acceptance. If I start to get willful, it will hurt even more. I had stomachaches as a little girl, and with the anorexia, I have chronic constipation, bloating, and gas. I was diagnosed with gastroparesis, irritable bowel syndrome, and pelvic floor disorder, but my team keeps telling me that I can reverse any damage by reducing behaviors and following a consistent meal plan.

Fortunately, I have no other purging episodes at the program. I even meet Aidan and Beth for dinner one night in the city when they are visiting from California. Beth, just like Grace, fits effortlessly into our family. And when she has a few drinks and speaks in her Southern drawl, I love her even more. They order butternut squash soup to start. The aroma pierces my nostrils. I taste it and celebrate the creaminess, the thickness, the nutmeg, and the cream. Only one spoonful. We all order the fish special, and I eat it all. My healthy self shows up, and I am full of pride.

A few weeks ago, we completed a decision analysis exercise in group where we picked an unhealthy behavior (i.e., restricting a meal) and then filled out the immediate short-term positive and negative consequences of acting on it and then the delayed positive and negative consequences of that same behavior. Then we made another list filling in the same boxes for not acting on the behavior (i.e., eating a meal). The list-lover in me enjoys this exercise, and I fill out an analysis for each unhealthy behavior—restriction, purging, bingeing, skipping program, overexercising, and weight loss—that I am working to reduce and eventually eliminate. It is basically a detailed pros and cons skill. The exercise is tedious, but I am a visual learner, and it helps to see the chart with my handwriting in front of me.

With time, I notice that while, yes, the behaviors help to numb me out, reduce my anxiety, and allow me to avoid my feelings, afterward I feel ashamed and hopeless. The behaviors get in the way of engaging in life and maintaining relationships, and I physically feel terrible. I notice that when I do not act on the urge, I feel proud about breaking the cycle. I have more energy. My mind is clearer, and I prove to myself that my emotions will not kill me.

Once a week, we review "healthy self" versus "eating disorder self" dialogues. I write so many that my binder barely clasps shut. It is sometimes impossible for my healthy self to get in the last word, but I try, and with a lot of practice, my healthy self gets a bit stronger.

EDS: *Let's skip breakfast*

HS: *Wait, I am learning that my meals need to be balanced and satiating.*

EDS: *Hold up. Why are you listening to your treatment team? They are jealous.*

HS: *My treatment team wants me to be healthy. Let's eat an apple and slowly add more food as the program continues.*

PIZZA DAY

Fridays are pizza days. Slowly, I start to feel less edgy when Fridays roll around because I know what to expect, but come on, it is pizza. I trudge upstairs to the lunchroom. What will it be today? Thick? Thin? Veggie? Whole wheat? Two slices or one? Please be a salad day. On salad day, we eat only one slice. And no blotting allowed.

Usually, if you are like most families, you have your favorite local pizza place on speed dial, and due to the sheer exhaustion from the work week, you order a few pies for you and your family on Friday evenings. But at a PHP for eating disorder recovery, each Friday, they order from a different place. It is like fear exposure on crack. Each time the pizza box is opened at lunch, it is a surprise. The exposure is terrifying and, hands down, necessary for recovery. If I continue to eat salads with grilled chicken and salad dressing on the side, yogurt, apples, and coffee, my eating disorder will stay fully in charge. Gradually, the perpetual exposure starts to chisel the eating disorder chains off my hands and feet.

Meal support groups do get easier. I become aware that the grumbling in my stomach at the end of morning therapy group is hunger. I also realize that my despondency and irritability is hunger too. And my fatigue. I sometimes have a skip in my step—excited to know what is on the menu. I am happy to connect with the other girls and have conversations while we eat. I also start to enjoy the food—the tastes, the smells, the textures.

On Monday, Melinda, an old client, is back at the program. I noticed her in body image group earlier, and she sits next to me at lunch.

"Hi, Melinda," I say.

"Hello," she says with a British accent as her long, wavy brown hair falls behind her back. "I had a small lapse."

"It's good to see you," I comment.

"I am here only for a few weeks to get my bulimia under control," she utters.

I smile, knowing all too well about lapses and relapses. I am impressed that she traveled across the country to be here. I notice a fierceness in her eyes. We are having caprese sandwiches today— tomato, basil, and fresh mozzarella on herbed focaccia bread with a side salad. I cannot lie. It is tasty. My healthy self wins. The dissonance is uncomfortable, but I finish it—every bite. After the thirty minutes we have allotted for eating, we process the meal as a group to discuss feelings, thoughts, and urges.

"Sandwiches are so hard to eat," Dara says.

"Uh-huh." Most of the other girls nod in unison.

"I just have this message sealed into my head that carbs are evil," I say. "I mean, what did the poor carb do to me, really? It is freaking bread, but it is so hard."

"Me too," Dara agrees.

Melinda moves around in her chair. Her eyes dart to each one of us. She has a scowl on her face. She struggles to wait her turn.

"I deserve food, and it's normal to eat a sandwich for lunch. I am not going to feel bad for eating it. I want to get better," she says with an edge. "And it is really annoying to hear you guys complain about it."

She has a point. Melinda had tasted the gloriousness of recovery and then had a setback. She is not fooling around this time. She is going to do whatever it takes to get back on track. I am inspired by her strength. And Goddamn, her anger is refreshing.

TURNING POINT

David is working in his private practice office today across town. Torrential rain pulses against the cab so hard that the driver can barely see through the windshield. A bitter chill throbs deeply, and I desperately want to be in a scalding hot shower. I unsuccessfully dodge the bullets of rain but make it to the front door of a gray stone building. I shimmy into a compact elevator that takes me up to the third floor. I pull the door open with a heave. I step into a dark, narrow hallway. The floors creak. I close my drenched umbrella, and water drops to the floor and beads up. I hear murmurs from the office—a sign that David is still with a client.

My phone vibrates in the large pocket of my oversized turquoise rain jacket. If my clothes are big, there is less of a chance of feeling them on my skin.

"Hey, Mer," my dad says in a stern voice.

"Hey, Dad," I answer, my body immediately tensing.

He is angry with you. You cannot do anything right.

"I'm waiting for David."

"Okay. What are your plans this weekend?" he says tersely. Gone is the teddy bear. He means business.

"I was thinking of doing something fun with Liam and Noah—maybe take them bowling or to the movies."

"You are not allowed to be alone with either of them. You especially cannot drive with them in the car," Dad comments in his you-have-to-do-what-I-say voice.

"Ah . . . what?" I question with a sting in my voice. "That's ridiculous."

"You could pass out. You should not even be driving yourself."

"Are you freaking serious, Dad? I am fine. I am eating. I've been going to the program for four months."

"I don't care, Mer," my dad says firmly.

"I would never hurt them. This is not fair. You are trying to control me," I cry.

"I don't care what fair is."

My body shivers and stands up straight at the same time. My body vibrates with fear. A stranger passes me in the tight hallway—my cue that David is ready for me.

"I've got to go, Dad. David is ready," I say with a huff and press the end button.

I walk into David's office, visibly shaken with wet, pink eyes. I feel like I was just punched in the gut. My thirty-five-year-old self falls onto the old leather couch the color of whiskey, and I place my pocketbook on the camel-colored rug, frayed at the edges.

"My dad said that I can't drive Liam or Noah. This is bullshit!" I voice, scanning his office and noticing the multiple diplomas framed on the wall.

"Okay . . . tell me more."

"My dad said some crap about me being weak and that I should not even drive myself."

"It sounds like you are upset."

"I'm an adult. He cannot tell me what to do!" I shout. "My parents have controlled me my whole life!"

"Maybe instead of being infuriated at your dad, you should be angry with your eating disorder."

THE PURGING INCIDENT

Deserving recovery is tricky. I have such little self-worth. I do not think I deserve to recover, or to live, for that matter. For me, my anorexia is just a slow way to die. A long, drawn-out method to leave the gnawing, constant pain. However, as I start to restore my weight and eat more, my brain slowly begins to function better. I have these small glimmers of joy, and I start to decrease my behaviors.

Some weekends, I stay at Conor and Grace's instead of making the trek back to New Jersey and sitting in rush-hour traffic. My mother persuades me to stay this weekend. And part of me knows I should not be alone. Spending time with Liam and Noah is good for me. The one good part of recovery is seeing them every day.

I eat Trader Joe's organic brown rice and microwavable steamfresh vegetables for lunch. I add a spoonful of chickpeas for protein. I sit at the dining room table, my plate lying on a pretty placemat. I finish my entire meal, fill out my eating record for the nutritionist at the program, and put my dishes in the dishwasher.

The sky is covered with dull gray clouds. *SportsCenter* plays in the background. Conor flips through cooking magazines, and Grace is enthralled with her latest book. Liam and Noah listen to college basketball highlights. I go to the bathroom, then grab my newest Elin Hilderbrand book, and sit on my maternal grandmother's blue-and-red-striped, newly recovered chair. The bottom of the chair has sharp edges, so Conor puts a yellow tennis ball cut in half on each corner to protect their hardwood floors.

I read and rock gently back and forth, noticing the light squeak. I see Grace glancing at me, giving me weird looks. I start to burn up as her judgment pierces through me. Immediately, my fight-or-flight reactions flare. *What did I do?*

You are too much. You are a burden.

I feel fat, uncomfortable, and frightened, and I pull my legs into a cross-legged position. Grace motions me into the hallway. I slowly get up and tiptoe toward her.

"I heard you."

"You heard me what?"

"Purging, Mer."

"I did not throw up," I say meekly.

"I heard you running the water for a long time."

"No . . . I didn't. I promise," I say adamantly. I am innocent, but my body feels like an alarm went off.

You are so bad, Meredith. You are so bad.

"I would never throw up in your house. It's a rule I have."

Grace's face, which usually gives off warmth, is full of disappointment. I am completely rattled. Even though I know I did not throw up, the second-guessing starts. Maybe I did throw up and forgot? I start to create stories in my head. But wait. I did not do this. I would never do that in their bathroom—it is too intimate, too personal.

I am trying so fucking hard to recover.

The accusation stings, and the self-critical narrative that I have on repeat starts to send me over the edge. My brain gets loud and fuzzy. I disconnect from my body. Everything around me mutes into slow motion. I am too fragile to fight back without bursting into tears. To this day, I think Grace thought I was lying to her—I was not.

I am not sure if it was the powerful allegation that woke me up that day. Maybe I wanted to prove Grace wrong even though I did not purge that day. Maybe I was embarrassed we were even having the conversation. Maybe, I wanted to get the hell out of their life and into my own.

GRADUATION

I make the decision to stop going to Columbia on my own. My weight is stable and sits in the suitable recovery range. I eat most of my meals. My restriction, bingeing, and purging reduce. Six months of treatment has a nice ring to it, and I latch on to the round, even number. Looking back, I leave prematurely. I do not give my illness the space to stabilize. I devalue the seriousness of it. The eating disorder is still embedded into me, but I crave normalcy. I arbitrarily choose a day to stop because I do not want to take the train into the city again.

My last day is on a balmy, spring day in May. I am not sure what I am expecting, but the day feels lackluster. I guess part of me yearns for a celebration. While I do not like being the center of attention like I did as a young girl, part of me wants to stick out that day. I could have died, but I chose to live. My eating disorder is still loud, but my healthy voice is more solid, durable. It makes more noise. It helps me make the next pro-recovery choice. I feel more robust. Resilient. I start to feel a joy in my body that is not immediately sidetracked by despair.

"Today is my last day," I announce to my lunch group.

We eat vegetable sushi, vegetable dumplings, and edamame.

"It is?" the clinician asks, looking up, surprised.

"Yup. I spoke to my therapist earlier in the week. I am going back to outpatient."

"I am proud of you," Dara voices as her face falls. We are a team, and I am jumping ship.

"Thanks." I half smile.

I want to tell her how important she is to my recovery, but I hold back. I am scared to be vulnerable. Most things still scare me, but I leave the treatment bubble anyway.

PART 3

RECOVERY

THE POST-IT

My way of navigating life pre-PHP brought my life to a jolting halt. So, it is time to do things differently. I must slow down and connect and focus. It is not just a friendly suggestion. It is life and death. Anything I put in front of my eating disorder recovery, I will lose.

I move out of my place and into my parents' beach house. They are in New York, so I have space to focus on recovery and have some independence. Every Wednesday and Friday, I attend my individual sessions with David. My current job is to follow my meal plan (three meals and two to three snacks per day), not engage in eating disorder behaviors, and strengthen my healthy self. Pre-PHP Meredith would find a full-time job with benefits in less than a week, but in-recovery Meredith takes a deep breath and slows down.

My typical switch is turned to "on." I have often been compared to the Energizer Bunny by many boyfriends because when I form a task in my mind, I do not stop until it is completed . . . perfectly (or so I think). I obsess over it until I can cross it off the list. Oh, the dreaded list. The to-do list. I would still love to hug the inventor of the Post-it; however, that small, three-by-three-inch, yellow sticky paper is a blessing and a curse. While yes, it is helpful to organize my life, it can backfire when my entire day is centered around finding satisfaction by drawing a straight black line through a word. Believe me.

Slowing my mind and my body down is critical to recovery. And it is hard as hell. I pride myself on "doing"—running the errands, returning the clothes, picking up my meds, and getting the oil changed. "Being" scares me. "Being" means sitting with my thoughts and feelings. It means not running away from them by restricting, purging, overexercising, or methodically completing my to-do list in an organized, timely fashion (that means today).

Routine is helpful, so I volunteer at a family resource center in Asbury Park. I help with a program called Youth With A Purpose, which gives underprivileged girls educational and recreational opportunities. Each Saturday, I take the girls to different activities, and it is a chance to get out of my own head and focus on other people.

• • •

I drive past the Trader Joe's in the Shrewsbury shopping center and pull up to an available parking space. I walk down the dark, shabby hallway to the third door on the left and walk into my psychiatrist's office. I sigh, relieved that her office is adorned with comfy couches, water fixtures softly dripping, and a coffee and tea station.

She and I have worked diligently to find the right cocktail of medication that can alleviate my depression and manage my anxiety. Waiting, I have a flashback of me sitting in a mid-length white eyelet skirt two sizes too big and a V-neck shirt the color of the ocean. I loved that no clothing material touched my body and the skirt fell off my waist like after you stretch out a sweatshirt with your knees. I sat zombie-like, detached from the moment. And now, with some recovery under my belt, I sit in her small office and feel slightly more confident. I have more energy. I am still anxious about my future, but strands of hope are visible.

"Tell me how you are," she asks with concern.

"I'm okay. I finished the program. I am seeing David twice a week. I am working with a nutritionist, and I go to the support group too."

"Okay. Good. It is important to keep that up. And your anxiety?"

"Hmm. Not great. I always think that something bad is going to happen. It is like I am constantly scanning for danger even when I know I am totally safe. I can be sitting on my couch, watching TV, and this wave of panic overtakes me. It is like I am on a roller coaster on repeat. I think the Wellbutrin helps a bit."

"Any particular new stressors?"

"Eating on my own is tough, but I'm doing it. Each week I go out to lunch with my friend, which helps get me out of the house, but I am following my meal plan."

"Any behaviors?"

"I have urges every day. Mostly restriction. Breakfast is the hardest. I keep pushing it off until I am starving, but I'm trying to eat it earlier."

"How are you sleeping?"

"So-so, but the nightmares are awful. Pretty much every night, my dad dies. Last night, we were at this resort, and he came back from his walk and was breathing heavily. He told me that he was going to go swim in the pool. I told him no, that he needed to take it easy. He swam anyway and he had a heart attack in the pool and sunk to the bottom. I dove in and brought him to the surface. I was yelling for help, but no one heard me. I tried to dial 911 but could not find the buttons on my phone. I was screaming, and then he died and no one cares except for me."

"Sorry to hear that. Sounds rough. You have been having these dreams for a while?"

"For years. And it is always my dad," I say, grabbing a small tube of Aquaphor from my pocketbook and placing a tiny amount on my lips.

"I can give you medication that can help. It can reduce them."

"Nah. No more meds. I am medication-ed out."

"Okay. Are you still taking your Trazadone?" she asks as she scribbles a note in my chart.

"Yep. Usually two to three pills. It puts me to sleep, but then I just wake up from the nightmares. The Prozac is helping. I have suicidal thoughts, but it feels more under control."

"Any active plan? Intent?"

"No. Some days I just want to be anywhere but here. I just want to rip off my body," I say, shifting awkwardly in the folding chair. "But overall, I am doing better. I have some hope."

"Keep it up. You have come a long way."

"I know. Thanks." I grin.

We schedule a follow-up appointment. It is a gorgeous day, and I can feel the warmth of the sun on my face as I leave the office building and tilt my head to the sky. I sit with her comment briefly. I worked my ass off to restore my weight. I sat through endless psychotherapy groups and meal groups. I reduced behaviors. I am outside the "PHP bubble" and, while part of me wants to run back, I also know what I need to do. I am on autopilot, sprinting through life with blinders on. I rapidly pinball from the past to the future, entirely missing the present and literally missing my life.

SLOWING DOWN

I unpack my luggage after a trip before sitting down or even taking a shower. I buy every color of a tank top just so I do not have to sit with some possible future discomfort if I do not have the right color for the exact outfit that I want to wear in the precise moment. I heat up ice cream in the microwave. I lock my keys in the car with it running. Yes, running! I open the door so quickly that I forget to grab them. When my Keurig tells me it's time to descale, I order a new one. The present just seems too scary. It is easier to obsess about the past or the future, but recovery is about being in the present moment—really sitting with all the crappy feelings and not running from them. Staying put. Tolerating the distress.

I was introduced to the concept of mindfulness when I was an intern at New York-Presbyterian Hospital in White Plains, NY. I was randomly placed in the borderline personality disorder (BPD) unit. Mind you, I did not know what BPD was—my diagnosis class was not until next semester. But I was told to show up at 9 a.m. sharp at the adult dialectical behavior therapy (DBT) day program. I did not know what DBT was either. My main responsibility was to teach DBT skills to people who struggled with symptoms of BPD.

So, like a perfect student, I read Marsha Linehan's book *Cognitive-Behavioral Treatment of Borderline Personality Disorder* cover to cover. I learned that DBT is a treatment based on concrete coping strategies to help those with emotion dysregulation. I reviewed the skills manual diligently (back then it was only a forty-page book with a cheap plastic binding). I memorized the four modules: mindfulness, distress tolerance, emotion regulation, and interpersonal effectiveness. The underlying goal was to "live a life worth living." One major concept is that physical and emotional pain are part of life, but suffering is optional depending on how we deal with our circumstances.

Years later, I call this internship a "God moment"—one of those moments that is placed in front of you before you realize the actual impact that it will have in your life. First off, I eventually got comprehensively trained in the treatment. I thought it would be a good resume booster, but the reality is that I use the concepts with most of my clients. DBT was a life-changer and became one of the major building blocks of my own recovery too.

"Mindfulness is intentionally moving away from thoughts and judgements to a more open, accepting awareness of what is." It is observing, describing, and participating (the "what" skills) with a nonjudgmental stance; doing one thing at a time; and being effective in meeting your goals (the "how" skills). I take deep breaths and feel the sensations of the air passing through my mouth or nostrils. I mindfully shower and feel the heated water on my skin. I mindfully eat and really taste the food, smell the smells, and notice the textures and tastes. I practice taking a moment to pause by mindfully checking in with what I feel inside my body and noting my outside surroundings multiple times each day. I download and use guided meditations. I attend trainings. I read books.

Through daily mindfulness practice, I eventually start to sit and take long deep breaths. I begin to let go of my judgments. And, believe me, I have a lot of them. Some against others, but mostly judgments about myself. I notice discomfort and sit with it instead of escaping by doing anything but feeling it. I crawl out of my own skin, but I stay with it. I slow down, pause, and simply observe—without acting on my urges. It is a miracle!

It is obvious that I also need a major overhaul in my thinking. I often think in extremes. All or nothing. Black and white. All good or all bad. I can catastrophize myself into a paper bag.

This is the worst day of my life.

I'll never be happy.

I'll be alone forever.

Slowing down allows me to observe my thoughts instead of wrapping myself up in them. I imagine myself standing on top of a large mountain, looking down. With the distance, I can gain different perspectives, see the gray, and really ask myself if my thoughts are helpful. Are they effective? Are they even real or factually correct?

I trudge through recovery with a focus on pausing—that beautiful hiatus before a thought turns into an action. That lovely rest while I process. That awesome lull when I sit with urges booming through my body without acting.

DBT also teaches us about the three states of mind—the emotional, the reasonable, and the wise mind. The emotional mind is motivated by intense emotions. Our minds can be volatile, enabling us to say things or act in ways that feel good in the moment without recognizing the potential consequences. Ah-ha—so that is what my impulsivity is. Usually, reason or facts are not acknowledged. In the reasonable mind, we are ruled by reason, facts, and logic. In this state, we access the part of our mind that plans, completes tasks, and evaluates. Sometimes we dismiss or deny the emotional needs of ourselves and others. The wise mind integrates the emotional mind and the reasonable mind. In this state, we can think, feel, and act from a balanced place, sometimes called the middle path. I was taught that our wise mind is like our intuition or "gut-feeling," and it leads to effective choices that help us reach our goals. We strive to be in wise mind, but the skill is to notice what state of mind we are in.

My intuition is nonexistent. I have no gut in my stomach to listen to. I doubt my decisions at every turn. I make one decision and then ruminate about it and then change my mind and ask others what they think, and by the end, I feel defeated and confused. In terms of my relationship with body, weight, shape, and food, I listen to the external rules of my eating disorder or diet culture and am blind to what I want or even what I like. So, I think I am in control, but it is an illusion. To recover, I need to attune my mind to my body.

ADIRONDACK CHAIRS

Today, I drive down River Road in Fair Haven to a hot yoga class. This is yoga in an extremely hot room. I repeat—an extremely hot room. The first time I took a hot yoga class was years before, after one too many glasses of wine the night before, and I was hungover. I only left the burning-hot room once to gasp for air, but overall, it was not incredibly fun (but I checked it off my to-do list). However, afterward, me and my eating disorder went to multiple classes to stare at my disappearing body in the steamy mirrors and to hear comments from teachers about how disciplined I was.

In recovery, I embark on a new journey with mindfulness and yoga. I practice yoga to slow down. I press the pause button on my frenetic life. I slowly reconnect to my body. I breathe through the poses and stop comparing my fitness level to others. The day I do a child's pose instead of another sun salutation in class is exhilarating.

See, I can listen to my body.

My life is not a competition with the yogi next to me.

I stop at the red light on the corner of River Road and Fair Haven Road, noticing the time on my dashboard (do they even call them that anymore?)—11:46 a.m. Simultaneously, I note the Fair

Haven Hardware store diagonally across the street. Vertical piles of Adirondack chairs in rainbow colors are stacked out front. Last week, I bought two white ones even though I wanted four. I scan the colors quickly and see white.

If I take a quick left, I can easily run in, purchase the chairs, and still be on time to my 12 p.m. yoga class.

And then, after a glorious lull, I continue straight to the yoga studio. My healthy self centers, and I carefully unwrap my aqua-blue mat and sit down quietly. I stare at the floor-length mirrors that are already hazy from the steam from the prior class. I reframe the negative self-talk that still gets stuck in my head and lie in child's pose. Breathe in. Breathe out.

In treatment, I learned that a thought is just a thought. I will have them all the time—over 60,000 per day—but I do not need to necessarily act on them. I can practice letting them go. I can tell you exactly what would happen if my eating disorder was in charge.

My body would fill with adrenaline as I sharply turned left and then right into the gravel parking lot. I would open my door before even turning the car off. As my feet hit the ground, I would grab my keys aggressively, almost pulling my shoulder out. I would run into the hardware store and skim the shelves like laser beams as I beeline it to an employee. I would tell him that I need two white chairs and, as he scooped them up for me, I would scan my mental to-dos like a computer generating a list—anything that I could potentially buy in that moment—light bulbs, bird seed, double-stick tape. I would frantically grab and pay for everything and drive to yoga like a woman on three espressos, arriving late and stressed.

Without the ability to observe and notice my thoughts and then let them float away, my thoughts would be like cement blocks banging over and over. My mind would race on overdrive during yoga:

Did I get everything I need?

Is white the best color?

Maybe I should buy two more . . .

Is white boring? Maybe it's boring. Maybe I should buy the pink ones ... or the orange?

Did I get batteries?

I need to go back to the store after yoga.

When is this class over?

Did I keep the receipt?

God forbid I actually be.

God forbid I actually feel.

God forbid I actually take a break.

FEELINGS

Feelings are a form of communication. As a little girl, my emotions felt too big, so I shoved them down and disconnected. Then my eating disorder started, and it took over the job. Restricting and purging and bingeing and overexercising were the ultimate numbing machines. And now, as I continue to reduce these behaviors, guess what is resurfacing—yes, the feelings! Lucky me. I come to accept the fact that feelings scare the hell out of me. They are intimidating and daunting. I desperately avoid them.

But a critical part of recovery is to feel. It is vital that I learn to identify what I am feeling, actually feel it, validate it, and express it. And to let go of judgments about them to boot. This is a tall order, and my initial reaction is full of willfulness. It is like I am a two-year-old having a temper tantrum, screaming in the middle of Toys "R" Us because my favorite Barbie is out of stock. I have been numbing out my emotions for most of my life and now, just as I reduce behaviors, I must feel. This is crazy! I have been duped. Can I please get my money back? Oh, shit, I pay you for the therapy?

I'll be honest, I have no idea what I am feeling. A term coined by Peter Sifneos in 1972, alexithymia "is when a person simply cannot describe what they are feeling because they cannot identify what their physical sensations mean." The meaning is rooted in the Greek words for "lack of words for emotion." And while part of me thinks my headshot should be placed in the dictionary next to this definition, a part of me wants to have the ability to understand and to know my self-experience. I do not want to walk this earth emotionally blind.

I begin by connecting to my body and noticing bodily sensations. Initially, this is threatening, and it seems easier to keep my mind and body split, disjointed. But with my increasing sense of hope, I do the work. I "avoid avoiding," as they say in DBT treatment.

Am I hot? Cold? Is my heart beating slow or fast? Do I have a headache or stomachache? Do I feel tense or relaxed? Am I restless? Do I feel like I am crawling out of my skin?

Then I slowly put words onto these sensations and feelings, even using a feeling wheel as an aid. Then I allow my feelings to rise and fall in my body without trying to block or suppress them. I also practice letting go of judgments because what I feel is valid. Say what? I missed that memo. I thought a feeling was valid if someone else agreed with me or gave me the permission to feel it. I believed in a myth that there was a wrong and right way to feel. DBT and therapy give me permission to feel in an authentic way and to challenge the myths that were reinforcing my disconnection.

Most times, as I navigate my way around feeling, I have emotionally driven urges to act on my eating disorder. Understandably so, because it is an entrenched, automatic default. After the program, I struggle a lot, but again, with exposure, I learn to sit with the urges, ride the wave of my emotions, and not self-destruct.

THE LOVE STORY OF APPLES

Courage is eating a meal when everything in your mind is telling you not to. Courage is picking up the fork and nourishing your body and brain one meal and one snack at a time. Courage is eating foods that do not feel safe and, honestly, terrify the hell out of you. I have to say, each day it gets a little easier, a little less scary, a little more normal.

In the beginning, I eat for Liam and Noah. I love being their aunt and I need to stay alive to do so. I want to love them. I want to make ice cream sundaes at our sleepovers, read them bedtime stories, and see them in concerts, plays, and talent shows. I want to cheer at the top of my lungs at their basketball games (yes, at times, I am embarrassing). I want to be there to see them accomplish their goals, graduate high school, and go to college if they choose. I want to be mesmerized by the things that they say, let their cuteness fill my soul, and have my heart jammed with joy until it almost explodes. I come to realize that this is part of what I am recovering to.

As time goes by, there is also a small, almost undetectable part of me that knows this life is too crippling even for me—the almost-perfect anorexic. Anorexia brings me down, controls me, suffocates me, and consumes me. It zaps away any small piece of joy or happiness or sense of worth. I have these rare occasions where I think there must be more. I want more. I deserve more. I have a brief surge of energy to conquer this disease and think that my whole life is going to change for the better, and then, seconds later, I feel fat and disgusting, and the anxiety within me is nearly impossible to tolerate. The disease wins, but with each meal and snack, my healthy core self gets bigger and louder.

Unquestionably, the meal support groups saved my life. Each meal I ate or partially ate was a small victory. Each new food I tried was a conquest. Each food rule that I disassembled was a triumph. They prepared me for real life. And even if I kicked and screamed, without them, I would still be sick.

Apples—from a young age, I adore them. A perfect, compact, and portable snack. I love apple picking. I enjoy baking homemade apple pies each fall and delivering one to Uncle Pete on his birthday. I revel in picking out what kinds will be sweetest—Gala, Fuji, Ruby Red, Crispin, Cortland, and the sweetest of the sweet—the Pink Lady. I delightfully slice them into slivers, eating them one by one.

They taste like sugar. Crispy, juicy sugar. For me, no sweet can compare. Usually, I buy two huge plastic bags of apples at the food store; however, it is not odd for me to come back with four or five bags of different types of apples. And I eat the whole kit and caboodle. The skin, the core, the seeds—even the rusty brown and green ends. The whole thing goes into my mouth. Sometimes I even get an eye roll or a furrowed brow from a stranger.

My ritual usually starts an hour after dinner. I choose the two rosiest, juiciest apples from my stash and lay them out on a Christmas cutting board that, for some reason, I keep out all year. Santa's face is half-peeled away, probably from putting it in the dishwasher instead of handwashing it. I rinse the apples gently with water and pat them dry. I grab a sharp knife. I take one apple and slice off a piece. Now comes the sweet-meter taste test. I pop a piece of the fruit in my mouth and mindfully decipher the texture and sweetness level of the bite and then choose what pile it is going in—the "yes" pile, the "maybe" pile, or the "no" pile. If it tastes bland, I throw it away. If it tastes soft and mushy, I chuck it. And if it is not sweet enough, then out it goes. I then try the apple slices in the "maybe" pile to give them one last chance to make the cut. Often, they enter the trash too. So, after my "yes" pile is complete, I take the slices and drop them into one of the apple-decorated bowls my mother bought me on one of our yearly apple-picking trips. I shove the whole core and seeds into my mouth, swallow it, and then bring my bowl to the couch and eat each slice slowly.

I name my family fantasy football team The Apples. I spell it wrong on the roster, so to this day, my team is Thge Apples. When I run into old friends, they ask, "What is that fruit you would eat all of the time at the beach? Oh yes, apples." Each time I walk into my parents' house, Mom says, "There are apples in the fridge, Mer." Looking back, I can see how the obsession grew. How it innocently started as a favorite fruit and snack and gradually became a meal-stealer, a preoccupation, an obsession, an excuse.

Eating an apple each day on the train to my program was a good start, but I know it is time for a challenge. I start eating yogurt and granola for breakfast. I eat cereal. Eggs. I challenge dessert by eating cookies or biscotti. And in my recovery, I eventually lose my lust for apples. I start to lose the taste for them. I start to eat blueberries and other fruits. Sometimes, I feel angry at the apple. Sometimes, I want to crush it into little pieces or smash it against a wall. However, I buy them on each grocery shopping trip because it is a habit, even when they turn brown and mushy in my wire apple basket, and I throw them away.

LUNCH DATE

n recovery, I learn I can express my feelings from the mountaintops. I can reduce restricting, purging, bingeing, and overexercising. I can challenge my eating disorder until I am blue in the face, but if I don't sit down and eat, I will not recover. Ever. Ever. Ever. Even after completing the PHP, my relationship with food is tremulous. I still see food as the enemy. I see food as something to use to self-destruct. I see food as something to restrict or to binge. It brings me comfort when I am sad. It gives me a sense of control when I am fearful. So, an integral part of recovery is to continue to heal my relationship with food.

I create my own meal support group with my dear friend Amelia. We met on the local swim team as children and have been beach buddies since. She is on maternity leave after having her third child. Her oldest is in school, so for three months, Amelia; her daughter, Charlotte; her newborn, Emma; and I meet out at a new restaurant in Red Bank for lunch. It is a natural progression of my program. I get to socially connect with her and expand my food horizons.

Today, we meet at Temple, a Chinese food restaurant right on Broad Street. The sun is out, and we sit under the pergola, watching people and cars go by. Emma quietly lies in her detachable car seat, and Charlotte colors in her high chair. Amelia and I catch up until the young waitress stops at our table for our order.

"I'll get the chicken, vegetables, and white rice," I say, breathing deeply, having already scoured the menu online that morning.

You got this.

"I'll get the beef and broccoli," Amelia decides quickly, giving no thought to her choice.

I shift uncomfortably in my seat, anticipating the meal. I focus on Charlotte's tight brown curls framing her adorable face. Amelia's presence grounds me.

I look at the food in front of me after the waitress delivers it. The chicken and vegetables sheen with soy sauce. The softball-sized mound of sticky rice calms me. I like its perfection, its order. I eat most of the meal. Amelia and I talk about everything but food and schedule our next date.

• • •

What I come to know is that structure is critical. Eating regularly (every three to four hours) is essential. I act oppositely to my urges multiple times a day and choose recovery. I realize that if I skip meals, I am more likely to skip the next one or binge and possibly purge. I prioritize my eating schedule above everything else. I respect my disease, knowing that other people may be too busy to eat lunch or skip meals, but to me, that is kryptonite.

• • •

I throw on a fleece before I bop down the stairs to our beach house basement. It is our yearly clean-out day—remember, more hands make light work! My dad obsessively organizes the aluminum shelves that hold numerous board games and larger kitchen items like a Crockpot, a Mixmaster, and a pancake griddle. My mom tackles our Costco corner of cleaning supplies and toiletries that I usually "shop" at. I sweep the cement floor and consolidate the large shopping bags by filling them with smaller shopping bags—you never can have too many bags!

At 12 p.m. on the dot, I hop up the stairs and grab my lentil soup and tossed salad from the refrigerator. As the soup heats up in the microwave, I pour balsamic vinaigrette over the lettuce and add some feta cheese and garbanzo beans. I set the table, sit down, and eat my meal. I have a brief flashback to meal support group. We often ate soup and salad, and the consistent exposure helped me to challenge my food rule that soup is too filling. I think about the welcome support I received from the girls. And even though I cannot remember all their names, I know if we made eye contact on the city sidewalks, we would wink at each other in solidarity.

Eventually, my parents saunter up from the basement, stunned that I stopped a task midway to eat.

• • •

Along the way, I build a toolbox of strategies. Through trial and error, I find coping skills that work. I always carry a water bottle with me to stay hydrated. I become the queen of snacks. I leave snacks in my car, pocketbook, beach bag, workout bag, or really any bag. I leave them at work. I leave them in jacket pockets. I realize that eating is my issue, no one else's. It is my responsibility to stay prepared. I need to prioritize eating, or before long I will be back in a program—a place I never want to go back to.

The "restart the clock" strategy is my favorite. It means eating your next meal or eating your next snack. Simple. Straightforward. Nothing fancy. I expand it to mean doing the next pro-recovery thing. Eating disorders love slipups. They love to sit on our shoulders, waiting for us to stumble. Not on my watch. The new narrative in my head gradually changes to *Will this decision lead me to recovery?*

In the same vein, I use cognitive restructuring. Cognitive restructuring is a therapeutic process of learning to identify and dispute maladaptive and/or irrational thoughts. Each time I have a self-critical or distorted thought (and in the beginning, I do a lot!) I alter it in a neutral or positive way. I challenge the thoughts— sometimes one hundred times each day.

You are nothing to *You have value.*

You are not lovable to *My mother loves me.*

You need to skip dinner to *I am going to give my body the nourishment it deserves.*

No one likes me to *Darcy, my best friend, loves me.*

Your life has no meaning to *I am a super aunt!*

Another tool is positive affirmations. Positive affirmation is the practice of positive thinking and self-empowerment that helps to foster a positive affirming attitude. My first positive affirmation is SHH. I came up with it during the program one day when I looked in the mirror and my eating disorder self started spewing criticisms and names at me like a machine gun. The acronym stands for—I am strong, healthy, and hot. I can be strong in my recovery. I can strengthen my healthy self. I can be hot like fire to burn the lies and the criticism that the eating disorder tells me. SHH helped to drown out the eating disorder thoughts that, at times, sounded like a rock concert in my head.

I start to come up with others like, *It is okay to not be okay; I am enough; Recovery is a process;* and *Be kind to yourself.* I write them down on Post-its and cover my bathroom mirrors, walls, and my office desk. I shout them out loud. And with consistency and determination, I slowly start to change the way I think.

I write out dialogues between my healthy core self and my eating disorder self frequently. If I do not have a pen or paper, I mindfully decipher the two voices in my head. I ask myself, *What is your last eating disorder thought?*—and then journal about it, making sure that my healthy self gets the last word.

EDS: *Time for breakfast. Let's just have an apple.*

HS: *Wait, it is time to expose myself to new meals. I am going to have eggs, avocado, and a bagel with cream cheese.*

EDS: *Hold up. You are going to eat all that food?*

HS: *All that food is a regular-sized breakfast. The more I eat now, the less my obsession with food will be. I am going to give my body the energy it needs, and a fresh hot bagel is delicious. Remember all the bagels you have skipped in your life? Not today!*

Eating disorders love patterns. Routines. The familiar. The comfortable. Recovery is about breaking them one by one. It is about taking the ineffective patterns and changing them.

• • •

After two months of volunteering, the itch brews. I am bored. I need to be productive. My new, slightly slower version of myself is cranky. I call my old agency, and within two days, I have a full-time job counseling children and families. Back to the grind. So, now I need to work forty hours and prioritize my meals. As diet culture continues to be thrown into my face, I must follow my meal plan. As friends and family talk about their new paleo or vegan diets, I must eat consistently. When coworkers complain, "I am so bad for eating this cookie," I need to eat the cookie. Every few hours, I need to put food into my body, even if I have a difficult session or mounds of paperwork.

MOTHER'S DAY

I have a hate-hate relationship with jeans. Yes, hate-hate. Trying on a pair of jeans can ruin my day instantaneously. One moment, the jeans feel comfortable, and then five minutes later, I rip them off in a fit of disgust and put on sweatpants to manage my anxiety. I spend hours out to dinner, solely focusing on the jean band against my waist. I drink to the point of intoxication to forget about how fat I feel. In the rare situation I think a pair is "perfect," the feeling is fleeting, short lived. I spend night after night trying on pair after pair in my bedroom, my floor covered with blue, dark, and black denim.

Presently, I own about forty pairs of jeans. I have owned more. All different brands—the GAP, Old Navy, Levi's, Mavi, Lucky Star, Liverpool, Free People, Express, Joe's, Citizens of Humanity, M. Rena, Ann Taylor, Loft, Anthropologie—in all different styles—bootcut, button fly, slim, relaxed, boyfriend, baggy, jeggings, straight. I have had them shortened to fit my five-foot-three frame. I pinned the acid washed ones back with safety pins in the eighties. I bought ones with holes in them in the nineties.

In recovery, one goal is to stop trying them on obsessively, to put on one pair and move on with my day. I wear the jeans that fit me (which changes gently, but to me feels drastic) and put the others in plastic storage bins under the guest bed and in the basement. Sometimes, I think I could be a full-time jeans organizer on the side. In recovery, I hear the statement "Celebrate your here-and-now-body." So, I go on a mission to wear jeans repeatedly, desperately hoping that I will like the feel of them. That with enough exposure therapy, I can think away the discomfort and possibly become a person who likes wearing jeans.

• • •

I jump on a midmorning train heading to New York City. I slide into a free seat, staring out the window at the passing homes, stores, trees, water, and the light-blue sky. At Penn Station, the chatter is deafening, and I hurriedly climb up the steep stairs two by two to the fresh air outside. I hail a cab and take it to the American bistro to meet my family for Mother's Day lunch. I wear a shimmery gold tank top, tan pants, and a cardigan. I tried on jeans earlier, but I panicked and tore them off (they are crumpled on my bedroom rug). I walk through the front door of the restaurant, immediately noticing the banter of conversation and tables filled with people. I take a deep breath.

You can do this.

We sit at a large round table so my parents, Conor, Grace, Liam, Noah, and I can fit comfortably. The menu is digestible with only two pages, and I say, *You got this* to myself on repeat. By the time the waiter pulls up to my side, I feel some confidence, even though it is a big deal for me to be out to lunch in the city with my family. I order an arugula salad with cranberries and almonds with a vinaigrette dressing and salmon with quinoa in a lime butter sauce—no sauce on the side for either! A small win. Exposure is ripping off the Band-Aid. Feeling more comfortable in my body, I engage with my family. I have a small desire to connect with them despite feeling anxious. I feel my anxiety and validate it. I feel proud of Conor as he talks about coaching Liam's baseball team. I feel joy when I hug Noah tightly, telling him that he is the best godson in the world. I feel joy when I tell my mother that I love her and hand her a gift and card.

In the past, my eating disorder would tell me what to order—a salad with grilled chicken and balsamic vinaigrette on the side. I would try to listen to the conversations darting from one person to the other; however, my mind would jumble. I would feel uncomfortable in my skin and clothes. I would calculate how much exercise I needed to do after the meal, literally feeling my thighs and stomach expanding with each bite. I would feel guilty about ingesting the calories and panicked about how this meal would affect me for the rest of the day, tomorrow, and next week.

But not today. Instead of sitting on my couch, eating frozen string beans heated up in the microwave, I am out in the world. Recovery starts to bud like a flower, and it feels glorious.

FOOD RULES

I could write an entire book on food rules. I started creating them as a little girl—pretzels need to be unsalted, no real ice cream, only one portion of rice. The commands give me a false sense of control and become rooted in my brain. *No carbs, no desserts, no white flour, no rest days, only fruit, only vegetables, nothing processed, no food after 8 p.m., no food before 12 p.m., only organic, only protein, no fat, "clean" days, fasting days.* They keep me in this disordered bubble. In recovery, I challenge each of these rules—every single one. I ask myself, *How did I come up with this rule? Do other people need to follow the rule? What do I gain and lose by following the rule? How does the rule impact my life and my relationships? Will I follow the rule forever? What needs to happen to give up this rule?* With time, I start to trust my body, not my rules.

• • •

As months pass, I feel bold and adventurous. I join a meal program where the company sends you all the food in a cardboard box to cook a specific recipe. At first, I am excited over the pretty laminated recipes and colorful pictures. I like shiny things. I feel happy when I see the miniature bottle of mustard or mayonnaise, a few stalks of broccoli, or one clove of garlic. I take pride in cooking. I feel some mastery after I sit down to a homemade grilled cheese sandwich and tomato soup. I feel proud of the pasta and chicken dishes. But eventually, the awe and excitement wear off. Before I know it, I throw expired ingredients into the garbage with my apples. Enthusiasm over. This is typical behavior for me. I become obsessed with something or someone and then, one day, I just lose all interest.

For months, I go to Whole Foods to get my meals. It is pricey, but worth it. Then I order meals from a chef who delivers them to my home. I learn that convenience is key. I see big poster ads on the New Jersey turnpike for Eat Clean Bro. I hear they are a new meal delivery service in New Jersey. Ironically, the first store opens at the exact location of that no-name convenience store. I hate the title with a passion, so I ignore it. Eating is eating—it is not clean or dirty—and this mindset has the potential to undo my hard work. I learn that all food in moderation fits. I learn that if I feel deprived of a food, then it has the power. I learn that food is not a moral issue or a power play. It is food! What a load off my shoulders! You mean I can eat without guilt? You mean I can eat the muffin? I can eat without telling myself I am bad and worthless? Hallelujah!

But following the conscious eating guidelines is tough. I visit the Eat Clean Bro website and see a full menu of choices. I still hate the name, but coming home each night to heat up a meal in three minutes in the microwave is a saving grace.

SAYING "YES!"

"**T**wo plain slices to go?" "Yes."
"Want to share dessert?" "Yes."
"Do you want croutons on your salad?" "Yes."
"Butter on your bread?" "Yes."
"Would you like to go out to lunch?" "Yes."
"Would you like to join the cookie swap?" "Why not?"
"Whipped cream on your hot chocolate?" "Absolutely."

For recovery to work, I turn into a "yes" girl. I roll up my sleeves, toss my dyed blonde hair back into a colorful hairband to get any fraying wisps off my face, and concentrate. I dig deep and say yes to everything that scares me surrounding food.

"Sure," I text Amelia, knowing that every cell in my body does not want to leave the safety of my house today. I agree to meet her at Dunkin' Donuts for coffee. The last time she asked, I said "yes" and then bailed at the last minute, my anxiety swallowing me whole. Today, the critical thoughts start to fall like dominoes. I am having a fat day to boot, and I want to hide from the world.

Just say no. Then turn down your shades and go to bed. You will be safe there.

I dress in jeans and a sweater. I repeat positive affirmations out loud—"You can recover. You can recover"—on my drive over. My stomach drops with anxiety as I push open the coffee shop door, smelling the sweet aroma of donuts sitting on shelves behind the counter. I see Amelia at the small laminate table by the wall. I walk over, and as I slide into the seat, I feel the material of my jeans on my stomach and thighs. I feel like a caged tiger. I either want to jump over the counter and shove Munchkins into my face or bolt out of the shop, crying hysterically while cutting my jeans off with a pair of sharp scissors. As both of those ideas go through my head, I smile, breathe out, and say, "Hi, Amelia."

You can do this.

"Hi, Mer."

I order a coffee with almond milk. Amelia gets a chai latte and blueberry muffin. The urge to burst into tears sits in my throat, but I breathe through it. I do my best to be mindful and present, but my mind constantly wanders. It drifts to the physical feeling of crawling out of my skin. It strays to the thought of ripping off the top button and then unzipping my jeans. It digresses to the desire to be sitting in my bathtub with steaming-hot water beating onto my back. But I sit there and drink my coffee, sip after sip. I talk with Amelia, and even though my mind is racing, I come back to the present.

I tear off my clothes violently as soon as I get home, relief washing over me as the jeans roll off my thighs. I feel liberated when my loose black sweats and my tattered, gray Loyola sweatshirt graze my skin. Then a huge smile forms on my face.

I was uncomfortable, but I did it anyway.

• • •

Exposure therapy is putting yourself in situations that are fear inducing and then doing them anyway. It is a psychological treatment that was developed to help people confront their fears. According to Tamar E. Chansky, "It includes practicing new behaviors one step at a time in the target situations," such as eating a snack or sitting with an urge to purge. Usually people avoid their fears, which may help temporarily in the short-term, but over time this makes the fear even worse. If you fear spiders, then hold one in your hand. If you fear social settings, then go to a concert. If you fear eating, eat—all foods, not some foods.

If I am at a [insert any kind of party] and they serve cake, I have a slice. If my office orders pizza for lunch, I eat it. When my mom puts out her platter of Christmas Eve cookies, I eat them. If there are bagels for breakfast, I grab a sesame. If I am at the movies, I share a box of Junior Mints. If my friends order Jersey Mike's Subs for the beach, I eat one—the way it is ordered.

It is hard and I continue up the lofty mountain with cement bricks in my pockets anyway. I start to feel like I am on an adventure, experiencing life in a totally different way. Eating some foods feels like it is for the first time. After so many years of restricting, a strawberry feels like a sugar cube on my tongue. Full-fat milk is decadent. Peanut butter pretzels taste like salt mounds. And through each exposure, I start to see the world as a less scary place. Even when every bone in my body says no, I act in the opposite way. Opposite action is a DBT emotion regulation skill. Opposite action is to do the exact opposite of your emotion-driven urge if acting on your emotion will not be effective to your goals or if your emotion does not fit the facts. I also publicly—well, to my mirror—make an apology to the poor carbohydrate. I have demonized it for so long, and now I add carbs to each meal. It becomes a building block of my nutrition.

• • •

Today, we take the girls in the Youth With A Purpose program to Longstreet Farm in Holmdel. I feel the dark-blue T-shirt and capri pants I wear hug my body. I stretched out the waistband with both hands that morning because I could not tolerate it on my skin. After we look at the farm animals, we stop at an old farmhouse to make homemade vanilla ice cream. The girls are giddy with excitement as we each take turns churning the ingredients—the butter, cream, sugar, and vanilla. It is a hot, luminous August day, and each girl digs into the ice cream before the sun melts it away. I grab a small bowl and spoon. I take a bite. Then another. The vanilla and fat and sugary sweetness erupt in my mouth.

• • •

One week later, another exposure presents itself. Liam has a baseball game and I decide to attend. I wear tan cotton Gap khakis, a white tee, and a lemon-colored sweater. I sit in my Toyota Corolla, tears wetting my cheeks. I feel the material of my clothes on my skin like bugs crawling up and down my spine. I want desperately to cancel, put on loose-fitting clothes, and retreat to my bedroom. But it's Liam—my first-born nephew. I cannot let him down. I drive sixty miles to his game and sit on the uncomfortable silver bleachers with Grace and Noah. Siblings play tag as their brothers hit or play the field. Families sit on the bleachers or in backpack chairs. Soda and chips are quickly bought at the snack counter.

I feel proud of Conor, who is taking time out of his career to really enjoy the small moments as Liam's coach. I hold my breath tightly when Liam strikes out the last player for a win. I feel calm sitting with Grace, even in silence. I feel happy when Noah places his beautiful, blond mop of hair in my lap.

• • •

Mom and I fly out to California to meet my new nephew, Henry. Aidan and Beth are thrilled. As we walk from the hotel to Aidan's house, I feel the material of my cropped Ann Taylor Loft jeans on my skin. I start to take deep breaths to work through the discomfort.

You can do this. You could be dead. You can stand this.

And if I had died, I would not be here. I would not be holding my third, tiny, perfect nephew nestled in my arms. Little Henry's minute fingers wrap around my index finger. A bond is set.

I am going to be the best aunt for you. I promise.

Two years later, my nephew James is born, and he is quite the firecracker.

BFFS

After Darcy gives me an extra-long hug, we sit down on the front steps of my beach house. Her extended hugs used to make me feel uncomfortable, suffocated. But through the years, I have softened, and after the year that I just had, I relax my shoulders and feel her embrace. It is a sunny day with a cool breeze making its way from the beach.

"Hi, Mer-Mer. It is so good to see you."

"You too," I say, smiling. I shift uneasily on the paved stairs. The rest of my family is on the back porch, so we have some privacy. "So, I have to tell you something."

"Sure."

I stare down at my mother's *Bonjour* welcome mat, which she purchased after a trip to France for one of her and my father's wedding anniversaries. The fuchsia hydrangeas in big pots on each side match it perfectly.

"I'm not actually doing that great."

Darcy's face falls and she grabs my hand softly.

"Last December, I started a PHP to get help for my eating disorder. I wanted to tell you, but I felt so overwhelmed, ashamed. I felt too depressed to pick up the phone and talk," I divulge. "I stopped in May, and I am definitely getting better, but I have a long way to go."

"Oh, Mer-Mer. I wish I was there for you. I am here now," Darcy says as she grabs my other hand. Her eyes fill with tears and her face scrunches, showing her concern.

"I could barely tell anyone. I wanted to pretend that it would just go away with a poof," I say, fanning my fingers out in front of me. "But it did not go that way," I say, laughing, always cracking a joke to defuse the tension. "I know God gave me straight white teeth, but he threw in the bunions and the crappy mind just to keep me on my toes." I grin.

Darcy bursts out laughing and wraps her arms around me. I place my head on her shoulder. I think about our Barbie shows and our Cabbage Patch Kids and when we wrote letters to each other over the summer, signing them LYLAS (love you like a sister).

· · ·

I move into an adorable two-bedroom apartment blocks away from the center of Red Bank. I have a front porch, granite countertops, and multiple large closets for my shopping addiction. As I methodically put away my groceries, the doorbell rings. My immediate response is to ignore it, but I go the front door and open it with trepidation. A woman with long dark-brown hair tied back in a bun stands there with a bouquet of red roses in her arms.

"These are for you. They were delivered to me by mistake."

"Thank you," I say as I gingerly grab the flowers.

"Someone must love you."

"Ahh . . . yes," I say, distracted.

I put the vase on my kitchen table and read the card.

"Congratulations. A year later and you are continuing to fight the good fight. We love you dearly. Love, your only mom and dad."

TROUBLED WATERS

A few months later, I sit on my tan leather chair, inches away from my home desk. Five new books lie on the middle bookshelf, but lately, I have been too restless to read, and they remain untouched. I turn to the computer and press print. As soon as the blank calendar page spits out, I know I am swimming in dangerous waters.

Just write down what you are eating each day. No big deal.

The sharks are circling me.

Three apples, one bag of string beans, coffee.

I am in deep water. I can ask for help or sink.

You can only eat fruits and vegetables.

I sink.

Only do it for seven days. Just to get some control back.

On day fifteen, I am weak and shove a handful of pretzels into my mouth.

Now you need to do more cardio.

• • •

My anxiety is crippling. I wake up with a looming pit in my stomach. I start to skip breakfast, letting even the apples turn brown. I go back to my psychiatrist, but the water features in her office do not help this time.

"I feel paralyzed. I can be sitting on the couch, and this sense of dread overtakes me, and I think that something bad is going to happen, even if I am totally fine and safe."

"I am worried about putting you on a benzodiazepine with your addictive personality."

"I can't function. I need to go to work."

Hesitantly, she grabs her prescription pad and writes a script for Klonopin. I drive straight to the pharmacy, and within seconds of taking the small, snow-white pill, my body softens like I have taken a shot of vodka. A warmness soothes me. I feel like I can take on the world. I am thrust into super-chill Meredith. My anxiety is washed away like someone sprayed Windex on a glass door and wiped it with a clean towel, leaving no streaks. My therapist, David, mentions that I seem a bit manic in our session today—talking in circles, talking quickly. I feel like a brand-new, much better, more composed version of myself.

A few days later, the suicidal thoughts start. They are intense, extreme. An array of active plans flitter around in my brain—I can cut my wrist, take a bottle of Tylenol and wash it down with wine, jump in front of a train, put rocks in a backpack and walk out to sea. I pause to realize that I am in my emotional mind. I tap into my rational brain and grab my phone.

"I want to kill myself," I cry to my parents on speaker.

Two hours later, Dad stands at my apartment door. I fall into his arms and cry.

"Why am I so sad?"

"I don't know, sweetie. I'm here."

I notice the duffel bag by his side—he is staying the night. My father's presence is grounding. My brain rests when he is around because I know he will take care of me. I promise him in the morning that I am okay. And, for a few days, I am.

· · ·

It is Friday night. I do not have plans and feel like a loose cannon.
Stay in the present. Relax. Use your skills.
My cell phone dings.
"Want to come over?" Amelia asks.
"Sure," I answer, relief parachuting over my body. I open a fresh bottle of pinot grigio, grab an oversized white-wine glass, and fill it to the top. This is one of the first times I have had alcohol since the program. I signed a document that I would not use alcohol or drugs while I was there, and like a good rule follower, I didn't.
But you are not in the PHP anymore.
I sit at my vanity, happy for a project. My overfilled makeup bag lies next to the brown wooden jewelry box Matt bought me for our first Christmas together. I apply some light cover-up to my face, blush to my cheeks, and contour my lips with a berry lipliner. I get another glass of wine. Next is my hair. I re-wet it by putting it under the shower spout, use a pick to get the knots out and brush it straight. I dry my shoulder-length, dirty-blonde hair using a wide brush to curl the ends, even though, in five minutes, I will throw it back into a ponytail.
I go back and forth about going to Amelia's house—part of me wants to be social and the other wants to isolate. My third glass of wine goes down easy. I go back to my vanity and reapply my makeup. I darken my lips with pink chocolate lipstick. I deepen the caramel eyeshadow on my lids. I blacken my eyelashes. I am tipsy and start to feel bold. Invincible. The more I drink, the lonelier I feel. I restricted today because of the anxiety, and the wine goes straight to my head.

No one wants you around. You have no life.

The thoughts start.

You are going to be stuck with your eating disorder for the rest of your life. You may as well just end it. You will never get better.

I pour another glass of wine, finishing the bottle to the last drop.

"Hey, Amelia. I'm going to stay in tonight," I text.

"Okay. Maybe next time," she replies immediately with a heart emoji.

I walk to the kitchen counter and see four pill bottles side by side by the oven timer, a mini teapot. I pick up the Wellbutrin and slowly unscrew the cap—it is full. I raise the bottle to my lips and empty about half of them into my mouth. I take a huge slug of water. I stand still briefly. Within minutes, a warm calmness spreads from my head to my toes.

This is what I want. Relief. No more war with my body.

I slowly walk down the foyer and into my bedroom. I slide off my tight dark jeans and my black "going-out" shirt and slip on my black velvet pants that I wore to the first day of my program. I place my old Loyola sweatshirt over my head. I wipe off my makeup. I methodically take off my jewelry and place it into the box piece by piece. I sit on the edge of my bed, my feet not touching the floor because it is on risers to store clothes underneath. I call Amelia.

"Hey, Amelia."

"Hey, Mer. What is going on?"

"Umm . . . I'm good. How are you?"

"We are good. Just finishing up dinner. What are you up to?"

"Umm . . . I took some pills."

"You just took some pills?"

"Yes. I did. Okay. I am gonna go now." *Click.* I lay the phone down on my bedside table.

I hear the low buzz of an ambulance siren. It quickly becomes louder and louder, like I have an action movie on in the den at volume ten. The bright-red lights of the police cars fill my driveway. Two police officers arrive at my doorstep. I do not remember opening the door, but they stand in my apartment entrance.

"Hi, miss. How are you doing tonight?"

"I'm okay."

"What is your name?" one asks, reaching into his pocket and taking out a small notepad.

"Meredith O'Brien," I slur, sitting down in a kitchen chair to catch my balance.

"Your friend Amelia called and wanted us to check in on you. Said you took some pills."

"I did."

"Do you know the date?"

"Hmm . . . Friday . . . Umm . . ."

I want more pills.

My body floats over the table, and I squeeze my eyes tightly to jump back to reality. I get up nonchalantly and shimmy past the cop to the counter. Before I reach the pill bottle, he stops me with his arm and shows me back to the kitchen chair.

"We need to take you to the hospital, miss."

"Okay," I say softly, looking down and feeling loose in my joints, like wet spaghetti. I sit in the back of the ambulance. By the time we get to the ER three blocks away, the left arm of my sweatshirt is ripped up to my bicep. I go to rip it more and a paramedic stops me by lying his hand softly on my forearm.

"That is enough, hun. No more," he says as he takes the tie from my pants and my sneakers with the laces and places them in a clear bag.

The hospital is quiet, I think. All the sounds I hear are muffled like I am underwater. I put the hospital gown over my head and wobble into the sterile bed. A nurse places a large white Styrofoam cup filled with charcoal on the wooden table and turns toward me. As I drink, I make teeth marks in the rim. I sip the dark liquid slowly. It tastes like concrete. As it slides down my throat, nausea begins to pull it back up.

I see my parents enter the ER door. Quickly thereafter, Conor runs in too. He is the big brother coming to the rescue. As soon as he got the phone call from my parents, he jumped into his car and started to drive south toward the Jersey Shore. After I medically stabilize days later, I am admitted into the inpatient psychiatric unit. Conor visits again. He pulls me into an embrace. I want to cry, but no tears come.

"Liam and Noah need you, Mer," Conor says, grabbing my shoulders lightly and looking me dead in the eyes.

"I know," I say, bowing into his shoulder and whimpering. Due to the heavy medications that I have been administered, I do not feel much of anything.

"We love you, Mer," Conor says, wrapping his arms around me.

• • •

As soon as I get released from the hospital one week later, I start purging up to three times a day. Sometimes five. This time, I purge blood. It does not stop me. I need the release. I need to purge the shame. Embarrassment. Disgust. And then I flip-flop, grabbing onto a sliver of hope. I clutch my journal and start writing in black ink: "Enough is enough! My life is passing me by and I need to focus on recovery. I need to focus on me. I need to throw every damn excuse out the window and fight to find peace."

This suicide attempt has woken me. I have a newfound faith. I want to be present in my life and see my nephews grow up. I want to beat this eating disorder and live life. I want to feel empowered, worthy, and comfortable with myself. I want to experience joy, real joy. But first I need to meet with Amelia and thank her for saving my life and apologize profusely. I have a nervous feeling all day. I know that Amelia will be compassionate, but also blunt.

"I am so sorry. Thank you."

"Mer, I did not know if you were alive or dead."

THE MONSTER IS BACK

I try my best to get back on track, but the purging takes over. Today, my goal is to have a "purge-free" day. I break the cycle. I do not purge! I acknowledge my success, knowing that it is no easy feat. I receive an email from Aidan, which helps me to stay on a compassionate path: "Mer, please, please, please break the cycle. Next time you feel like you are going to purge CALL ME. You are too important and vital to do this to yourself. If you can figure it out on your own, that is great. But don't just write it down. Do it! I know you can. I believe in you. I love you."

The words "you are too important to do this to yourself" hit me powerfully. Each time I purge, I am in danger of dying. I could be the end of an after-school special on *Lifetime*. I could die without reaching forty. Or having children. My parents could find me dead of a heart attack, lying on my kitchen floor with empty cookie bags and ice cream wrappers around my sink.

I rededicate myself to recovery. My depression is high, and most days, I do not want to get out of bed, but I act oppositely. I get out of bed. I take a shower. I go to work. On some days, I feel a little brighter and continue the fight, reminding myself that I am recovering so I can be the best aunt I can be. Now, with four of them, I want them each to get the attention they deserve. I also want to have a family of my own. I want to connect with others. I want a partner. My life must be more than my eating disorder.

I hear the crackle of my white pebble driveway as my parents' forest-green Mercedes pulls up behind my car. I walk to the bay window and watch Mom and Dad get out. Mom pops open the truck and grabs a white shopping bag I imagine is filled with small gifts for, well . . . no reason at all. I also know something is wrong as soon as I see my mom's face through the screen door.

"Hey, Mer," she says, straining a smile. Her voice says it all.

Something terrible is about to happen.

I peer into the bag. It is filled with Dots candy, scented candles, a new scarf, and a gift card to Anthropologie. My hands tremble as I put the card into my wallet.

"Hey, honey," my dad says. I notice the bags underneath his eyes. "So, I have something to tell you."

Tears stream down my face before he says anything else.

"Something is bad, isn't it?" I ask.

"Everything is fine. Everything will be fine. I have tongue cancer."

The tears fall more forcefully, and everything goes into slow motion.

My dad is going to die. My dad is going to die.

"I called Conor and Aidan, but I knew I needed to tell you face-to-face. We are concerned about your recovery, and we need you to stay on track. I am getting surgery in two weeks by the best surgeon in the city."

I fall into his arms, smelling his musty aftershave. I hug him tightly, scared to let go. Dad makes everything better, but he needs me to be strong now. I know how to cope—go back to my faithful companion—but it feels disrespectful, like a betrayal. I garner a strength I do not know I am capable of.

Two weeks later, he has his surgery. On the train into the city, I try to mentally prepare myself, but no preparation is adequate for the dad I see in his recovery room. Tubes and IVs stick out from his arm and chest. His face is so bloated that he looks like a stranger. His lips are chapped and bleeding. He has a large bandage on his left arm. I want to burst into tears, but I don't. I reach out my hand and rest it gently on my dad's hand. I am his rock today.

• • •

It is midday. Saturday. Dad is recovering at home. I mindlessly scroll through Facebook. My doorbell rings. A jolt of anxiety fires in my body; but I get up, walk to the door, and open it. Two girls in lawn-green Girl Scout uniforms stand on my white porch. They unfold the large cookie purchase list three times. I am quickly brought back to a memory of Dad buying over twenty boxes of cookies so I could earn a circle badge that my mom sewed onto my green sash.

I take the list and fill in my order. I buy a box of Samoas. Thin Mints. Do-si-dos. Trefoils. All my favorites. It was Girl Scouts, for God's sake. No one at my door ready to attack. I place my order and go on with my day. I open the door.

IS THIS HAPPINESS?

string a few encouraging months together. I eliminate behaviors, challenge my eating disorder thoughts, and follow my meal plan. I have small bursts of positivity, feeling a tingle in my fingertips. It feels unfamiliar but pleasant, light, and free. I sit with the feeling.

I have an unusual desire to be social, and I invite my friend Peter from Connecticut to visit for a night. We met a few years ago when we worked at the same marketing company. Our firm had weekly happy hours, and his vibe was endearing. He was always in the center of a crowd, telling sarcastic and funny jokes. He can make me laugh hard. He also has this knack for making me feel like I am the only girl in the room. We flirted a lot but never dated. He is the perfect male friend, and I don't want to jeopardize the friendship.

I make reservations at Via 45, a small rustic restaurant in the middle of Red Bank, my favorite one in town. It is run by a female couple who change the handwritten menu daily. It is impossible to get in, so I make reservations weeks in advance. It feels weird to get dressed up. But it also feels new. Fun. I slide on a new pair of skinny jeans and a new blue satin blouse that brings the blue out in my eyes. I feel pleased when I look in the mirror, turning my mind toward body acceptance, but I still feel squeamish in jeans.

Decorative, colorful plates and framed pictures fill the walls. Each table has different styles of chairs surrounding them, and a velvet purple curtain ropes off the restaurant from the kitchen. As soon as we sit down at the bustling restaurant, the waiter drops a basket of fresh doughy bread on our unique table, which has decorative flower designs at the corners. Next to it, he places a small bowl filled with herbed olive oil. Peter grabs a piece and dips it into the oil.

"So good." He smiles. I grab a piece of bread and dip it into the oil too.

"Delicious." I taste the garlic and herbs. Peter makes eating fun, and in this moment, I feel happy. Really happy.

"We will get a bottle of your house merlot," Peter says to the waiter, and I nod. I feel safe and know that I will moderate my drinking with him. I am completely myself.

"Everything looks amazing," Peter says as he scans the one-page menu. "What are you going to get? This place is awesome. Good choice."

"Thanks. I know, isn't it? I'm thinking the fish special or the risotto."

"That bacon app is calling my name. Want to share?"

"Sounds great," I answer excitedly.

As we catch up with each other's lives, the waiter sets down the appetizer of asparagus and potato wrapped in bacon in the middle of the table. I relish the crispy bacon in my mouth. I get the skate Francese. Peter orders the steak. We share a decadent chocolate brownie with vanilla ice cream. He grabs my hand as we leave the restaurant, and we both stare at the moon glowing over the Navesink River.

MY ANGEL TREE

collect angels. They adorn my bookcases, desks, doorknobs, mantels, and built-ins. I dislike malls, but I go twice a year specifically for the Hallmark store. I have the angels of serenity, wisdom, Irish charm, good health, courage, love, and remembrance. As a young girl at Christmas time, I went to the Woman's Exchange, a store run by the woman's club in our hometown. I was fascinated with the handmade ornaments—angels made from walnuts, starfish, pipe cleaners, ribbon, and cloth.

My favorite part of Christmas Eve each year is sitting down to a magnificently decorated dining room table with our fine china. Sitting next to each place card is a holiday ornament Mom buys specifically for that guest. Each ornament is personalized. The year Liam is the captain of his basketball team, he gets a basketball ornament. My uncle Pete is very handy, and one year he gets a toolbox ornament. My cousin Fred is a surfer, and he gets a colorful orange surfboard. For me, though, it is always an angel. And each year, I add the delicate ornament to my angel Christmas tree before it is stored in my "angel ornaments" cardboard box that somehow holds up year to year.

This year, I am excited for the holiday season. Dad is completely healed from his surgery. My recovery is solid. I run up the garage stairs two by two to the upper floor where I store my Christmas decorations. After carefully hopping over clear bins and shopping bags filled with old pictures, trophies, and outdated clothes, I grab the two large parts of the artificial tree and carefully walk down the stairs because there is no railing. I squeeze my abs to stay balanced.

"Need help?" Ben asks, taking an oily rag and putting it in the back pocket of his jean overalls. Ben rents out the garage attached to the apartment I rent and refurbishes old cars. We run into each other from time to time.

"I'm good," I answer, blushing because I think he is cute.

"Getting ready for Christmas, huh?"

"Yes. I love this time of year."

"Well, let's exchange numbers just in case you need anything. I'd be happy to help."

"Sure," I answer.

Is he flirting with me?

I take the tree inside, snap the pieces into place, and situate the three-foot-tall tree on a small table by the bay window. A Kelly Clarkson Christmas album plays in the background. I open the brown cardboard box, daintily unwrapping each angel bursting with memories. I hang up about twenty angels, plug in the white lights that are wrapped around the tree, and smile. It is my tree of hope. I place a small, red blanket at the base and continue with my decorating.

• • •

Ben stands about six feet tall, and I am intrigued by his ruggedness. No one in my family is a "car person," and he piques my interest. Each Saturday, he spends almost the entire day in the garage. Within a week, he texts me to go on a date.

So, he was flirting.

I am feeling stronger in my recovery and ready to start dating.

I wear dark jeans, a fitted pink tank top, and a tight black sweater knotted at my waist. He picks me up like a gentleman. He walks into my kitchen in light-colored jeans, a light-blue button down, and a cream-colored cap. No coat, even though it is December.

"Wow, you look beautiful."

"Thanks." I half smile, tickled by his genuineness.

Our first stop is a small and cozy bar in the next town over. Since I have only been focused on my eating disorder recovery and work at the clinic, I am excited to explore the town. I crave novelty and newness. I get a vodka club and he orders a bottle of Budweiser. He challenges me to a game of shuffleboard, and I am taken aback by his playful personality. As I push my pegs to the other side, I feel the vodka warming my body and easing my nervousness. He is big—the type of body I can fall into. The type that is safe and can eliminate my self-consciousness.

Before we leave, I check my face in the bathroom mirror, reapply my rose lipstick, and wipe down any hair wisps with some cold water. The vodka has gone to my head, and I am already feeling toasty. We head to another bar. On the left side of the restaurant sits a large, rectangular bar. A full set of glass windows cover an entire wall with a view of the Navesink River. On the right, there are scattered brown tables where a few people finish their dinners. We eat large raw peanuts from small brown plastic bowls and throw the shells onto the floor. I feel a sense of liberation just chucking them with abandon.

"I come here all the time. It is a local hangout."

"I've never been, but the peanuts are a nice touch," I say, popping one into my mouth. "Do you work?"

"Yes, I am an electrician. You?"

"Yes, I am a therapist. I work at a mental health clinic and am thinking of starting a private practice soon."

"Woah. A therapist."

"Don't worry, I have already diagnosed you."

He laughs out loud and smiles widely. I know he is smitten with my sarcasm and wit.

"Do you always wear a hat?" I ask, staring up at the faded hat that he has worn all night.

"Yep. Always," Ben answers.

"Okay." I shrug.

Ben pauses and says, "I lost my hair early and I am self-conscious."

I touch his rough hand softly and our eyes meet. Ben removes his hat slowly and places it on his knee.

"I love it," I say, grinning wide.

Ben quickly returns the hat to his head, bowing in embarrassment. His vulnerability is refreshing.

And even though I know something is amiss when he finally kisses me after our third date, we fall for each other quickly. I have just spent years breaking free from a self-destructive pattern with my body, weight, and food; however, I have no idea just how vulnerable I am to fall right into another.

· · ·

When we are in love, we are passionately in love. When we drink, we drink a lot. When we fight, we fight hard. We have dramatic disagreements that end in upheavals of conflict. Within a month, I break up with him. He is not stable. I need to continue with my recovery undisturbed. The excitement of dating someone with such a different upbringing fades. He is clingy and I need alone time. I also obsess about the potential judgment from my parents. He flees my apartment abruptly. After five minutes, my phone pings.

"I just quit my job," Ben announces.

"What? Why would you do that?"

"I am going to move away. I cannot live without you."

My gut tells me to walk away. His behavior is erratic. My healthy core self screams at me to listen, but I ignore it. I am probably being impulsive, too hard on him. He deserves a chance. We deserve a chance. Within a week, we get back together, promising that it will be forever.

We become drinking buddies. Even though I continue to eliminate eating disorder behaviors and eat more, I am still uncomfortable in my body. The vodka elixir decreases the doubt, the insecurity. We are from two quite different worlds, and we try our best to meld them together. We have a deep connection, and despite the turmoil, we keep coming back to one another. I am fresh out of recovery. He has recently gotten divorced. He is self-conscious. I am self-conscious. We quickly become codependent. We take turns being "sick." When I feel positive, he is depressed. When I have daily anxiety attacks, he thrives at work. We are so in love but cannot find a consistent rhythm.

DANCING

Ben shows up to my mother's birthday party in a white Hanes T-shirt, baggy cargo shorts, and a worn baseball cap. A few days before, I told him to pick up a small hostess gift.

"What is a hostess gift?"

"It is a gift that you bring to the people hosting the party. This is the first time you are officially coming to my home, and it is good etiquette to bring a gift. Just pick up a bottle of wine."

"What kind? I don't drink wine."

"Any kind—red or white. Don't spend over $20."

He walks in with a brown paper bag in his arms, looking so uncomfortable that he seems like he's about to jump out of his own skin. He awkwardly drops the bag on the kitchen table. I quickly pick it up, remove the two wine bottles, and briefly show my parents the gift.

"Thank you. How nice," Dad says.

Mom smiles uneasily—another boyfriend is in the house, and she looks like she wants to throw up but takes a large sip of her pinot grigio on ice instead. The caterers pass around appetizers, and the band finishes setting up in the living room. The band starts to play some oldies—Dad's favorite genre of music. My parents, uncle and aunt, and my brothers and their wives get up to dance.

Ben sits like a schoolboy on our beachy tan-and-red couch.

"Will you please take your hat off?" I whisper, leaning into his cheek.

"No."

"It's rude, babe."

"No," he says firmly, and I smile big to pretend that everything is fine. After a few songs, I turn to Ben, "Are you going to ask me to dance?"

"I don't dance."

"You don't dance? Like ever?"

"Never."

"Okay. Well, I would like to dance, mingle with the family, talk," I say, embarrassed that we are so cut off from the rest of my family.

"No, Mer. Please. I can't," he says seriously. "Can I please just sit here?"

His grimace is palpable, so I lay a soft hand on his shoulder and nod.

"Sure."

I get up to dance with Liam and Noah, who are twirling on our green carpet. We make circles as our index fingers point at the ceiling and our shoulders bounce up and down. Time stops momentarily and tension leaves my body, replaced with joy. Afterwards, I return to Ben's side on the couch. Eventually, the band starts the first few beats of my parents' wedding song. Dad takes my mom into his arms and sings softly into her ear. Conor swirls Grace around, and Aidan holds Beth tightly. Ben and I watch until I finally convince him to just stand and hold my hands and sway to the music. Our dance is short lived, and he hastily returns to the couch, pouting. He leaves without saying goodbye. As soon as I get into my car to drive home, I burst into tears.

• • •

He goes camping for a weekend with his childhood friends, and within a day, he drives back at midnight because he cannot be away from me. Yes, it is romantic but also unhealthy. The pattern of fighting and then making up continues. The fighting is awful. The make-up is beautifully overwhelming. When my hand slips into his hand, the sky turns blue and the sun shines.

THE PAIN IN MY MIND

I t starts out as a relatively normal day. My body is buzzing with indecisiveness about my relationship. It is the opposite of stable, but I push the feelings away. Recently, Ben and I discussed moving in together. Part of me feels exhilarated. Another part feels inharmonious. I know I am an adult and I need to make my own decisions, but the anticipated judgment from my parents is stifling. And deep down, I know it is not what I want.

I cannot handle it if my parents are angry with me. Disappointed.

As the thoughts consume me, I start to feel fat. Then ugly. Then I open a cold bottle of white wine and drink a generous glass. I want the feelings to stop. The alcohol begins its job of numbing me, anesthetizing me.

Ben finished work early and stopped at a local bar to get drinks with some friends, but we agree to get dinner afterward. He says that he will make reservations. I get dressed and wait patiently by the phone, but he never calls. He does not return my text messages. Radio silence. I finish the bottle. By now, the feelings of excitement are deadened, replaced with feelings of exclusion and shame.

I guess he just forgot about me.

The suicidal thoughts emerge from out of nowhere so quickly that I am not even sure if I just swallowed a handful of Prozac. I am dazed but dial Conor for help.

"Conor. I took some pills," I say bluntly. By this time, I am disassociated from reality.

"Okay, Mer. Everything will be okay. I am going to call the police."

Conor is the older brother—he will save me. He will protect me. He jumps in the car, heading for the George Washington Bridge, and comes directly to the hospital, calling my parents on the way. I do not have the ability to recognize the impact I may be having on him, but after things settle down, I am mindful of the grave disturbance. I am also cognizant that in crisis, I call him—not my parents, not Ben. Conor is my rock.

This time, I get my stomach pumped.

I miss Halloween and Hurricane Sandy, which demolishes the Jersey Shore, leaving people's homes in shambles. While the East Coast is being destroyed, I lie in a hospital bed, hallucinating for what feels like weeks. I see bugs coming out of my mother's eyes and nose. Ben's face looks warped—like I am looking into a funhouse mirror. The ceiling tiles change color. The laminate hospital floor turns into frogs, then snakes, then monkeys. Ben brushes my greasy, matted hair as I try to sit up. He is tender. Accepting. Mom is tense. Her eye rolls and austere face reveal that she is furious that Ben, an intruder, is here at this intimate time. But he comes every day. He sits with me. He holds my hand.

The hurricane has the hospital in mayhem. They have backup generators, but the lights and power still flicker off and on. After a few horrible days in intensive care, I shower. The water is freezing, but it is exactly what I need to bring me back to reality. I quickly wash my body with the bar of soap Mom hands to me as she stands inches from the curtain to make sure that I do not fall. I wash my hair in record time. I dry off my shaking body.

They keep me in the psychiatric ward for a few days but ultimately discharge me.

"You are smart. Educated. You are not like these other people," the psychiatrist announces, and he swings his left arm, palm open toward the door, gesturing to the patients out in the hall through the tiny window.

Who the fuck belongs in a psych ward? I did not know that there was a "type" of person who needs mental health support.

I guess it seems like I am put together. I am a White, privileged, employed woman with a support system. But did everyone forget that I just tried to overdose? Again? For the second time? Mom drives me to my apartment. We are silent. She pulls into the gravel driveway, puts the car in park, takes a breath, and turns directly to me.

"Mer. I cannot take this anymore. I am one day away from flying to a deserted island and never coming back home. We don't know how to help you anymore."

"I'm sorry. I can do this, Mom. I'll start eating more. I'll stop drinking. I have to try harder."

As my mom pulls out, the lights somehow turn back on in my apartment. I take a hot shower and blow-dry my hair, the heat filling my core. The effects of Hurricane Sandy are subsiding, but the hurricane in my head is buzzing.

• • •

The next day, Ben and I get pedicures. He hates people touching his feet, but he sits next to me and gets his feet washed, scrubbed, and massaged. He jokes with the nail salon employees, and they all love him by the time we leave. His charm is undeniable.

We walk down White Street in Red Bank. Ben runs ahead to Char. They can take us now for dinner. The restaurant is just getting full as we sit down. Here are two people in love trying to make sense of life. Another crisis. I will never forget this day. It is etched onto my heart, but the sweetness does not last.

DECEPTION

When someone constantly tells you that no one will love you the way they do, you start to believe it. Each time I question Ben about the toxicity of our relationship, he tells me that I am emotional, dramatic. He says that I am jumping to conclusions and that other people are jealous of our love. That people stare at us when we are holding hands in a restaurant, gazing into each other's eyes. Maybe Ben is right. I will probably be "too much" for other people. Maybe because of my eating disorder and depression, I cannot trust myself. Then why did my body initially resist when we kissed for the first time? Why did I end our relationship after four weeks? A glaring red flag flew ferociously, but I wished it away.

"I cannot pay rent this month," Ben says calmly over dinner one night.

"Um . . . okay . . . why?" I ask, my body filling with heat.

"I just had some unexpected bills, and I did not get much work this month."

"Um . . . okay," I say, my jaw clenching, and I push my dinner to the side.

"I know you can cover me."

"Yes, I can, but why did you wait until today to tell me? It is due tomorrow."

"It's not a big deal, Mer."

"I feel like I need to take care of everything," I say as my body tenses like taffy. "I am the only one who has any savings. You rarely have money. I am not sure what you do with all of it." I hate confrontation and alarm bells go off, ringing in my ear and drowning out my thoughts. They all jumble, and I start to shut down, losing focus on our conversation.

"Mer, I am embarrassed as it is—do not make this more difficult for me. I would cover you," Ben says tersely.

"I'm not saying that I won't cover for you, but what if this happens again?"

"It won't," Ben says. "I promise."

And even though I know it is going to happen again, I write out the full rent check and pop it in the mail to our landlord.

• • •

After about six weeks, I tell Ben that David, my therapist, says I am stable enough to drink again. After the second suicide attempt, I promised to stop drinking since it was a common denominator. Even though the hospital never brought up my use, I know alcohol and I are not a good mix—it's like my reasonable mind gets wiped out entirely. Ben pulls his neck back and crumples his face. He does not buy it.

"No. He said I am okay. Really. He told me at our last session. You can call him if you want," I say, signaling to my cell phone on the kitchen counter.

I know he won't call. He'll believe me. Those words were never uttered from David's lips.

Ben takes me to a new restaurant that opened in Atlantic Highlands. He buttons my jacket up one at a time and gives me a kiss on the head. It is blistering cold. Frigid. There is a fifteen-minute wait, so we both grab a stool at the mahogany bar. Before we even sit down fully, the bartender places a drink napkin in front of each of us.

I am just going to do it.

I order a glass of pinot noir.

Please be a big glass.

He orders a beer. Ben shifts on his bar stool, looking out of place—it is like he knows I am lying but going along with it because he loves me. The red wine sends a warm glow through my chest. The tension that tightens my neck and shoulders slowly dissipates. The negative self-talk is drowned out by the alcohol. I order another glass of wine as we sit down at the table. Ben orders another beer.

See, just like old times.

The waiter forgets to bring out our appetizer of fresh mozzarella and tomato, so we skip it. I get the salmon. Ben gets the lamb chop. The food is mediocre, but I rarely go out for the food. I order my third glass of wine.

Okay. No more, Meredith. You need to prove to Ben that you can socially drink.

We get up to leave.

Please suggest that we go back to the bar.

We leave.

Please say we should go get a drink. It's early.

Ben remains silent in the car. I am freezing and pump up the heat, rubbing both of my hands together. Ben presses on the brakes as we near the stop sign one block from our place. Right, we go home. Left, we go out.

"Want to get a drink?" I say nonchalantly, like I literally just thought of the idea.

"No. I'm tired. I don't want any more to drink. Let's go home."

Defeated.

As Ben gets undressed in the bedroom, I fill up my *Annie* plastic tumbler with white wine. As it goes down my throat, anxiety floats away, but the alcohol never satisfies the pain inside, so when I drink, I do not stop. I want to feel nothing.

"What are you drinking?" he asks, tilting his head in that way he does. I take one last sip from the tumbler before replying, "Water."

WE'LL HAVE TO WAIT
AND SEE

I wear dark jeans, a tight cream camisole with lace at the top, and a fitted red sweater with gold buttons. A bottle of Ben's favorite whiskey sits on the counter. He is not aware of the vodka hidden in the freezer. I bought it a few weeks ago. Sometimes I take a shot at night. Sometimes I put some in my morning orange juice.

Ben comes in the door smiling, "How is my sweetie?" he asks, wrapping me in a hug.

Let me just get some alcohol in him. He'll loosen up—forget about the suicide attempts, forget about my eating disorder, ignore my drinking.

We sit down on the brown bar stools flanking the breakfast bar. I have finished a bottle of wine already and feel unwound. The cranberry spice candle lights the room with a soft hue and gives off a pleasant fragrance. I pour another glass of wine and Ben drinks the whiskey. Ben zips up my brown velvet jacket and places a pink hat on my head as the cab beeps outside. We head to a boisterous Irish pub in town. As soon as I walk in, I wish I was home in my pajamas with my nephews, watching a movie and snuggling. We get a booth in the corner. He orders a burger. I order a turkey burger. Now that I am drunk, my mind allows me to get a burger and fries. When I am drunk, calories do not count. By the time our meals arrive, I am despondent. I text Conor and Aidan. I need reassurance that someone loves me even if, at this moment, I hate myself. My body. My life.

The ride home is unclear. I go straight into my bedroom without taking off my coat. I open my nightstand drawer and grab my bottle of Prozac. I pick up a large bottle of Smartwater. The pills slide down my throat. I call Conor immediately.

"I took more pills, Conor."

"Okay, Mer. Where are you?"

I really cry after hearing Conor's deep, yet gentle and firm voice. I hand the phone to Ben.

"Oh my God, again! I cannot fucking believe it. I got to get the hell out of here," Ben says sharply.

"I don't care what you do. Get Meredith to the hospital. Now!" Conor yells with a stable authority.

I vaguely hear the sirens of the ambulance and police cars in the distance. This time, I don't remember going to the hospital. This time is different. Too scary. Too "we almost lost her." Too "she may have brain damage." Too "if you don't do something, you are going to lose your daughter."

I eventually hear the loud beeps coming from the hospital machines around me, the murmurs of the doctor talking to my parents. I slip in and out of consciousness. Suddenly, I am a smaller version of myself, and I need to swim through this underground tunnel to get to safety. I am trapped. This is my life now—completely different from how I once lived. I have no idea that I am hallucinating. It feels so real. I want to tell Mom about it, but I am unable to talk.

"She may have some permanent brain damage," the neurologist says. "We have to wait it out. We still need to run more tests."

Oh my God, my life has changed forever.

I am back in my miniature size, sliding down this dark, winding slide. My eyes are closed. I hold my breath to get under the cliff to safety. I can breathe now, but I'm scared. I'm a tiny version of myself, and I cannot get out. I'm paralyzed. Stuck.

. . .

"Who is the president?" Mom asks as I eventually sit up with her help two full days later.

"Obama," I whisper and then my head turns to the left in slow motion. It feels like an hour has passed. I stare blankly at the walls. *Where am I? How did I get here?*

I want to tell my mother about the new world I am in, but the words are cemented between my brain and my mouth.

"Who are your nephews?"

"Liam, Noah," I garble as my eyes fixate on the white ceiling. I cannot move my body.

What was the question?

I flail down the slippery tunnel again. This time it's behind boxes and furniture. It's harder to get to. Someone is after me. I plunge into the water, desperately seeking the surface. I make it. I can breathe. I'm uncomfortable. I'm jumping out of my own skin. I'm unable to move. Is this my new life? Will my brain ever be normal?

"What month is it, Mer?" Mom asks calmly, holding my hands, which I have no control over.

"January," I mutter and then slip back.

I have no idea why Ben is not here. Each day, I just wait for him to visit. After three days, I feel a bit clearer.

"Mom, where is Ben?" I ask. Mom looks to Dad, who is standing at the end of my hospital bed with his arms crossed.

"We kicked him out of your apartment, Mer. He is not good for you. He was drunk and belligerent when we got here. We told him to leave. And he left. We told security that he is not allowed in to see you."

"Okay. I was thinking about ending the relationship anyway," I say, shrugging without an ounce of emotion.

At the age of thirty-eight, my parents end my relationship without a peep from me. But like normal, I just go with it. I must get myself straight before I can focus on a relationship, right? I negotiate with the on-call psychiatrist. We feel like friends now.

"The psych unit will not help," I say to the psychiatrist. "I know what to do. Trust me."

• • •

The day I am discharged, I attend my first Alcoholics Anonymous (AA) meeting, conveniently located three blocks from my apartment. I see people standing in the small yard, smoking cigarettes and talking. I pass through the cloud of smoke and head up the steep stairs. It is loud with chatter. I get a seat right by the door—an easy exit. The meeting is in a small room next to a Presbyterian church. Chairs line the long rectangular table in the middle of the room, and another square of chairs is formed against the four walls. The leader—or that's what I guess he is called—talks about how to get sober, what AA is, what the twelve steps are, and what worked for him.

"You need to be honest. Honest to yourself and honest about your drinking. I finally realized that my behaviors were not normal. I never wanted to feel like that again. I was out of control. Crawling out of my skin."

I perk up slightly. My body feels like I got run over by a truck, but I relate.

"Any last shares before we end?"

I timidly raise my hand, hoping he will not see it—that it will be blocked by the large man sitting next to me.

"Ah . . . yes. Please go."

"Um. Hi. I am new," I whisper. "My name is Meredith. And I am an alcoholic." As soon as the words come out, my throat relaxes and tears swell in my eyes.

THE RIFLE

Ben moved his stuff out when I was at the hospital for a week but continues to come over and bang on the back door. I stare at the knob, knowing that if I turn it, I am choosing to go back to the chaos. The instability. The relationship between us is lethal.

Open the door. Don't open the door.

"I will call the police!" I shout.

"Mer, please just open the door. Let's talk. I love you."

"Please just go."

Our relationship is toxic. Do not open the door.

I want to rip open the door and hug him tightly. I also know that it is a gateway into the quicksand.

Focus on your wise mind, Meredith. The definition of insanity is doing the same thing over again and expecting different results.

• • •

Tonight, my friend from AA is celebrating one year of sobriety at a local diner. This will be my first time attending a celebration meeting with my home group. I feel nervous, but I also feel centered and focused. I have been sober for eight weeks. I re-engaged with my treatment team, and I have been focusing on strengthening my healthy self. I have no eating disorder behaviors or thoughts, and each day, my mind sharpens. As I back out of my driveway, my cell phone chimes. It is Ben. He sent a video. I press play, and as soon as I see the defeated expression on his face, I know what it is—it is a goodbye video.

I immediately call Ben. It goes to voicemail. My heartbeat quickens.

Okay, Mer. Take a deep breath. Calm down. What do you need to do?

I frantically dial Ben's brother, not having any clue what I will say.

"Hello?"

"Hi, it's Meredith. I think Ben is in trouble."

"Are you guys having a fight again? What did you do?" he questions with a tired voice.

"Umm . . . He sent me a video where he basically says goodbye. I think he is suicidal. I am on my way to his apartment right now."

I am so nervous that I miss the apartment and need to turn around. I slowly inch up the long, sloped driveway and park erratically. I leave the headlights on for some light because otherwise, it is pitch black. I jump out of the car and dart up the stairs to the front door. I knock.

"Ben! Ben, it's Meredith. Are you okay?" Nothing. Silence.

I knock again. "C'mon, Ben. Let me in," I say, twisting the doorknob, but it is locked. The night is still. I place my ear on the door, but I hear nothing.

I run down the stairs back to my car. I open the door, and just as I am about to get in, I sense something. A presence. A breath. I turn around slowly, and I see Ben sitting against a large tree trunk in a wooded area. The beam from my headlights shines, and his outline is foggy. As my eyes readjust, I see the long hunting rifle that he is holding toward his face. His hand is on the trigger.

"Ben," I whisper. "Oh God." My instinct is to go toward him, but

I cannot move my arms and legs. The gravel feels like thick, sticky molasses.

"If you come any closer, I will shoot," Ben yells.

I stiffen. My brain shuts down, full of nothingness. My surroundings become blurry. My body feels like Jell-O, and my legs crumple spastically underneath me. I fall into a squat on the driveway to keep my balance. My heartbeat thumps in my ears and the cicadas chirp loudly, but all other noises evaporate. I feel like I am swimming underwater while my fear fades away to blankness. I am paralyzed, but I hear myself utter the words.

"I love you, Ben."

"You are just saying that!"

Somehow, I slowly grab my cell phone and dial 911 even though my fingers feel immovable. A voice on the other end briefly snaps me to the present. I cannot remember the house number, but I repeat the street name multiple times. As I lay my phone down, I see a truck heading up the driveway.

Please be the police. Please be the police.

It is his childhood friend.

"Everything okay?" he asks as he rolls the driver's seat window down.

"Hey. Not really," I murmur, not knowing if the words came out of my mouth.

"Umm" I say louder, squeezing my stomach to get some volume out. "Ben is in trouble." He puts his car in park and walks toward me.

Under my breath, I utter, "Ben is in the woods with a gun."

"What?"

"Ben. He is in the woods."

"Holy shit. What?" He turns and sees Ben. "Hey, man. What's going on?" His voice is astoundingly calm.

"Do not come any closer!" Ben screams. "I'll shoot."

His friend keeps one eye on him and turns to me.

"Meredith. Back off. Get in the car," he says brusquely.

I slowly back up, praying that the police are on their way. He fully turns toward Ben. He edges forward one inch at a time. I hear mumbles as they talk back and forth. I see the line of police cars drive past the house.

I throw up in my mouth, swallow it, and call 911 again.

"The police just drove by. It is number 32," I say, clarity returning. "He has a gun."

I hear the crunching of the leaves as Ben jumps up, drops the gun, and runs into the woods behind him. The police finally arrive. There are four cars with sirens, and it looks like I am at a rock concert. A bunch of officers run into the woods to search for Ben. They find him and put him in a cop car and drive off.

A young policeman walks up the driveway to me.

"Who are you?"

"I am the ex-girlfriend."

• • •

As soon as I start to drive home, trembling, it makes sense. Ben came to the door earlier. He wanted to give me something. I told him to go away and that we could not get back together.

I find the suicide note in the garage. The letter is in an envelope left on a rusty table next to wrenches and corroded directions pamphlets. *Mer* is written in pencil on the top. Inside is a two-page letter on loose leaf. Ben tells me that he loves me and cannot live without me. He tells me that it is not my fault.

I call Conor for guidance. "Mer, do not go to the hospital. He is not stable. If you go, you are giving him false hope. Stay home. Be safe."

"Okay," I say as tears fall down my bloated cheeks. With every passing minute that I do not go to be by his side, my guilt grows and grows.

WHO AM I?

I t is a summer night in August. The weather is perfect—still warm at eight in the evening. I have on a long blue dress and a white cardigan. There is a slight, tepid breeze. Tonight, I am going out to dinner for my friend Kyle's birthday. Maggie, my friend who I met in middle school at the back of the beach, arrives in the lane by foot. I am the driver for the evening. I have been sober for seven months. My eating disorder recovery is robust. Secure. I want to live.

"It's good to have you back," Maggie says with a sense of affection.

"Yes, I was quite lost for a long time, but I'm getting there."

Ben is getting the treatment he needs. We have no contact. I am sober. I never want to be hospitalized again. I radically accept that even with a lot of recovery, my anorexia is still hijacking me, and I want more. My recovery was sidetracked by Ben and our toxic relationship, and even though I have been able to eliminate behaviors and thoughts, I have only scratched the surface with creating an identity away from the eating disorder. The layers of protection that my anorexia built served their purpose and I thank it tremendously, but it is time to heal. It is time to find my authentic self. As I start to build a little bit of faith in myself again, I start to create my identity.

Not the identity masked by my eating disorder or the identity controlled by what others expect of me or even the identity of what I think I "should" be. Maybe I do not want to be the "straight-A student." Maybe I do not want to be the "health nut" or the "workout fanatic." Maybe I am not seeking perfection. Maybe I am nothing like the person I have morphed into.

The first task I attempt is to make a decision. Yes, make a decision. My anorexia has made most of my decisions for over twenty years. My parents have made the others. Now, it is my time.

What if I make the wrong decision?

What if my decision disappoints someone?

What if someone does not agree with my decision?

What if someone judges me? Or God forbid, not like me?

At first, I flip a coin. An old therapist suggests this method, and I give it a try. As I sit stuck, wondering if I should wear a pink or purple shirt, I flip a coin. Stay in or go out? I flip a coin. It makes the decision for me. I trust a quarter before I trust myself. As I thrust myself back into recovery, I realize that I must stop the noise in my head long enough to listen to myself—to my healthy core self, not the eating disorder self. I really have no clue about who I am. Fear runs my life. I am filled with such indecision—such dread and angst over the smallest choices. Each day, I ask myself some basic questions. Instead of jumping into my doing mind on autopilot, I pause:

Do I want to sleep in or get up early?

Do I want to practice yoga or spin?

Do I want a salad or sandwich?

Do I want to stay in and have a quiet night or go out to socialize?

Do I want to go out to dinner?

With practice, I start to ascertain what I like. My body starts to like the gentle stretching of yoga as compared to running miles on the hard, bumpy street. My mind appreciates staying in the moment instead of pinballing back and forth between the past and the future. I like the compact way a wrap is shaped instead of always eating a salad in a large bowl. I enjoy listening to coffeehouse covers on my Alexa instead of pop top forty. I revel in sitting in nature instead of compulsively completing my to-do list. I relish waking up early to enjoy a leisurely morning instead of racing to work with my hair still wet from my shower.

At the PHP, I completed an exercise called the "eating disorder pie." To begin, you trace three large circles on a piece of paper. One circle represented my life before the eating disorder. One circle represented my life when I was most ill. And the third circle represented what I hoped my life will look like when I am recovered.

When I was most ill, I was obsessed with my body, weight, and shape. I was controlled by isolation and compulsions. I was infatuated with burning calories. I was preoccupied with the flatness of my stomach. I was fixated with mirrors. I even marked a sliver of the pie "broccoli, apples, and Starbucks coffee." Visually, I saw how my anorexia took over. In the circle of what I envisioned my life to be, I wrote the words "relationships, home, friends, career, charity work, leisure, vacations, and family." A fire sparks under me, and I know that I want and deserve more.

Each day, I practice the pause. I quiet the chatter in my head to listen to my healthy core self.

I love being creative. I try to read, write, or paint (yes, paint by numbers!) each day.

I have a lot of love to give, so I think one day I'll buy a puppy.

Shopping is a way I escape my feelings.

I really enjoy a steaming-hot cup of coffee.

I am still sometimes shocked when I get home after a long day and feel clear minded, energetic, and happy.

My four nephews are my joy.

I despise jeans.

I feel safest when I am in my PJs watching TV.

I like going out to breakfast and lunch. I will pass on dinner.

I love playing games of any kind (just not the relationship kind).

I like sleeping in my own bed with flannel sheets.

I like eating bagels with butter.

I usually never connect with other people because my eating disorder is in control.

I hate working a nine-to-five job.

The fact that I go out to dinner with friends tonight is exhilarating. After the beach, I shower and get dressed. I put on one outfit and spend time with my family on the porch before Maggie arrives. And yes, I did type that right! One outfit! I get ready with time to spare.

"Hey, Mags, can you take a family picture of us?" I ask when she reaches the porch stairs. My family and I gather on the back steps. I grab Henry into my arms. Beth places James in her lap, and everyone else takes a spot. I still cannot believe how big my nephews are. My heart fills with love.

"Summer!" we say in unison.

JOY

am not sure when my positive feelings start to surpass my negative ones. I continue to practice mindfulness and to sit with each emotion, pleasant or unpleasant, without judgment. I notice a combination of anxiety, mania, and excitement more often. I come from a place of compassionate curiosity. I feel these feelings bubble in my body like seltzer. I want to give my body over to it completely. To let go fully like an orgasm. And finally, one day as I drive past my AA home group church, it happens. Jubilation. The euphoria breaks through and I feel joy. I feel it in my head, my heart, and my soul. I hear the *Top Gun* soundtrack in the background—"Na na na na na na na na na na na na na na, nan nan na nan a nan a an nannnnaa." Some would call it ecstasy. I do. The grin on my face. The ease of my shoulders. The openness of my heart and hands. I imagine a sweaty Tom Cruise with his shirt off during the volleyball scene as my shackles break off.

I continue to get to know the real me, and I clarify what sustained recovery allows me to do:

Enjoy dessert. Get dressed once a day. Put other people's needs in front of my own.

Miss a workout. Enjoy the holidays. Listen to my body. Smile. Be present.

Feel peace. Love deeply. Be me.

Share a pizza with a friend on a Wednesday night.

Sit by my pool sipping coffee instead of going to a morning workout class that was on my schedule.

Add creativity to my daily life. I start to write, paint, and listen to more music.

Genuinely laugh. Drink sweetened iced tea to quench my thirst.

Drink a soda without the world ending.

Use self-compassion to silence the inner critic.

Connect and celebrate with my here-and-now body.

· · ·

The cooking class takes place in our expansive villa kitchen overlooking the light-blue sheen of the pool and the breathtaking vineyard in Tuscany, Italy. I look through the brick arc of the outside kitchen with a pizza oven and large hand-crafted table that sits ten. Bold, bright-pink flowers the color of the sunset and shades of emerald greens and violet purples line my postcard view. We are on a two-week trip. I am strong. I am eating. I am joyful.

Francesco Costagli, our private chef, leads the class. My family and I fill the edges of the white-and-gray granite island. The menu looks impressive and somewhat daunting since most of my meals still come from the microwave or are dropped off at my doorstep. The menu of the day is pappa al pomodoro, pollo in fricassea, focaccia bread, fresh vegetables from the garden, and hazelnut biscotti.

I roll the fresh pasta dough. I chop the bright-green zucchini. I knead the biscotti dough—or at least try to. It is harder than it looks! I smell the fresh herbs and the aroma of the garlic and rosemary. I mindfully taste the warm, buttery bread melting in my mouth. I am in my glory. I am rock climbing the mountain of recovery, cooking and eating pasta in Italy!

We visit Rome and the other small, exquisite towns of Pienza, Orvieto, Castellani, Chianti, and Siena. The country has so much history, coziness, and magic. We stay at a splendid villa in Tuscany. Our villa is called Tramonti, and even to this day when something incredible happens to me or one of my family members we ask, "Is it Tramonti good?" Is it a villa with eight bedrooms overlooking a vineyard good? Is it home-cooked Italian food for two weeks straight good? Is it getting a private tour of the Sistine Chapel good? Is it watching the sunset over a bowl of freshly cooked cacio e pepe good?

My trip to Italy marks a major milestone in my recovery. Through exposure—constant, exposure—my relationship with food changes. I see food as something to enjoy in different countries. I see food as energy to climb the steps of the Colosseum. I see food as something that connects me with family and friends. I also learn something new on this trip. I love pasta! I still cannot believe it took me over thirty years to eat!

INTUITIVE EATING

Many years ago, I read the book *Intuitive Eating* by Evelyn Tribole and Elyse Resch. At the time, I was swimming in my punch bowl of diet culture. I scanned the ten principles and quickly recognized that my anorexia would not get on board. I grabbed the *South Beach Diet* book instead and aggressively biked ten miles while reading it. I was always so future-focused. I operated under the deadly myth that if I could attain the "perfect, cultural, beauty-ideal" body, then I would be happy.

Now, with sustained recovery, I pick the book back up and read it cover to cover. A light bulb finally goes off. Fuck beauty ideals. Fuck diets and cleanses and gym challenges. I am not messed up or crazy. I have been brainwashed by diet culture since I was a little girl. Throw in genetics, a type A personality, competitive dance, trauma, and a people-pleaser persona and you have the perfect storm to get an eating disorder.

I want to reach body and food freedom. I am giddy with excitement. Maybe this is a next step—from the tenets of the "prescription for regular eating" that I learned in the PHP to attuning to my hunger and fullness. It makes so much sense that I need years to undo the coding—

to erase the flash drive of my diet-culture mind and start anew. Maybe the principles can guide me to an even better understanding of my relationship with food, my body, and my weight.

Intuitive eating has ten principles (principles, not rules, which means they do not need to be followed to a T). It works from the spiral of healing theory, where energy flows in loops up and forward, but not in a straight line. According to *The Intuitive Eating Workbook*, "These little loops represent moments of returning to past behaviors. These moments allow for reflection—time to examine beliefs and thoughts, self-care, and negative self-talk." Instead of labeling them as setbacks, they are opportunities to learn, coming from a place of curiosity and letting go of judgment.

1. Reject the diet mentality.
2. Honor your hunger.
3. Make peace with food.
4. Challenge the food police.
5. Discover the satisfaction factor.
6. Feel your fullness.
7. Cope with your emotions with kindness.
8. Respect your body.
9. Movement—Feel the difference.
10. Honor your health with gentle nutrition.

This time around, I connect to the principles. I am in the driver's seat, not my eating disorder. *Intuitive Eating* discusses self-compassion—being kind and caring, instead of treating ourselves with criticism and judgment. After beating myself up for ages, I am ready for gentleness. Tenderness. Self-compassion becomes a daily goal for me. I practice kindness. I validate my feelings. I accept my feelings. I realize that I am human and will make mistakes, but I can learn from them. I order the *Intuitive Eating* CD and listen to it on the way to and from work. I research the certification process and sign up. I attend the weekly teleseminars. I receive supervision from Evelyn herself. I take the test. I pass and I become a certified intuitive eating counselor. Another huge victory!

Intuitive eating helps to move me away from the pass/fail mentality. I try to accept that my life is a journey, and my experiences are opportunities to attend to my needs and to be curious about my feelings. We can learn from our mistakes instead of reeling in shame.

I love the principles—all of them—but giving myself unconditional permission to eat all foods is a major game changer. I have completed tons of exposure, but underneath there is this faint, almost inaudible voice that gives me a daily score like I did in my pink notepad as a child. I need to detangle morality from food once and for all. All foods fit. The intolerable guilt that I feel after eating is not justified. Food is not "good" or "bad." It is food. I should only feel guilty after eating a piece of cake if I intentionally trip the baker on her way back to the kitchen. Or if I stab the chef who prepared my grilled salmon and spinach with a steak knife.

Do you remember TCBY, the country's best yogurt? When I was in my twenties, I had a short love affair with it. Seeing the chocolate sprinkles evenly swirled in the yogurt shiver was tantalizing. It was not ice cream, so my eating disorder allowed me to eat it, but since it tasted so good, I felt nervous. It was like my eating disorder was giving me a pass, but the pass felt wrong. It was too pleasurable. Too indulgent. I did not deserve the gratification.

Each time I went to the yogurt store, I got the largest size possible because it felt like my eating disorder would create a food rule at any moment, telling me that frozen yogurt was bad and that I could never come back to this store. I usually bought two to three yogurt shivers at a time due to the sheer fear of some possible future deprivation. I felt like I was breaking the law. I was eating frozen yogurt.

Diets do not work. I will repeat—diets do not work. You do not fail at diets—the diet fails you. The billion-dollar diet industry does everything in its power to keep that from us. They continually make false promises. I was so desperate for an answer that I jumped on the diet bandwagon until I almost died.

Intuitive eating honors your hunger and fullness. I continue to trust my signals that slowly return. I use my mindfulness skills to attune to my body. I am gentle with myself. When I am hungry, I do my best to eat. When I am full, I pause to reflect on any possible feelings or urges that arise. Instead of silencing my cravings, I listen to them. If I crave sweetness, I eat a cookie. If I crave a sandwich, I eat one. And yes, sometimes I overeat and realize that the world will not end. I recognize the symptoms of low blood sugar that still plague me from time to time and make sure to eat every three to four hours to stabilize it. I am free.

I align with the philosophy of Health at Every Size (HAES), an approach to public health that seeks to de-emphasize weight loss as a health goal and reduce the stigma toward people who are in larger bodies. It promotes focusing on all aspects of health and not measuring health by body size. I read informative books and join Facebook groups and other organizations that are HAES-aligned.

CARMELITAS

My mom makes twelve different types of cookies for Christmas Eve: chocolate chip, coconut macaroons, raspberry foldovers, raspberry bars, oatmeal, oatmeal lace, snickerdoodles, lemon bars, spritz, brown rim, cutout, and carmelitas. Carmelitas are made with caramel, chocolate, and graham crackers. They are my cousin Katie's favorite.

Each Christmas season, Mom spends a few days baking up a storm. She wakes up before dawn, wraps her holiday apron around her waist, and takes out the laminated index cards filled with cookie recipes. As a little girl, my favorite part was decorating the spritz and cutout cookies with sprinkles, silver balls, and sugar that looked like red and green glitter. I also loved licking the cookie dough off the whisks.

"Hey, Mer, come down for a sec," Mom bellows from the first floor. My music is on loud and I don't hear her, so she tries again. "Hey, Merrrr, come here. It's time for you to put the cookies on the platters."

"Be right there, Ma," I yell. I swiftly walk down the stairs without holding on to the railing because it is wrapped with fresh garland and bright-red bows. It is Christmas Eve morning, and our entire house is trimmed with ornaments. We have so many decorations that Mom moves pieces of furniture and knickknacks to our attic to make room. Nat King Cole plays in the background. On the kitchen counter sits my grandmother's punch bowl, waiting to be filled with the special concoction made from orange juice, cranberry juice, seltzer, and ginger ale.

"The platters are downstairs on the ironing board. Make two— no, three platters—just in case. I want to give a tray to Uncle Pete."

"Alrighty." For some reason, this role falls to me each season and I love it. As a little girl, I felt a sense of pride and responsibility, and I'd much rather organize cookies than take out the garbage or the recyclables.

I bounce down to the nippy basement, careful not to knock into the various items that hang from hooks on both sides of the walls— shopping bags in shopping bags, a strainer, the broom. The cookies are neatly stacked on top of one another on wallpapered shelves that hold our board games and other toys. Each kind of cookie is wrapped tightly in a holiday tin. It takes me multiple tries to pop the tins open without ripping the aluminum foil or catching my finger. I bunch together each kind of cookie on part of the trays until they're all fanned out. I cover them each with two pieces of saran wrap. They chill in the cold basement until dessert time. After dinner, I run down to get two trays and place one of each on the two exquisitely decorated tables, the adult table and the kids' table, proud of my accomplishment.

What my family may not know is that each year, as my eating disorder got worse, the cookies created an unnerving feeling. I walked down those creaky steps to the basement, and as I saw the three empty platters sitting on the ironing board, I would flinch.

Do not eat a cookie. You will get fat. You have no willpower.

As I carefully placed the cookies on the sheets, I ate a cookie.

You are so bad. Weak.

Then two, then three. Sometimes I felt like I could not stop, but I always did—I thrust back into control. I needed to escape the feeling of mortification if someone found out. With sustained recovery, the power of the cookies fades. As I attune to my body and eat cookies when I want them, they do not ignite fear or terror. I practice habituation, and cookies lose their pull.

My role of cookie tray organizer is passed on to my dad, since most Christmas Eves I arrive right before afternoon Mass. This past Christmas, I ate some cookies. I really tasted them—the sweet raspberry bursting in my mouth. The old familiarity of the chocolate chip. The crunch and caramel gooiness of the carmelita.

Now a cookie is just a cookie.

RELATIONSHIPS

My recovery maintains equilibrium, and I start a private practice. I rent an office the size of a closet and see clients part-time. As my career finds its footing, I decide to do some hard but important work on my romantic relationships. Having a true, meaningful connection with a man was nearly impossible before because of my eating disorder. I tried to be fully present, but there was a piece of me that was hijacked. I was truly terrified of being rejected. I was also fiercely independent and usually had one foot out the door. My eating disorder put up an impenetrable armor around me. As men tried to get close, they ricocheted off me like I was a Teflon omelet pan. *Stay away. Do not dare get too close. I'll turn into a pumpkin.*

When I was struggling with bingeing and purging, my relationships were chaotic, brief, and intense. I met people, spent a short but fervid time with them, and then I left. I ended it abruptly. No heartfelt goodbye or mindful evaluation of the relationship. I simply got up one day and ended it. I even broke up with a boyfriend while eating Chinese food together. I was eating some sticky rice, and next thing, I ended the relationship and asked him to leave. We did not even finish our food! We did not even make it to the fortune cookie telling him,

"Something bad will happen in the next few minutes. You will probably need to take your food to go."

Strong impulses fired in my body and all emotions disappeared—complete disconnection. It felt like a stranger was sitting next to me. I could not catch my breath until the person left and the door was closed and locked. Finally, relief showered over me, and I never thought about them again, like they were never a part of my life. Remind you of anything? Binge and purge until every morsel of food is out of me with absolutely no indication that I ever ate.

During periods of restriction, my isolation peaked. I stopped going out with friends. Once a loud, boisterous friend, silence saturated me. I stopped spending time with my family. I ignored phone calls, texts, and emails. At the height of my disorder, I only left the house to go to the gym, treatment, and Starbucks. I raced back to my place, closed and locked the door, and turned off the lights to pretend that no one was home. The sound of the doorbell sent alarms off in my body.

In my twenties and thirties, if I was dating someone, I only saw them face-to-face if everything was "perfect"—my hair, my outfit, the emptiness of my belly, my skin. When I was drinking, I needed a slight buzz to silence the self-loathing. And if I had an inkling that things were not "perfect," I canceled. I canceled the morning of or ten minutes before our date. I sat paralyzed with fear until the other person said, "Okay." Then I'd let out a breath because no one would set eyes on my fat, disgusting self. I would be alone with my anorexia. Joyless, but safe. Hopeless, but in control. Fading away—just the way I liked it.

Part of recovery is to build connections with others—to nurture relationships and create new ones. Since I flip-flopped between short, chaotic ones and severe isolation, I had my work cut out for me. I never wanted to get close to someone because, if they knew the real me, they would be disappointed. I was damaged goods. I could never share my secrets, my deep-rooted shame. So, I always kept a distance. While man after man fell in love with me and opened up, I would close up like an oyster, the shell encapsulating me.

So, it will come as no surprise that Ben and I got back together. Even with the joyous tastes of recovery, intuitive eating, and connecting to my feelings, my self-worth's default is to please others. Maybe I can heal this chaotic relationship by loving him more? Accepting him more? Trying harder? Taking responsibility for my volatility? I desperately want to go back to our first date when there was so much promise and pretend the toxicity does not exist. Perhaps start over and have a happy ending.

He moves back in and, within three months, we purchase a colonial home in Fair Haven, two blocks from the Navesink River. I pay the down payment, and Ben promises he will pay his half back.

Ben finishes his mental health treatment program but is too depressed to work. I pause to think of how much I have progressed in our time apart. I feel like a new person. Ben has regressed.

I'll take care of him. My love will heal him.

The house reminds me of a beachy cottage. The house is one block from the center of town. Booskerdoo, the local coffee shop, sits at one corner, and the picturesque Navesink River and the boat club are at the other. The house is lemonade yellow with black shutters. I place two white rocking chairs on our large front porch. The house has three bedrooms and one and a half baths. The downstairs has vaulted ceilings, old built-ins, and a fireplace in the center of the living room. My favorite room is the kitchen. It is covered in two walls of windows that allow the light to shine in. A vintage Garland stove with a salamander broiler sits in the corner. We have a large backyard; a garage with an attached, run-down room; and a rectangular swimming pool.

The day we move in, Ben is in a mood. Flustered. Annoyed. My gut senses that something is wrong, but I am too filled with excitement to listen. I unwrap each packed item with anticipation of where it will go in our new home.

THE READING ROOM

see this move as a new start. My private practice is underway. I courageously transition to it full-time, seeing over thirty clients weekly. I continue with recovery and weekly therapy sessions. Eating starts to find a neutral place in my life. I have a desire to connect to other people and excitedly sign up for a writing class at Project Write Now, a writing studio in Red Bank. One of my favorite classes in college was creative writing, and as I seek to find my authentic self, I have a hunch that it will serve as a grounding hobby.

I constantly hear from the eating disorder community that journaling is a major component of healing. Even though I have a small scar from my diary fiasco, I grab a notebook and write. I write about my feelings, thoughts, and dreams. Each week, I attend class and connect with other imaginative and introspective writers. The journal prompts at the beginning of each class stir up creative energy, focus, and motivation. I share my intimate work. I practice being vulnerable. I yearn to hear ideas, suggestions, and even critiques. I spend time doing something I love. I take a break. Hallelujah!

I designate the dining room as the "reading room" and decorate it with two oversized chairs, a gray ottoman, a standing lamp, and two brown bookshelves filled to the brim. My love for reading is back, and I sit by the fire or in a lounge chair by the pool and read an entire book in one sitting.

One fall day, I pick out the book *Hunger* by Roxanne Gay. She has suffered with an eating disorder, so I am excited to read it.

Let's do some bonding, Roxanne.

I grab a cup of hot coffee from up the street, put a soft, turquoise fleece blanket over my legs, and sit down in my maternal grandmother's wingback chair. I reupholstered it with colors of blue, yellow, and honey. The brand-new paperback lies in my hands. Little do I know that in chapter eleven, Gay shares that she was gang-raped when she was a young girl in a cabin in the woods. She eloquently describes the horrific scene when "something terrible happened."

I stop breathing. My heart thumps as the room closes in on me.

THE BEACH
HOUSE FLOOR

The next day, I sit on my therapist's couch, the type of couch you just fall into, and when you place your body in the middle, both cushions pop up from the sides. Due to my height, my feet bob up and down as my back rests shakily on the back cushion.

"I was raped when I was thirteen."

As soon as the words come out, they sound wrong. Maybe assault is a better word to use. Rape sounds utterly awful, like it should not be coming out of my mouth. Assault is softer, more palatable. Rape is violent and crude. Christine, my new therapist, nods gently. Her face softens, showing me compassion. She is not surprised. Trauma and eating disorders are often linked.

"It was by a so-called friend of mine. We were home alone. My parents had gone to church."

I take a deep breath.

"We started kissing. We had kissed before. But then he pushed me down onto the floor in the kitchen. It felt weird. I had never had a boy on top of me like that. I stared at the orange flower overhead light. I really did not even know what was happening."

She nods again. She is hearing me.

"I banged my feet against the wine refrigerator to get leverage and shimmy out of his grip. I said no. I pushed his chest, but his pressure was too much, and my body fell back. He overpowered me." I pause to catch my breath and to hold back tears. "As soon as the back porch door opened, he stopped. I jumped up quickly, trying to pull up my shorts, and ran into the bathroom. That back sliding-door noise still makes me jump to this day. I saw blood. I grabbed a bunch of tissues and shoved it in my underwear."

"Go on," Christine says gently.

"The sliding glass door opened again. My parents came home. They were talking to my friends. I made myself stand up straight even though I was like literally shaking." I pause. "I just decided that this did not happen and if I did not tell anyone, it would disappear. So, I opened the bathroom door and put on a fake smile. My eyes darted to him. His head was down. My eyes flitted to Kelly. She looked confused. I kissed both of my parents goodbye and walked the two blocks to the boardwalk with my friends. I never uttered a word to anyone . . . until today."

• • •

Bessel van der Kolk writes in *The Body Keeps the Score: Brain, Mind, and Body in the Healing of Trauma* how trauma rewires the brain and shifts the way we see the world. In a nutshell, trauma impacts your mind and body. When I was not able to share my feelings, I pushed them down. When I was raped, I thought it was my fault and the shame festered. Hypervigilance became my default. Panic was the only button. I did not have the voice to say, "Mom, I need you. Something bad just happened. I cannot handle it alone. I need help."

As a little girl, I had two reoccurring nightmares. In one, a mean old witch with mangled teeth and puke-yellow eyes chased me from my bedroom, down the tan-carpeted stairs, and all the way out the front door of my childhood home. I gasped, looking for a glimpse of light in one of the homes that lined my suburban street, but all I saw was darkness. I skidded on our front walkway, wiping the blood haphazardly from my skinned knee onto my bubblegum-pink mini skirt. The sky rolled violently with gray clouds so huge I could almost touch them. I sensed the witch's hot, sweaty perspiration on my neck, and fear invaded my body. I sprinted across the street to my neighbor's large colonial ranch and knocked on the door frantically. I screamed and rang the doorbell in desperation.

In another dream, a cascade of multicolored flowers fell from the ocean-blue sky. Purple lilies, red roses, white daisies, and yellow tulips. I manically shifted sideways on my white Tretorns, catching each petal before it hit the ground. From the corner of my eye, I saw a delicate fuchsia daffodil bud falling. I was too far away. I extended my small pale hand. It snuck through the cracks of my fingers. I watched it flounder in the air as dread filled my chest. *Boom!* It smashed to the ground. The world blew up with me in it. Just like the scene in *Superman* when Lois Lane gets pulled into the earth.

The anxiety, rape, puberty, insatiable guilt, fear, poor self-image, diet culture, perfectionist tendencies, obsessiveness . . . it was like the eating disorder was just waiting for me.

NO HEARTBEAT

"Let me put it to you this way. There is a .001 percent chance that you will carry a baby to full term. Now, we can investigate egg donors or adoption," Dr. Gallagher, my fertility specialist, says nonchalantly.

My face falls. The air goes out of my lungs. Tomorrow, I am going to the Bahamas for a family vacation, and in less than ten seconds, my world turns upside down.

"I don't understand," I gasp into the phone.

"Your FSH levels are up and your AMH levels are down, and they should be the other way around," he explains.

"Can I keep on trying?"

"You can, but at your maternal age, there will most likely be something wrong with the baby—birth defects. See . . . your eggs are not viable."

"My eggs are not viable?"

What the fuck does that mean?

After having two miscarriages at eight weeks, I had made an appointment with the specialist. I waited anxiously to hear the small, thumping heartbeat of my child, and both times, my gynecologist could not find it. My dreams of being a mother were sucked away with each loss.

For years, I did not trust my body. But I did the work. Now my body is supposed to do what it's meant to do. Have a baby. Reproduce. Ben and I investigate egg donors. I spend hours upon hours on websites. I look up athletic and intelligent women with blonde hair and blue eyes. I scan their baby pictures to see if anyone looks like me. I look up their SAT scores and personality traits—outgoing, of course, and confident. Funny. Someone with a strong sense of self. I do not want my child to suffer like me.

I scroll through adoption applications and even start filling one out, but never finish it. I want to grow my child in me and create an unbreakable bond. I never imagined a world without a baby. Never. I want to help my kids with their homework after school, put notes in their lunchboxes, and shower them with love just like my mom.

I go to another specialist. I become resolute on having a baby instead of radically accepting that my relationship with Ben is falling apart. We barely speak, never touch. My uterus is scanned. I run blood work three days into my period. Same exact news. Chances are .001 percent. My body is broken. I know it. This is all my fault. Oh my god. I shrunk my ovaries. I starved all my viable eggs.

Meredith, take a breath. You are in emotion mind.

I go to a new gynecologist, and she tells me to just have lots of sex. She says it only takes one good egg! I hold on to her hopefulness for a long time. All I really want is to hear the heartbeat. To hear the heartbeat of my baby inside me. But after miscarriages three and four, I never do.

THE COURTHOUSE

Ben proposes in our kitchen. He gets down on one knee. I say yes; however, the dissonance in my body ignites.

You are an adult, Meredith—make your own decisions.

But isn't this day supposed to feel magical? Shouldn't I feel over the moon?

The ring is gorgeous. Absolutely perfect. But I am in a relationship that my family does not approve of. I feel like I am walking on a tightrope over a stormy sea. At any moment I can slip, and the sharks will eat me whole. My parents do try. They take Ben and me out to dinner for our engagement and start to become part of the wedding plans. My mom even hires a day-of wedding consultant.

I notice the depression slipping over Ben. The previous breakups were too hard for him. He is devastated. He stops eating. The miscarriages do not help. The familiar pattern starts to unfold. I start to grow. I am strong in my recovery and in my career. At the same time, Ben falls apart.

Our wedding invitations eventually arrive on a fall day in October. I grab one and place it in my purse.

"Hey, want to go get coffee?"

"Sure," Ben says, disinterested.

As we sip our lattes at a table by the window, I pause, waiting for the perfect time to show him the invitation.

"So, I have a surprise," I say. Ben's face is blank. I slip the invitation out underneath the table and whip it out. "It's our wedding invitation!"

Ben shakes his head with apathy.

"Well, do you like it?" I ask

"It's fine," he answers.

It's fine!? I have seen a lot of romantic comedies in my day. I think he should be a little interested.

I place the invitation back into my pocketbook, feeling defeated.

• • •

Our intimacy stalls to a halt.

We try couples counseling. During our last session, Ben storms out without saying goodbye. I sink into the puffy couch.

My life is at a breaking point.

I cancel the wedding.

Ben and I break up.

I hire a lawyer.

I move into my beach house until I pay Ben a lot of money to leave.

I move back into my home in Fair Haven. Now I am the sole owner.

I buy a scale from Amazon. It comes in two days. I just want to check my weight. I do not reach out to Ben, but he shows up on the front porch like I knew he would.

I will try harder. I will be more compassionate.

Ben moves back in. It is a secret. We get married by a justice of the peace in Rumson. We spend a quiet but happy weekend in Pennsylvania. We keep the secret from our families for a few weeks. I am desperate to revel in my happiness and stand by my decision, but my mind and body will not relax. I finally tell my family, and they are beyond disappointed that I lied. The guilt eats me up inside. I walk on eggshells.

I thought that if I just decided, all my doubt would disappear.

Four months later, I ask for a divorce.

After three grueling months, the divorce finalizes. I think he will be at the Freehold courthouse, but the judge tells me that Ben showed up earlier. He signed the paperwork. My legs shake underneath me as I answer the judge's questions. I am not sure how I stand. My legs shake ferociously, and I use my core to keep me erect as I walk out.

We have opposing values that, in the long run, cannot balance out. We love one another and are toxic for one another. Altogether, we got engaged twice (the first time, I gave him the ring back after a couple of days), there was one bridal shower, one wedding dress, hundreds of invitations, one canceled wedding, one set of vows at the local courthouse, one weekend honeymoon, and—seven months later—one divorce. A chapter of my life is over.

PRIVATE PRACTICE

After the divorce, I throw myself into my career. I outgrow my small office and rent an entire second floor with three offices. I hire four additional affiliates. Building my practice is a happy distraction from my sorrow. Even when you want a divorce, it is tremendously sad, like a death.

From out of nowhere, my face falls and tears stream down my face. I feel relieved and free, but it is sprinkled with cheerlessness and gloom. I practice radical acceptance by turning my mind and not fighting reality.

You made a wise-mind decision.

I increase my caseload. I hire a social media team. I build a new website, create a logo, and design new business cards. I write a monthly mental health column for a local magazine. I take educational trainings—learning grounds me, helps me to put both feet on the earth. I notice that I am in "doing" mode, but it helps me tolerate my distress without self-destruction.

As I hang my Fordham University social work degree on the wall of my new office, I exhale deeply. I walk across the office and sit on the honey-colored corduroy couch. Next to the couch, I have four chairs flanked by wooden side tables. I straighten the lavender candle, box of tissues, and bowl of Jolly Ranchers that I leave out for my clients.

A flashback to the first family session my parents and I attended years ago comes to mind. The gray-and-white-striped pants I wore are now packed in a bin in the basement—they do not fit, and I plan to donate them. Now, I buy clothes that are comfortable and fit my here-and-now body. It makes sense that the memory arises. That second floor that I now rent is the same exact location my mom, my dad, and I sat in nervously many years ago.

Each day when I walk up the narrow staircase to my office, I think about just how far I have come.

Full circle number one.

A BRILLIANT IDEA

So, back to the jeans. I tried my experiment. Years of exposure. The results are not promising. For years, I exposed myself to wearing jeans, and all the data goes against my original hypothesis. I thought that if I just wore them repeatedly, the anxiety would subside just like eating. I was wrong. To be honest, I was perplexed about what to do. Everyone wears jeans. It is the staple of everyone's wardrobe—right? Jeans and a tee. Jeans and a sweater. Just throw on a pair of jeans and then we can go.

One day, I wake up with a brilliant thought. And it is not a thought to buy twenty-five pairs of sneakers again. (Did I mention that when they were delivered, they were the wrong kind? And as my mother returned each box, I cried on my Barbie pink rug?) No, this is my thought, and I think it is appropriate to sing the theme song from *The Greatest Showman*, "This Is Me" by Keala Settle.

I never have to wear jeans again. I can choose what clothes I put on my body!

So, now, some of my jeans sit in my bedroom, which I re-painted the color of sand after the divorce, on a vertical white wire shelf that I bought from HomeGoods. I pass them every day on the way to one of my three custom closets that hold my thirty pairs of LuLaRoe leggings, ten maxi skirts, multiple dresses, and pants made of spandex. I still own over forty pairs. Most of them are stored in the basement in clear storage organizers under empty Amazon boxes.

BODY ACCEPTANCE

For some reason, I get triggered when I get blood work. And it is not the needle; it is my arm splaying out, resting on the pad while the nurse prods to find a vein. The tourniquet wrapped tightly. My skin bulging. I desperately want lady arms. Petite and defined and slight, like a ballet dancer. Even after recovery, they make me uncomfortable.

However, I continue to let go of the unattainable beauty ideal that has been drilled into our heads from our warped, thin-obsessed society. I make it a mission to challenge this bogus beauty standard. I will not be a robot anymore. Fuck that. And fuck you, diet culture! All bodies are worthy. I start to focus on what my body can do for me—the functions, the pleasures. I even start having gratitude for it.

Eyes: *I can look outside my window and see the pretty, vibrant green trees.*

Ears: *I can hear the soft hum of my computer and the birds chirping outside.*

Legs: *I can walk, run, climb up stairs, and dance.*

Arms: *I can hug people (especially my nephews)!*

Mouth: *I can taste the french roast coffee that I am drinking.*

Hands: *I can type these words that may help those who are suffering.*

Nose: *I can smell the apple spiced potpourri that sits on my bookshelf.*

My first affirmation SHH helped me during one of the hardest times in my life. I wrote it down on yellow Post-its and stuck them on walls, mirrors, and daily planners. I stood in front of the mirror and shouted it out loud.

And with consistency and determination, I eventually change the way I think. Yes, it takes years of regular practice, but it works. Our brains are neuroplastic. They can refire and rewire. They are flexible and ever changing.

With time, I can see that my body is a part of me, not something I desperately want to detach from. My body deserves to be loved, respected, and cared for. I was not born with body shame or body hatred. The oppressive messages I received from living in this world became deep rooted, unshakable. I know these thoughts do not come from my authentic, healthy self. I practice being a friend to myself. I come from a place of compassion and curiosity. I tap into my earlier experiences of joy when I laughed out loud, completely free; when I twirled my baton for hours; when I was at peace with myself.

My AA meetings ground me. I have been attending religiously since I was discharged from the hospital the third time. Even though I have been sober for a few years, I know that the meetings and being part of a sober community are critical. It is Sunday afternoon. I sit on an old wingback chair the color of mustard. Different styles of chairs and couches create a large circle. I grab a cup of coffee with cream and an oatmeal cookie from the kitchen. The meeting fills quickly, and participants go down the hall to the church auditorium to get extra seats, forming a back row. The group leader reads a page from *As Bill Sees It*. The topic for the meeting is gratitude. The meeting is an open-share format and, one by one, members start to raise their hands. A woman with long brown hair pulled back in a scrunchie raises her hand.

"I heard this at a meeting last week, and I have been using it since then. The person suggested that we change the words 'I have to' to 'I get to.' I get to go to a meeting. I get to be sober. I get to go to work. It's really simple and so life changing."

I listen intently, knowing that this is the golden nugget that I will receive today. There is always one—always a tidbit of information that helps my sobriety and makes every meeting worth attending. I want to thank the woman personally; however, I lose her in the shuffle after we hold hands and say an Our Father to end the meeting. I chalk it up to another God moment.

• • •

I love my writing class. It helps me to reconnect with my self and my body. There was always a part of me who knew that healing would be finding my voice that I lost after childhood. For so long, I felt too scared to use it, but the writing softens my thoughts. With practice, I can pull them from my mind, untangle them, and get them onto paper without judging, just simply noticing.

I sit at my memoir writing class on a Wednesday morning. I block out two hours to write two days a week, and it feels amazing to attend a class entirely for myself. It is not for a grade. Or a degree. Or a certification. It's purely for me. I grab a blank notebook stacked in the middle of the long table and start writing with a freshly sharpened pencil.

DEXTER—THE BOYFRIEND

Dating Dexter is easy. And no, he is not a blood-splatter expert and a serial killer. We dated briefly before I met Ben. He was my personal trainer (so cliché). I was feeling brave, and I asked him to the movies. We saw *Moneyball*, starring Jonah Hill and Brad Pitt. Then we drank and talked for hours on my couch, the newness buzzing in my muscles. He was my type, which I have come to know is a short and solid male with facial hair and glasses. He did not want anything serious, and I was fresh out of my PHP, so we naturally stopped texting.

One day, we reconnect over Facebook. Even though he just returned from a business trip in Chicago that morning, we meet for coffee. I feel at home with his witty and sarcastic style. He has dark wavy hair and piercing hazel eyes. He boasts a quiet confidence that I find sexy. He stands only a few inches taller than me, so he is the perfect height to hug and kiss. He is funny. He is also a nerd, which is a perfect combination for me. He loves outer space and numbers and logic. He likes Marvel movies, *Jurassic Park*, and *The Martian*.

Knowing that Booskerdoo closes at 2 p.m. and I want to spend more time with him, I ask, "There is an open house a few blocks away.

Want to come with me?"

"Sure."

We saunter into the large, freshly built home, and the real estate agent welcomes us. There is soft elevator music playing and chocolate chip cookies in the kitchen. The sweetened whiff reminds me of childhood. We look up at the tall ceilings and move around the home.

"The playroom will be perfect for the kids," Dexter says loudly as I touch the granite island in the kitchen.

"How many children do you have?" the realtor asks.

"Two. Honey, come over here; this bedroom will be perfect for her," I say, playing along. Pretending to be a family makes my heart smile.

That same night, he comes over for pizza. I guess he wants to spend more time with me too. *The Notebook* is on television.

"What movie is this?" he asks.

"*The Notebook.*"

"I've never seen it."

"You probably have. Nicolas Sparks? Love story? Noah and Allie?"

"Nope," he replies.

"Um . . . it's like the most romantic movie out there. This is the part where Lon proposes to Allie and Noah is fixing up their dream home."

"Never seen it," he says, sitting down next to me on my brown suede couch. Dexter does not mince his words—he says what he means, and I am not used to that.

We watch the rest of the movie, and I find out that he is quite the movie buff, just not with romances. The credits roll on the screen, and then the same movie starts again. I guess it is fate that he will watch it from the beginning. I think we are also relieved that we have a distraction, both feeling the edgy excitement of a first date.

"Can I kiss you?" he asks after our conversation standing by the front door comes to a natural stop and the movie credits roll again.

"Yes," I say eagerly but with restraint.

It is a soft kiss. It feels unfamiliar but lovely. He has soft pink lips.

"Thank you for kissing me. My ex-husband stopped kissing me a long time ago."

"You're welcome."

THE NEXT STEP

E ven though a small part of me misses the chaos and the ups and downs of past relationships, Dexter moves in. His lease is up, and we genuinely love spending time with one another. He is a man of few things, and his clothes fit seamlessly in the guest room closet. He positions his camping equipment and mountain bike efficiently in the garage. He sets his tools in the basement along with a few frayed bins holding old high school and college track and field trophies and workout equipment. I put up framed photographs of us in each room.

My eating disorder recovery is solid; however, we are in two quite different places in life. Dexter, nine years younger—or as he would say, "eight years, four months, one week, and one day" (he is not a rounding-up sort of guy)—is finding his path. I start to love so many parts of him, including his sense of humor, analytical mind, laid-back attitude, love of movies, and ability to fix pretty much everything. We hold hands when we fall asleep. We authentically make each other laugh out loud. He does the laundry. I put the clean clothes away. He takes out the garbage. I order the trash bags. We balance each other out. I am content. Peaceful.

But eventually, my depression starts to percolate. I feel too good, and feeling too good feels wrong. I start to feel bored, antsy, restless.

Isn't something bad supposed to happen?

We celebrate Thanksgiving. No drama. He spends Christmas Eve at my parents'. We watch the annual Christmas shows (his favorite is the original *How the Grinch Stole Christmas!*). We see *Dear Evan Hansen* in New York City and visit the tree at Rockefeller Center. On New Year's Eve, we literally just laugh and kiss all night and watch the shining ball drop. We make love on the couch. We are happy.

So yes, maybe that is it. My life is good. I feel free from my eating disorder; have a successful career and a beautiful home; and I am in a serious, intimate relationship. I continually wait for the other shoe to drop but tell myself to stop being so silly.

FULL CIRCLE

know I am going to go as soon as I see his picture on the screen. Immediately, memories flood back. There he is—David, my old therapist—the one who held my hand as I navigated the partial program at Columbia years earlier. I poured my soul out to that man. I do not care what he is going to talk about. I just want to see him. He is speaking at the FREED sixth annual conference, entitled "Future Directions in Eating Disorders," in Boston two months from now.

I will just rearrange my schedule.

His topic is "Emerging and Novel Approaches to Treating and Managing Eating Disorders."

I must go.

David was a sturdy, solid rope when life was taking me down like quicksand—the same quicksand I fell into playing *Pitfall!* on Atari for hours in a row as a child. Sometimes, I was just about to go under, and David would say something small that I would hold on to desperately. He never got excited when I raced into our sessions full of hyper-restlessness combined with palpable panic or when I walked in slowly, riddled with apathy.

I buy train tickets. I reserve a room at a bed-and-breakfast near

Boston's South Station. On the day I leave for the conference, it is chilly but sunny—a crisp fall day that energizes your soul. I breathe deeply into my lungs. I have a leisurely morning drinking coffee and watching *New Amsterdam,* a medical TV show (I am slightly obsessed with medical shows). I go to a spin class down the street. I wrap some Christmas gifts (yes, I know it's October, but this is how my organized self operates). I take a hot shower and dress in layers—four to be exact. Even at my fully restored and stable weight, I get cold quite easily, so I throw some toe warmers, gloves, and a scarf in my bag.

Recovery helps me to cope ahead of time in most situations. Since my compulsion to overpack has subsided, I fit everything into my baby-pink backpack. I pack an almond butter and honey sandwich; a few KIND bars; and a white chocolate pumpkin spice scone, a new flavor of pastry that the coffee shop has for the fall season. An hour before the train's departure, I drive to the Metropark Station. At 2:45 p.m., the train doors open, and I walk in.

Recovery teaches me to sit still and appreciate the moment. I have a six-hour journey, so I pick a window seat and hunker down. I spend the ride writing in my wide-ruled notebook, coloring mandalas with colored pencils, and listening to Dawes. I arrive in Boston quite late. The food court is just about to close, so I quickly order a salad and sandwich for dinner and hail a cab.

The room is homey and adorable. Hand-painted side tables flank the queen-sized bed. I place my luggage on the wire rack near the rocking chair. A small desk and lamp sit by the window looking out onto the Boston streets. Cute, tiny soaps lay in a wicker basket by the sink. The heat is low during the night, so I sleep in my pajamas plus two additional layers to keep me toasty. I put on three pairs of socks to stop the chill in my toes.

. . .

The conference starts right on time. I am a few minutes late due to the Boston traffic, but it is nice to see the city in the daylight. I see David as soon as I walk in through the double doors leading into the meeting room. He sits at a round table up front with the other speakers. He has on a shirt and tie. I pick a chair close to the door, which is my preferred seating choice—even after recovery, I like a quick getaway.

David talks about the role disgust plays in anorexia nervosa. He discusses interoceptive awareness and mirror exposure. He talks about enhancing appetite and exposure to cannabinoids—yes, weed. His calm voice soothes me. My plan is to talk to him at lunch.

"Please ask your questions now since I need to leave right after my talk. I am flying to DC. I will not be here during the lunch panel."

I alter my plan without catastrophizing. I immediately get up and walk briskly to David, who is standing next to one of the other presenters. Quickly, a large line forms behind me, like we are at a book signing. I move a little closer to David, feeling possessive. I stretch out my legs to take up more room.

"Meredith, I saw you when you came in."

We hug. The small doubt that he will not remember me fades. I take a deep breath and focus on this moment. Full circle in the making.

"I wanted to thank you for being on my recovery journey." My eyes brim with tears and my legs are weak, but I push into the ground and stand with pride. "Thank you for helping me. I could not have done it without you."

"Of course," David replies. "You did the hard work."

"It was hard, but I did it. And I'm so grateful."

"How are your parents?"

"They are good. Everyone is good. Here is my business card. Do you have one?"

David checks his shirt pocket, his pants pocket, and briefcase.

"Of course not," he chuckles, slightly scattered but calm.

My heart beats fast. My mission is complete. So, here is my second full circle, right? Everything has been tied up with a fancy red lace bow. This is how my story ends. Perfect. Flawless.

PART 4

RELAPSE

THE SHOE DROPS

November starts, and I gravitate toward restriction with a vengeance. I try on the jeans that I do not wear, and they fall off my body.

LET'S GET A PUPPY

have been on fire for the past few years and especially this last one—surviving my first year of divorce, building my practice, starting a wonderful new relationship with Dexter, and eating! Gloriously eating! Practicing body acceptance and self-love. Helping others—using my firsthand experience to have compassion for them. Feeling so strong . . . and then . . .

It does not take a rocket scientist to detect transitions are hard for me. Even if they go astoundingly well, there is a shift, and on cue, the anxiety bubbles. Good anxiety or bad, my alert system goes on overdrive, and I need time to simmer, like soup.

I step on the scale that has been hiding under my bed on top of the clear bin labeled "summer pajamas."

I am just curious.

I come down with a terrible stomach virus. Romaine lettuce from California is the culprit. As I sit on the toilet for an hour, I am not aware of the slippery slope that is ahead of me. For the next few days, I sip from mini Ginger ale cans and eat unsalted pretzels and dry Cheerios.

I know what will make me happy. A puppy!

"Can we see that one?" I ask, pointing to a golden doodle in the window of Bark Avenue Puppies. The employee goes around back, and in seconds, she places her in my arms.

"She's precious," I say.

"She is," Dexter agrees.

For the past few months, I have this growing itch to get a dog. My maternal instincts intensify. I feel this need to take care of something, to love something, to cuddle something, to parent something.

"Okay. What do we need to do next if we want this dog?" I ask, moving the pup into Dexter's arms.

"Mer, take a breath. We are just looking. This is the first dog we have seen."

"We just need you to fill out some paperwork and leave a deposit," the employee answers.

"I have never bought a dog before. What does she cost?"

"Two thousand dollars."

"Okay. Sounds fine to me," I say as Dexter mouths "What?!" under his breath.

We leave the store five minutes later with a $500 deposit slip folded neatly into my pocketbook. Dexter pays the rest as an early Christmas present. I order a leash, dog food, a water bowl, a medium-sized crate, and a few toys from Amazon.

We name her Sandy. My heart opens. As she sits quietly in my lap as we drive the mile home, I am full of nervous energy and excitement. *Oh my gosh, she is all ours!*

PUPPY TRAINER

Having a puppy is a lot harder than it looks, especially if you have done absolutely no research before you purchase one. The puppy store clerk tells us to put Sandy in her crate on the first night and then go to sleep upstairs undisturbed. As soon as we hit the first creak in our hardwood stairs, Sandy lets out a purr—or something like a purr. Maybe it is more like a whimper or cry. And then as our heads strike our pillows, the wails come. It sounds like we are torturing her, but all we did was put her to bed.

"I'll go downstairs to check on her," Dex says.

"Yes, maybe give her a T-shirt that smells like you—I read on the internet that that helps," I say. The cries continue until Dexter reaches the crate and then she quiets. I fall asleep within minutes. Dexter unsuccessfully sleeps on the cold kitchen floor with his arm touching the crate.

We think it is separation anxiety, and within a day, I hire a puppy trainer. Her name is Jen, and I feel the perky energy bubbling from her immediately as she stands at the front door, ready for our first training session. I grab a red, Moleskine notepad and label it "dog notes." Little do I know that the small pad will not suffice. After she leaves, I rewrite the notes on loose leaf and color code different subjects. I am an amazing student, and I can learn how to take care of a puppy.

I am also a rule follower, so when we are told to take Sandy out every hour, we do. We quickly become two ships crossing in the night. Dexter is getting his associate's degree in electronics engineering and falls asleep in his car between classes. The fatigue weighs on us. Each night, Sandy wails when we leave the kitchen, so Dex stays with her. Each night, she soils her blanket, and Dexter cleans it in the middle of the night. I come home in between clients to let her out. The loose-leaf pages pile up on the kitchen counter. Instead of talking, Dexter and I write down Sandy's pee and poop times in black ink to communicate.

Another transition. My anxiety boils over.

I get my annual physical. I ask for a blind weigh, but the nurse comments anyway.

"You are so good. Always so consistent with your weight. I wish I could be like you."

Do you even know what that comment does to someone with an eating disorder? And yes, I have a history of an eating disorder—it is in my chart!

I ignore the comment, but my eating disorder self lights up like a neon sign.

SMASH!

en days later, we give Sandy away to our trainer, who thankfully lives on a farm. We know she will be with other dogs and animals, but I regret the decision within an hour and fall into sadness. It is the first time I see Dexter cry. We get into a disagreement over something trivial. My anger brews. I skip dinner.

The next day, I do not eat—not one thing.

That night, I go to bed hungry—the old, comfortable illusion of control rears its ugly head. Like always, my bladder wakes me up in the middle of the night. I slither my feet out from the covers and onto the floor.

Woah. I am dizzy.

I place a hand on my side of the bed to steady myself. Dexter is snoring. I walk past the front of the bed slowly and turn toward the door. I lift my hand and my focus turns blurry. I fall into the wall.

I will just rest my head on the wall, like a ledge. That's a good idea.

A wall has no ledge.

SMASH! My head bangs face-first into the bedroom door. I barely miss the radiator.

"Are you okay?" Dexter asks with his arm somehow already

wrapped around my body.

"I lost consciousness for a few seconds. I think so. Ow." I say, bringing my right hand up to my right eye, pulsing with pain.

• • •

I continue to weigh myself every day. The anorexia slips in silently—sort of like a spy—but I notice. It is too obvious not to. I do not need to look back to see the red flags. The scale. The skipping of meals. The transition of Dexter moving in. Giving away Sandy. Work stress. Extra time at the gym. My pool house renovation project.

I feel the fatigue instantly. My healthy self knows that my body is devoid of energy. Malnutrition and starvation have a particular tiredness—I know that if I shift my body too far left on the gym stepmill, I will tip over and just crumble.

I stare mindlessly at the TV. Hunger gnaws at me. The loud cravings gurgle in my stomach. I want to crawl out of my skin. I am restless and move my legs—legs crossed, uncrossed, underneath me, back to crossed. The emptiness will not go away.

Why is it so hard to restrict this time? I am not feeling better. I feel worse.

The next day, my body shakes and tingles during my two o'clock client. I squint my eyes almost closed in hopes of focusing. It is not working. I nod, staring at my client, and swiftly rise off my chair, grab a protein bar from the small wicker basket on my bookshelf, and sit back down. I continue nodding, making eye contact as my hands quiver and my fingers falter on the plastic wrapper.

Please open.

I take a deep breath and rip it open using all my strength. I shove the bar into my mouth. I continue to smile, still listening, nodding. And at the same time, praying that the sugar will go directly into my bloodstream.

I continue to see my therapist, but there is no immediacy about it. Every two weeks is good. I am a therapist. I know what to do. I got this.

IT'S TIME

I t is a frigid Saturday. I get up at seven, earlier than normal, and enjoy the stillness of the day blooming. The grass thawing in the sun. The fog lifting over the river. I buy a large coffee, leaving room for almond milk, and top it off. I drive the five minutes to my new, even bigger office, which is empty and tranquil. I painted the walls light blue, chose beachy oak hardwood floors, and placed a big picture of a beach from HomeGoods over my new off-white couch adorned with two aquamarine pillows. There is a private kitchen in the back where I hope to run meal support groups one day.

I do the billing in silence. Doing payroll is a methodical, straightforward task, and it is perfect for me since I thrive on organization and small, manageable chores. It is why I still pay some of my bills by check. I sit down at the kitchen table and mindfully sign each one. Placing the address label and stamp on each envelope is soothing. Satisfying. It brings me back to when I was a little girl and watched Dad write checks at our wooden dining room table, a pipe in his right hand and a pen in his left.

• • •

I meet Mom and Dad for breakfast. The week before, they were startled at my weight loss at Noah's birthday celebration. I wore an oversized sweater to hide my body. I even ate a cupcake! But they have been put through the wringer. My mom can tell just by looking at my eyes. Are they clear or dead? They are dead.

We get right to the issue—there is no darting. The severity of the issue is tangible, sitting heavy on our chests. The elephant in the room is at the table with us. I bring up some recent stressors in my life—the exciting but expensive pool house renovation project; Dexter moving in, which is fun and overwhelming; expanding my practice, which triples my stress; buying and then impulsively giving away Sandy, which devastates me; and the holiday season is just coming to an end to boot.

"I started to see Christine for therapy again. I increased my Buspar. I'm trying to eat more. I'm trying to talk back to the eating disorder. I know I can do this."

"We know you can," my parents say in unison.

I notice a softness in both of my parents. They are not angry. They are scared. Gone is the rage. Gone is the exasperation. It is replaced with compassion. Love. Understanding. After closely pondering the menu, I order the special "protein" sandwich—egg wrap with cheese, tomato, and avocado. My dad gets the avocado toast. My mom orders an omelet. I eat half of the sandwich.

"I'm going to finish my sandwich. I'm just sitting," I say, jumping to justify my actions.

"Okay," my mom says. Tension releases from my shoulders. I am not a young child. They cannot make me do anything. They cannot chastise or punish me. This is my fight.

I do not plan to tell my parents at breakfast. Like, no part of me. None. I simply look down at my napkin for a moment and know that it is time.

"I have something to tell you. It is not that good, but you need to know. Maybe just to make sense of my craziness. My life . . ."

My mother's face falls. My father stares intently at me.

"When I was thirteen, I was raped."

"Oh, Meredith," my mom blurts out with a crackle in her voice.

My body tenses up. Time slows down, but I stay in the moment and stare at the coffee droplets next to my saucer.

Stay in the moment. Feel your feelings.

"Oh, honey. Thank you for telling us," Dad says and reaches for my hand.

"I thought it was my fault. I did not even know what was happening." Light tears fall down my face.

"Who was it?" my dad asks.

"I don't want to talk about that."

"Did you know him?"

"Uh-huh. He was a friend. I did not understand what was happening."

"I'm sorry, Mer," my mom says in a gentle voice.

"It's okay. It's okay."

"You didn't feel like you could tell us?" my mom asks bleakly.

"I thought it was my fault. That I would get punished. That I was bad."

"I wish you told us."

My dad gets up to go the bathroom; however, I imagine he is dry heaving over the sink. My mom stays still, desperately trying to keep her sadness in check. I take the sandwich to go. That night, I finish the sandwich and send my parents a picture for proof.

Then the purging starts. I tell Dexter that I am nauseous from dinner and quietly tiptoe to the downstairs toilet. The secrets emerge. My head pounds. Wow, that came back easily. A familiar friend, but I need to stop.

This will only make things worse.

I weigh myself at the gym. The scale must be broken. This is just ridiculous—freaking ridiculous—so ridiculously low. I notice the almond milk on the counter. I have been coming to this shop for almost three years, and now I notice the calories of the almond milk. My heart flutters; however, I pour the milk into my coffee—I am not going down.

I focus on what I am recovering to. To be an amazing aunt. To find peace and serenity. To connect with others. To feel joy and feel free.

THE SCALE

The blistering water sprays down like bullets onto my brittle body. Minutes before, the biting cold forcefully penetrated my fingers, toes, and the tip of my nose. I ripped off my clothes, shivered with a chill, and turned the shower faucet to the left—the perfect place on the dial where the water is extra hot. After thirty seconds, I tested the water with my hand and quickly sat down on the shower floor. I wrap my arms around my legs and lay my head on my knees as the burning water gushes around me, warming my body. I breathe deeply, slowly, trying to calm the adrenaline inside me. I close my eyes.

From time to time, I pick up my head and examine my body, which has shrunk in the past few months. My arms slight. My thighs narrow. My stomach curved in like an ice cream scooper. I scrutinize. I criticize. I loathe. My thoughts clamor loudly, so I drop my head into the shower stream to drown out the blasting noise. Gush . . . Gush . . . Gush.

This is my second shower of the day. The less I eat, the more I shower in hopes of getting rid of the coldness that attacks my body. I put my heating pad, lying in between my bed sheets and blanket, to its maximum level. After I dry off and quickly put on multiple layers of clothes, I can sink into a warm bed to seal in the warmth—a protective barrier.

The digital scale lies on the white tile next to the toilet a few feet away. Before spin class or a sip of water or coffee crossed my lips, I stood on it naked. It was low. I already knew that. My restriction had escalated over the past few weeks, and I watched the fluorescent red numbers go down, day by day, lower and lower. I knew what I was doing. I was playing with the devil.

There is a low, repetitive knock on the bathroom door. Dexter walks in to check on me. Before my shower, I had a severe blood sugar crash, and he was the one that opened the blueberry yogurt, stirred it for me, and handed it to me with a spoon to eat. He is worried that the heat from the shower is going to make me dizzy. He pokes his head into the shower as I sit.

"I'm okay," I say. "Not dizzy."

"Good." He starts to walk away. I pull the shower curtain back and say meekly, "Hey, Dex?"

"Yes, Mer."

"Throw the scale out."

· · ·

Two days later, I order another one. Two. I carefully unwrap it and throw the evidence away into the recycling bin. I test it out and sheer panic arises when I think it does not work. Fortunately, I just need to put in batteries. Of course, I weigh myself. I then put it underneath my bed for safe keeping (and hiding). Eating disorders are insidious. They never rest.

Right now, I am at a crossroads. Recover or die.

You know what? I will get a tattoo!

I get my fourth and most noticeable tattoo at Front Street Tattoo in Red Bank. It is there for the world to see (my three other tattoos are more hidden). Exposed. Like it or leave it. I permanently etch another symbol of hope onto the inside of my left wrist, facing me. A semicolon surrounded by an open heart shaped like a butterfly, representing support to those who struggle with depression, self-harm, or suicide but also a representation of me blooming and coming into my own. This relapse will not break me. I have more to say. To do. To experience. To love.

INTERVENTION

My parents do an intervention. Dad in person. Mom on the phone. Dad arrives in a gray Brooks Brothers suit, having just finished a meeting in New Jersey. We walk into my kitchen and sit at the oak kitchen table.

"Would you like something to drink?"

"I'll have a coffee since I need to drive home afterward," Dad says in his work voice, signaling that this is serious. I jump up nervously, happy to have something to do. I grab the Keurig pod and press the button. The coffee spouts out into a green Loyola mug. He dials Mom and puts her on speaker.

"Grace told us that you are purging again."

"Dad, I . . . um . . ."

"Let me speak," my dad says curtly, cutting me off. "Grace told us about your purging. You need to eat, and when I say eat, I mean three meals every day," Dad says, getting straight to the point. "We are not going through this again, Mer. And we are not sitting back to watch you die."

"I know. I'll start eating more."

"That is bullshit!" my dad yells.

"Dad, yelling at me is not going to help," I express calmly. Even as tears well up in my eyes, I stay composed and use my voice. "I know what I need to do."

"So do it."

We nail down a recovery plan. I assemble my treatment team— my psychiatrist, a new therapist, and a nutritionist who specializes in eating disorders. Now it is time for action. Time to be uncomfortable and still move forward. To set small, manageable goals. Recovery is an action. It is movement. It is tangible. It is alive. I am back in the ring. (Did I ever leave?) Both feet are planted firmly. I know I will get knocked down. And hell over high water, I will get back up.

LIFE OR DEATH

As my anorexia builds steam, my relationship with Dexter is on shaky ground. He stays silent as the weight drops from my body. He does not question me when I skip meals or sit down to a bowl full of vegetables. He does not say anything as the depression pins me down and I can barely crack a smile.

I disconnect. I place the mask back on my face.

Because you know that he is eventually going to reject you. You need to protect yourself by pushing him away.

I sit at Booskerdoo for five hours, sipping coffee, trying to read, and skipping breakfast and lunch. Five minutes before closing time, Dexter walks in and sits across from me. He lightly grabs my hands.

"I don't know how to help you. I do not want you to die, but I do not know what to do, Mer," he says.

Part of me feels furious and part of me feels compassionate.

I need you to figure it out. I am just so tired. Grab my hand so I do not drift away forever.

I ask him to read a few books about eating disorders. Sometimes, when we have conversations, I shut down, but this time I use my voice and pull three books from the bookcase. As I pile them up next to him, I do not know that I am steamrolling him. I am vying for control just like with the puppy and the tattoo because I am crawling out of my skin.

"Okay. I will read them," he says, but I hear the slight frustration in his voice, like I just gave him a research paper to write. Dexter hates homework.

· · ·

"How is the book so far?" I text one day later. He is visiting his sister in South Jersey for spring break. I have not been able to sleep since he left. I desperately grab onto my all-or-nothing thinking for a semblance of control.

If he has read the book, then everything will be okay. I will fully recover; we will get married and live happily ever after. If he has not read the book, then we have to break up.

This is life or death. I know that this time, but does Dexter know that? The black-and-white distortions blur my judgment. The recent malnutrition clouds my mind.

A perfect boyfriend would read the books right away.

Practice radical acceptance. You are not in control of him.

Make no rash decisions. Take a pause. Do it differently this time.

Use your voice. Have a calm conversation. Maybe he is scared. Maybe you are scared.

But it must be this way!!

"I have not had time to start it. I am on vacation," Dex answers. My stomach jolts inwards, and bile comes up my throat. At that moment, my body rejects reality. It is like I am having a temper tantrum in my brain without saying anything.

One day later, I text: "Did you get anywhere with the book yet?"

"GET OFF MY BACK," he replies.

I end my relationship with Dexter thirty seconds later. He did not answer the question correctly. Game over. Purge complete.

MY PARTS

As Dexter collects his things a few days later, I feel nothing. I am detached. I want to say that I was impulsive and apologize for my rashness, but I don't. My mouth is glued shut. I felt out of control, so I ended the relationship. I binged and then purged. Now I will restrict him. No connection. No feelings. I will wipe out any memory of him like a hard drive.

However, a few days later, I regret my decision. I feel incredibly sad. I miss him immediately.

Why are these feelings coming up?

This time, I know I made the wrong decision. I was feeling too vulnerable with him and pushed him away to survive.

This is a sole mission. Nothing will stop me.

I do eventually reach out to Dexter to apologize. But I get no response. Just as I am sometimes impulsive with decisions, Dexter is the same way about loyalty. After creating a family and home together, I kicked him out, and the trust is severed.

I desperately practice radical acceptance. The willfulness that I feel is almost impossible to tolerate, but I use my skills. I distract myself. I soothe myself. I stay in the moment.

My new therapist specializes in Internal Family Systems. This model of psychotherapy offers a clear, non-pathologizing, and empowering method of understanding human issues. It stems from the idea that we are made up of different parts. I start to recognize and acknowledge all the different parts of myself. I have parts of me that are scared to let go of the anorexia again and parts that want to fully recover. I have parts that identify with my anorexia because it gives me a sense of control and a part of me that wants to feel free. I have parts that want to please my parents and parts of me that seek independence and individuality. I have parts that are strong and unrelenting and parts of me that are sad and drained. I have a part of me that fears my feelings, and there is a part of me that knows feeling them is what I need to do. There is part of me that wants to use my voice and a part of me that numbs it out instead.

I know recovery is feeling my feelings instead of running away from them. Recovery is identifying them without judgment. Recovery is expressing my feelings out loud without justification. Recovery is using my voice instead of stifling it.

MY HEATING PAD

I sleep with an old, ratty heating pad on my stomach every night. It can be a cold day in winter or a hot day in summer. The temperature outside bears no weight on when I use it. It sits on the side of my bed, and each night, I turn it to high as I head to the bathroom to brush my teeth. By the time I unravel the very tangled cord and slip into bed, the heating pad is warm, inching its way to ovenlike. I lay it over my pajamas, and a relief permeates my body.

I took my heating pad to college, to boyfriends' homes, on trips, to each new apartment and condo, and eventually my adult home. There was a time that I even placed it on my bare skin and tied it tight with a sneaker shoelace. I woke up with bright-red heat marks that slowly faded away. When I am sad, I wrap it tightly against my body. When I have a chill, it warms me. When I am scared, it helps me to feel safe. The light weight settles me. It helps me to take a deep breath and fall asleep calmly, peacefully.

"Try the heating pad," my mom suggested when my stomachaches started as a little girl. My stomach felt like a rock. I did not know that it was my anxiety manifesting in my body yet. I did not know that each person has a weak spot and mine was my stomach. I also did not know that Mom was teaching me a self-soothing skill.

"Okay," I said, knowing that my mom was full of good ideas. My mom brought the heating pad down from the closet, disentangled its cord, put it down, and plugged in it. She then waited for it to get hot and called me into my bed, which she had already turned down meticulously. She kissed me on my forehead, patted the heating pad, and shut off the light.

Warmth creates safety. No wonder I take scalding showers. No wonder I wrap soft throws tightly around my body. No wonder I use my heating pad every day. No wonder I love the hot sun radiating on me.

Now I can also use my voice to create shelter, protection, a refuge. I can finally say farewell to my eating disorder.

PART 5

FULL RECOVERY

FULL RECOVERY EXISTS

Full recovery is sitting on a beautiful beach, feeling the sun warm my face.

My eating disorder embedded itself into my cells, my DNA. It firmly grew intricate, knotted roots deep down into my soul. I believed, even with years of recovery, that it would always be with me and could easily be awakened, provoked. That quasi-recovery was the end goal. That "co-existing" with my anorexia was the best available outcome. But that is not true. Full recovery is possible. I know I can get to that place in recovery where no stressful transition or anxiety-provoking change will wake it up because it will not be in there. My two parts will integrate, and I will be whole.

Carolyn Costin, my mentor, was the first person to avow that full recovery from an eating disorder was possible. She had recovered, and she knew other people who had as well. Her philosophy gave me the permission to see my life without my anorexia and to acknowledge that complete freedom was possible.

Costin believes that our healthy self will heal our eating disorder self. And eventually, both parts of our selves integrate, and we become whole, fully recovered. Then what used to be our eating disorder self serves as an alarm system—that part of our selves that says, "Hey, look over here. Something needs attention. Please respond."

This green light fills me with hope. I will break the cycle. I will heal my relationship with food, my body, and exercise and process root issues that I have avoided for too long. I use my personality traits of being driven, competitive, super organized, and somewhat obsessive and make full recovery my mission.

CALIFORNIA

Full recovery is feeling strong enough to go on vacation.

When I first hear about our "sibling" trip to California, it feels like an angel sending me a hopeful message. I am fully committed to letting go of my eating disorder. The future trip changes from a yearly vacation to a significant turning point in my life.

I dedicate myself to treatment. I sit on my therapist's chair each week and start to process the rape and my toxic marriage, and begin to heal the trauma of having an eating disorder for more than half of my life. I embrace the sessions with my nutritionist. I use the Rise Up + Recover app to record my meals, snacks, feelings, and behaviors. (Please check it out—it is amazing.) I get weighed weekly, and as the dial shimmies to the right, I see strength, freedom, and life. I stop my workouts, which have become compulsive since this relapse, and mindfully move my body with walking, yoga, and stretching. I have this insatiable desire to recover, and it is intense and beautiful.

I set some treatment boundaries immediately. The trip is a reward for staying on track with my recovery. And recovery means weight restoration, elimination of behaviors, and challenging my eating disorder thoughts. Another stipulation is to take a leave of

absence from my practice and go into a residential program if I do
not make gains in my recovery. I will use whatever support necessary.
I will not die. Hell no. I have too much to lose. Hell, I have too much
to gain. My beautiful life is right in front of me. I can almost reach
out and touch it.

• • •

Aidan sends me the Vrbo pictures from the home we are going
to rent in Ojai. I scroll through images of the rolling mountains, the
vineyard, the acorn-shaped pool, spa, gorgeous movie-set kitchen,
and cabana. I am recovering to this vacation.

I gather all my recovery building blocks and dive in headfirst.
I eat my meals, stop the purging and restricting behaviors, and
reframe the eating disorder thoughts. I sign up for another meal
delivery service. Not only is it convenient, but it is also imperative.
I slowly restore my weight by nourishing myself at each meal and
each snack. I reread supportive texts from my friends that say, "I'm
proud of you" and "Glad you are on your way up!!! You deserve it!!"

As I board the plane to Ojai, I feel stable and strong. I will not let
go of this momentum. As I fall back into the airplane seat, I know this
is where I am supposed to be. Each and every decision led me here—
to this moment. I grab a fresh hardcover book by Kelly Corrigan
from my knapsack and read it cover to cover, finishing the last few
pages on the descent.

I hold my head up high as I walk through LAX. I know I have
more recovery ahead of me, but the hope I feel is unrelenting. I make
the decisions now. I can use my voice to express my feelings and set
boundaries. I can use my voice to say no and speak my mind. My
eating disorder does not need to protect me anymore.

I hop on the escalator and head toward baggage claim to pick
up my luggage. About halfway down, I glance out and see the back
of Henry and James's heads below. Beth and the boys have surprised

me. As soon as I see their precious faces, gentle smiles, and small, beloved bodies, my heart expands. My eyes fill with tears of happiness as they both run into my arms. I bottle this feeling into my soul.

• • •

We pull into the expansive circular driveway of the vacation home two hours later. The home is bordered by mountains. The large, antique, wooden front door welcomes us.

"Wow. We are staying at a castle," Henry remarks. "Let's go swimming!"

We each quickly choose one of the six bedrooms available. I pick the room down a long hallway with a reading nook outside next to a large window overlooking the pool. I place my bag on the luggage rack and search for my bathing suit. I shimmy into my turquoise one-piece. It hangs loosely around my butt and thighs. As I walk, I feel light pockets of air rising into my suit where it should be snug. I reach for my black swim skirt that I bought a few seasons ago. It sags on my hips. Instead of feeling defeated, I feel motivated.

Just stay on track. You can do this.

While Henry, James, and I sit in the hot tub, warming up from the cold yet absolutely refreshing pool, the rest of my family arrives: Grace, Connor, Liam, and Noah—who were on a later flight—and Aidan, who drove from a work project. Finally, a well-deserved break. We are all together for an entire week. A time to relax and take long, deep breaths. A time to browse outside bookstores, lazily sit in the hot tub, read in the sunlight, sleep in, and cuddle up with my beautiful nephews.

The next day, the boys get into the pool early. After swimming for over an hour, Henry exits the pool dripping. I wrap him in a warm towel and hug his body tight. James continues to lie on the pink raft shaped like a donut.

"Thanks, Mer-Mer," Henry says, looking up at my face. "You would make a really good mother."

"Thank you, pal," I say, holding back tears. The words fill my heart. The determination rustles in my soul. Without a doubt, I know that I will not stop until I reach full recovery. Serenity fills my chest, causing chills down my arms. That evening, I wake up in the middle of the night with Henry softly lying in my arms.

CELEBRITY

Full recovery is playing board games with my family.

We love games in our family. Cards, Monopoly, cornhole, Kan Jam, Scattergories, Things, Code Names—you name it, we have probably played it. On trips, we usually get on a roll with a specific game and play it each night after dinner.

The lucky game on this trip is Celebrity. After dinner, we sit around an exceptionally large marble table in the dining room. It is so big that if I put my arm out straight, I barely reach midway across. We pass around my mother's chocolate chip cookies that she made from scratch and sent from New York to California. The cookies have broken into small pieces from the trip, and in that moment, I recognize that I like eating pieces of cookies instead of whole cookies. It is more enjoyable.

Maybe I could invent this. Wait, are cookie pieces already a thing? I am always thinking of new ideas. I learn to change my rumination into creative planning. And I always tell Noah that I will invest in his company one day because he is an entrepreneur in the making.

After I read Henry and James two books of their choice, their heads hit the pillows, exhausted from the day's events. Noah hands out small scraps of paper, and we each write six celebrities on them. Beth, Grace, and I take a little longer to finish. The boys wait patiently, minus Noah, who walks restlessly around the table. This is how the game works—during the first round, you use words to get your team to guess the person. In the second round, you do charades (no talking). And then, in the third round, you only use one word.

Noah is competitive. I am goofy and laugh a lot, sometimes to the point of breaking down, where no sounds come out. Beth is theatrical. Liam is laid back. Aidan is funny yet spirited. Conor is creative. And Grace plays like a designated hitter.

"She is the queen of pop. Top female singer," Aidan says confidently.

"Ariana Grande. Madonna!" Conor yells out.

"She is the queen of pop!" Aidan says again, louder this time.

"Umm . . . Kelly Clarkson?" Liam blurts out.

"Oh my God! How can you not be getting this? She makes the most money of any female musician," Aidan howls as his assurance turns to astonishment with a hint of rage.

"Katy Perry?" screams Noah.

"She is the queen of pop!"

"Say something else!" Noah squeals.

The sand timer runs out.

"It was freaking Taylor Swift!" Aidan says, crushed by his team.

I sit and observe my favorite men (minus Dad, Henry, and James) in the world. Did I mention I was eating cookies?

• • •

We check out the small, quaint town. We browse the shops; saunter around Bart's Books, an outside bookstore; and enjoy yummy lunches. We spend most of the time in the house because we are homebodies— every one of us.

"I just want to snuggle with all of you and read *Tree House* books," my mom says regularly, especially when we got older and moved away. Home means safety. Comfort. Protection.

I also listen to myself intently. When I need a break, I take a nap. When I have a penetrating chill, I take a long, steaming-hot shower. When I need quiet, I read in the library that has the cool ladder that rolls past the long bookcase wall bursting with books. When I am overwhelmed and not physically feeling great, I stay home to get some alone time. When I feel invigorated, I play with my nephews in the pool and hot tub. And during all of it, I stay present and repeat the mantra that *I am safe. I can use my voice.*

We dub the large, ornate, and sunny wood room in front of the house the "yoga room." The walls are decorated with long, uncovered, vertical windows that allow the light to shine in, illuminating the trees and mountains in the distance. A stone fireplace blazes. Beth, Grace, and I do a yoga class set up on Grace's ipad on the Glo app. The class focuses on intentions. As soon as the teacher asks what our intention is, the word "nourishment" pops into my mind. I need to nourish my body and brain, not just now, but forever. For the next thirty minutes, I repeat my mantra.

I choose health. I choose life. I choose nourishment.

On the last day of vacation, I try and rope my family into yoga again. Beth and Liam feign interest right to the end. Beth chooses to sit on the couch to watch a Beyoncé documentary. Liam decides to sit in the hot tub. Can you blame them?

So, it is just me and my mat today. The teacher talks about how everything has a beginning, a middle, and an end—our breaths, each yoga pose, life. My mind quiets. Curious. Intent. I envision a pot of gold next to a colorful rainbow after a summer storm. The rainbow is leading me to the gold. For me, the gold is loving myself, trusting myself, feeling my feelings, being present, and using my voice.

As the sunlight warms my face, a huge sense of faith explodes around me. The room is drenched in light. I smile. I smirk. I am grateful. So grateful. At that moment, I know that I am alive on this earth to fully recover and to help others to see the light.

I decide to do another video, but my body has other plans.

"Conor, can you bring me a cup of OJ?"

He rushes in with a small glass of freshly squeezed orange juice that he made earlier that morning.

"You okay, Mer?" Conor asks caringly.

"A little shaky," I say as I grab the juice with an unsteady hand and sit down on the oak step. My body is telling me to stop, and I listen. I stare through the wide-open door leading from the yoga room into the library, past the high shelves of books, and notice the mountains. At this moment, I feel tall and alive. My motivation and hope are intoxicating.

A WHOLE PERSON

Full recovery is feeling joy and shouting it from the rooftops.

The sibling trip kindles a fire beneath me. I use this renewed energy to slay the demons and acknowledge that anything I put in front of my recovery, I will lose. Each day, I do the work. I dig deep and break through my wall. This time, I use each and every strategy until it is my automatic default—until I become a whole person without an eating disorder. It takes me years and I do not stop. And believe me, it is miraculous.

I feel my feelings without judgment. The pleasant ones. The unpleasant ones. I feel every feeling that arises, even if it is shame, sadness, embarrassment, anxiety, or grief. I experience the discomfort with grace and respect and curiosity. Just like food, I stop assessing them as good or bad. All feelings are important. I surf the wave of my emotions because they are going to ebb and flow, rise and fall. All feelings are temporary. They do not last forever. They will eventually dissipate, and instead of seeking refuge with short-term self-destruction, I focus on the long-term goal of living a life worth living and being free. I listen carefully to what the feelings in my body are communicating to me. I sit with them with compassion and wonder. I validate that I have every right to feel what I feel, and no one must approve them. I proceed mindfully in accordance with my goals, which I see now with supreme clarity.

I eliminate all behaviors. I use my coping strategies—DBT skills, cognitive restructuring, self-compassion, positive affirmations, and Carolyn Costin's 8 keys to recovery and dialogues, ending with my healthy self. I reach out to my support team. I journal about my experiences. I reread my pros and cons lists and look at the tattered index card that sits in my wallet from the PHP. On one side is a list of consequences of my eating disorder and on the other is a list of healthy coping strategies. Eating regularly and consistently each day gradually eliminates my urges, and my obsession with my body, weight, and shape subsides. I know without a doubt that my worth has nothing to do with the size of my body!

I eat ALL foods. Not some foods—ALL. Pizza, chocolate, ice cream, bagels, butter, cookies . . . ALL. OF. IT. Each and every day. I realize that I love cream cheese—lots of it—and spread it on hot, fluffy plain bagels straight from the oven. I love fresh, bright-green broccoli and pair it with most meals. I realize that I love syrup and have waffles for dinner. I bake fresh chocolate chip cookies and make sandwiches with vanilla ice cream in the middle, drizzled with chocolate syrup. I love Greek yogurt mixed with cereal. I find that my body responds to high-protein cereal, so I listen to it. I melt large marshmallows at the outside firepit for s'mores. I attune to my body and listen to my cravings. I honor my hunger and fullness.

I also erase all morality from food. I repeat over and over that food is not good or bad. Food is food. My food choices are not linked to my decency or virtue. I acknowledge that I am a good and kind person, and my weight is not associated with my self-worth. Nada. Zilch. I dismantle my core belief that *I am bad* and change it to *I am lovable*. I feel angry at diet culture and how it brainwashed me as a vulnerable child. I feel irate that those messages could have killed me. I delete diet culture permanently from my life, choosing to follow positive social media, people, and philosophies, including intuitive eating and Health at Every Size. I stand on my own soapbox and scream messages of compassion, love, and respect.

I challenge my eating disorder thoughts at every turn. I bring awareness to what my eating disorder is telling me and talk back from my healthy self. I realize that the thoughts usually arise when I have an uncomfortable feeling or when I judge someone or some situation. I write out daily dialogues between my healthy self and my eating disorder self. My healthy self gets the last word, and eventually, it is the only voice I hear. My two selves merge and I am complete—unified with myself.

I gain the weight back—ALL OF IT—every pound. It is necessary for my recovery. I radically accept that I cannot stay at my "sick" weight and recover. It is not possible for me to stay that weight and have a healthy relationship with food. I tried for twenty-five years; believe me, it does not work. I carry my scale to my driveway, put on safety goggles, and smash it with a mallet into a hundred little pieces. Oh, the sweet victory.

I take my medications compliantly. Every morning. Every night. I accept that the neuropathways of my brain are askew and the Prozac stabilizes it. It places me in the middle of the balance beam. The Buspar sharply decreases my anxiety, and the rumination in my head dwindles. The Trazadone helps me to get adequate sleep, which is imperative to my healing.

I also make a sacred space to thank my eating disorder. It was protective during trying times. It was reliable and constant, but I know it is time to say goodbye. I write a goodbye letter to it and burn it into ash. The small pieces of black soot symbolize a death and a rebirth.

I practice mindful movement and decrease my workouts dramatically. Pilates feels soft on my body and joints. I like spinning— the music energizes me, and I find group camaraderie in the classes. They both help me to connect with others. I attune to my body daily and ask it how it wants to move today. I also rest a lot! My body has been crying out for it for years. I spend multiple weeks in a row taking a break. I engage in activities that bring me pleasure, such as going to the beach, reading memoirs, floating in my pool, and connecting with friends. I do daily mindfulness exercises to fully connect to the present moment.

Take a deep breath in and out.

Take another deep breath in and out.

Do a body scan from your head to your toes and notice any tension and body sensations.

Observe any feelings that arise without judgment.

Focus on the rise and fall of your belly as you breathe in and out.

When your mind wanders, which it will, gently bring it back to your breath.

I focus on what I am recovering to. My nephews are front and center. I am also recovering to connection, relationships, joy, and love. I am recovering to peace of mind—to the ability to let go of my thoughts like they are leaves floating down a stream and be fully in the now. I also reach out to friends and family. I act oppositely to my urges to isolate. I leave the house. I make plans. I do the hard work.

I sit down and prioritize each meal and snack. I set out my pretty placemats from Anthropologie that Darcy bought me for Christmas. I eat out of pretty bowls and from fancy plates. I light candles and dim the lights to set up a calm ambiance. I start to listen to classical music and sway to the effortless rhythm.

I find my voice again. My amazingly sweet voice. Making my own decisions is like lying down on cool, freshly laundered sheets that smell like Lysol. I feel a sense of liberation down to my soul. The heaviness of my shoulders falls away. Not caring what others think is like a cow being set free into a green pasture. I feel emancipated. I sense the guilt that rises in me when people want me to do something and then sit with it and make the most effective decision for me in that moment. I express my needs as clearly as I can. I set boundaries to protect myself. I practice self-care. I get out of toxic and harmful situations more quickly because I know they are not healthy. I trust my intuition more. I know that the world will not end if someone disagrees with me or is disappointed in me.

I am still polishing my voice. At times, I shout it from the mountaintops. At times, I need to give it more credit. At times, I need to use it more. At times, it is stifled by grief or is painfully shy. At times, I know I should say something, but I hold back. At times, I know what is best, but I do the opposite, then catch myself quickly. I then make the effective choice. I trust my intuition more consistently. And as my genuine voice gains power, I mend beautifully together. I am restored, healthy, and authentically me. Unapologetically. Unashamed.

MAVERICK

Full recovery is running around the beach with Mavi,
laughing out loud when she buries her head and full body
into the sand.

"I thought you did not like dogs. You said they were messy
and unpredictable," Kelly texts after I send an adorable
picture of my new mini golden doodle sitting in the palm
of my left hand. Maverick is the size of a cantaloupe. Her coat is curly
and fluffy. She is the color of multigrain Cheerios, the color inside a
Milk Dud. Soft as an old, frayed robe, her carrot-colored eyelashes
extend for miles. Her cuteness overpowers me, and as she settles
onto my chest, I know that my life has changed.

I pause before I text back. "I used to to think that." Back when
dogs signified clutter, chaos, muddy paws, annoying squeaky toys,
and unappealing early morning walks.

But I am ready. Maybe I was not ready for Sandy, but I am ready
now. I feel it in my gut. I can trust myself. A loving, furry companion
is what I want. And even though she is three times more expensive
than Sandy, she is worth every penny. When she sits on my lap,
something in my body shifts—a release, a calmness, a reprioritization
of obligations.

My first real introduction to dogs was meeting Pepper, Aidan and Beth's first dog, who they rescued. My mom never allowed us to get pets—unless you count goldfish. We won one each year at our annual grammar school fair, the fish swirling in the plastic bag as I carefully walked home. For some reason, we kept the small fishbowl on top of the oven, and one year, my dad heated it to death. Maybe that is why she did not want us to get a pet. Anyway, I will never forget the time I was staying at Aidan and Beth's first home. I slept in the guest room on the pull-out couch. I got up in the morning and we could not find Pepper. Maybe he was curling in a ball behind a chair. Maybe he was outside. As I went to push the couch back in, I found Pepper lying under the pullout. He had slept underneath me all night.

I bought Maverick from a golden doodle breeder in Rochester, New York. The night before I went to pick her up, the dog breeder called me.

"So, I wanted to call to tell you that you are going to be a great dog mom," she said. I had called and texted a few times this week with questions, so I imagined she was trying to put my nerves at ease. "The one I have chosen for you, a male dog, is quite the barker."

"He barks?" I cut her off. "My last dog did not bark. She whined softly. Sort of like a purr. She definitely did not bark."

"You know you are getting a dog, right? Dogs bark," she laughed with a sprinkling of passive-aggressiveness.

"Yes, I know I am getting a dog and that they bark, but do you have one that maybe does not bark that much?"

"Let me see. I do have a girl puppy who has not made a peep."

"I'll take her!"

I pick her up and bring her home in a small white laundry basket stuffed with fleece blankets. I can trust myself now. I can make my own decisions. After a week of deciding on names, I name her Maverick after Tom Cruise in *Top Gun*, a childhood favorite. For female flair, I give her the nickname Mavi, and it sticks.

That night, she falls asleep in my lap as I sit cross-legged on the kitchen floor. She is so tiny that I hold her up with both arms so she does not slip through the spaces between my legs. I gently place her in the wire crate padded with old bath towels. I creep upstairs to my bed and gently lie down. My ears perk up as I wait for Mavi to make some type of noise to communicate the separation, but no sound comes. She sleeps through the night. So do I.

I add Mavi to my family and I am ready to add more.

BUILDING A FAMILY

Full recovery is connecting to others with vulnerability and tenderness.

"I miss you," I write in the middle of doing burpees in my garage, that I recently got professionally organized. A country song plays loudly from the Sonos radio placed on a shelf by the treadmill, and it reminds me of him. Of us watching *Songland* together and Lady A deciding to record the song "Champagne Night." Of us drinking coffee on the front porch. Of us making s'mores on a summer night. The ping back is instantaneous. Dexter misses me too. I lie down to stretch with a smile plastered on my face in child's pose.

I have spent a lot of time putting my life puzzle together. Often, I tried to shove in pieces that obviously did not fit. It was like I was looking at a square-shaped puzzle but sabotaged myself by trying to cram in a circle wedge repeatedly, praying that somehow it would come together. Full recovery is taking a step back, looking at all the evidence, mindfully pausing, and then acting effectively. Dexter is one of the final pieces to my puzzle, and I am ready to accept him, love him, and invite him fully into my world.

Dexter and I meet up a few days later. His dense, warm body engulfs me in a hug, and I melt into his embrace. This time, I use my voice and tell him about my serious history with anorexia. My body is not a symbol of my pain anymore. I share with him how the eating disorder started as a child and eventually worsened. He listens. He is supportive. He tells me he is proud of me. He takes it seriously. I radically accept to be in the moment. To let our relationship unfold like a flower without judgment or control, understanding that we are two different people who love each other and can seek the middle path together.

I convey that I need a partner, a teammate, a companion to walk through life with, and he wants the same. We become aware of each other's needs. Dexter understands that when I compulsively start a new home project or work late into the evenings several days in a row, I may be experiencing anxiety. He gently shares his observations, and I pause, reflect. We practice problem-solving together. I acknowledge my initial reaction to "fix" his problems and learn to hang back, showing interest and support; I accept that he can guide his own destiny. We acknowledge that I tend to be more emotional, and he is more rational. We balance each other. We bring the best out in one another.

In general, we share more. We share our feelings and thoughts. We attend to them with acceptance. We learn about each other's perspectives. When my mind wants to jump to catastrophic conclusions, I pause, take a deep breath, and see the bigger picture. I learn to sleep on things and, as Dexter says, "let is marinate." I practice walking alongside Dexter instead of walking or sprinting ahead of him, steering him to what I think is acceptable. We are two people who care deeply about one another. We are happy. We are stable. And as our bond grows, my loyalty to him and us is fierce. We decide to walk through this life together. Dexter, Mavi, and I build a family and start to build our own puzzle. The pieces fit seamlessly.

SELF-LOVE

Full recovery is focusing on how I feel, not the way I look.

n full recovery, I wholly accept my body. At any size. At any shape. At any fitness level. I separate my self-worth from my body or appearance. I practice mirror exposure and witness the curves in my body with pride. I accept the roundness of my breasts, the fullness of my cheeks, the extra layer around my tummy. There is a softness in it now—without the war on my body, my shoulders sit farther from my neck. My stomach relaxes. My body trusts me.

I walk around in tank tops. Sleeveless dresses. I try on one outfit before I go out because what I look like is not as important as how I feel. Perfection does not exist. I let go of preoccupation and meticulousness. I leave the house without lip products and sit with the discomfort of chapped lips. I leave dishes in the sink overnight. I stop getting manicures and let the old gel polish disintegrate from my nails. I am messy. I am complicated. I am remarkable.

I accept my body. I wear clothes that fit my here-and-now body. I wear clothes that are fluid and comfortable. I stand naked in front of a floor-length mirror, usually after a hot shower, and sing or yell out loud, "This is my body fully recovered" and "I love that my legs can walk Mavi to the park" and "My body has nothing to do with my self-worth!"

I am not afraid of my body anymore. We are at peace.

I rest a lot. I radically accept that I am exhausted. Depleted. Recovery is difficult, one of the hardest things that I have done in this lifetime. I take a break from movement for weeks at a time. At one point, I stop attending my morning workout classes because I realize I enjoy lying in my bed, cuddling Mavi instead! I find other ways to re-energize myself, like reading in a safe place with my feet wrapped up in a blanket. I find pleasure in softly stretching my body.

I declutter (and not in an obsessive type of way). I clean out my drawers and closets, donating six very large garbage bags of clothes. I grasp that I do not need ten sweatshirts or fifty sweaters. Instead of feeling a false sense of control in having stuff, I realize that simplicity and a reduction in things are helpful to my sense of peace. I clean out my garage and basement. I get rid of vases, boxes, and old lamps. Decluttering helps me to feel lighter—less weighed down by objects. And overall, it assists me by making more room for purpose, meaning, and connection.

In full recovery, I feel safe—most of the time. At least once a day, I can still sense panic building, and I repeat my mantra, "I am safe," and practice paced breathing, inhaling for four counts and exhaling for six. I still regularly struggle with anxiety, but my body slowly begins to be more of a secure haven. I trust myself. I am aware of my gut intuitions and listen to the messages that my body sends me. I have an upsurge in my confidence and sureness. The second-guessing withers. My nervous system lightens. My flight-or-fight response eases. Finally, no one is out there waiting to hurt me. In full recovery, I feel assured, self-reliant, and poised. Mindfulness is my default—most of the time. I am keenly aware of the state of mind that I am in. Is it emotional, reasonable, or wise? I stay grounded in the moment.

At times, when I wake up feeling sad and depressed, I feel the feelings. I acknowledge that these feelings are temporary. I practice self-compassion and let go of judgments. I can be fully recovered from my eating disorder and feel depressed sometimes.

I recovered to make my own decisions. I recovered to making my own decisions even if someone, God forbid, disagrees with me. I will not combust if someone is disappointed about a decision I make. And even if they are disappointed, I can stand firmly by my decision anyway. I shed the layers of pleasing other people. I shed the layers of doing what other people want me to do. I shed the layers of my timidness and doubt. I shed the layers of asking multiple people what I should do. There are some decisions that I do not even share with others. Without needing constant reassurance or justifying my actions, I keep some parts of my life private. I set boundaries with others. I do not see them as selfish. They are pertinent to survival. I only have so much energy to give, and I can decide where my energy goes.

I will make the wrong decisions. I will make mistakes. But recovery has taught me that I can manage the consequences. The world will not blow up. Not everyone has to like me. I do not need approval of my life decisions. I make amends when I mess up. I take accountability. I erase judgment from my vocabulary. I replace it with compassion and curiosity, realizing that judgment destroys peace.

My dreams are less violent, less disturbing, and less turbulent. I stop having the recurring dreams of the world blowing up or the mean witch following me. In some of my dreams, I can get my father to safety. But in some, he still dies. And even though the majority of my dreams are negative, I feel like I process a lot in my dreams so I can be more present in my life. In most of my dreams now, I am engulfed by bags of stuff, mostly clothes, and it takes me hours to move forward while holding on to all of them. I believe this dream represents my continued work to let things go. To let go of judgments. To let go of the oppressive messages we are told by society. To let go of material items. To let go of regret and old narratives that do not serve me. To latch onto joy, happiness, and serenity. Sometimes I even have dreams that Zac Efron or Ryan Eggold is my boyfriend. I fasten onto those dreams, and I peacefully and soundly fall asleep.

It is no coincidence that my private practice is more successful in full recovery. I am a proud business owner. I am a hard worker. I thrive on structure. Mastery is rejuvenating. But I also prioritize self-care and rest. And when I don't, my body is my teacher. I also find meaning in my life. I eventually specialize in treating those with eating disorders, and it becomes the focus of my career. I became a Carolyn Costin Institute certified eating disorder coach and run a coaching business. I work with organizations like Project HEAL to help those who cannot afford treatment. I run eating disorder groups. I run meal support groups using the adorable table my parents bought me so many years before. Helping others on their eating disorder journeys brings me purpose. I share parts of my story with clients, and my recovery journey gives people hope. I write blog posts and articles to inspire others who are suffering. Talk about full circle.

DINNER ON A
THURSDAY NIGHT

Full recovery is meeting your friends for dinner on a weeknight.

I send the thumbs-up emoji in the group chat after Maggie suggests that we all go to a restaurant in Asbury Park that serves delicious, thin-crust pizza. I get dressed without thinking, throw on tan wedges, and drive over. My friends and I sit at a long, splintered wooden table outside on a warm July night. There are eight of us, so we grab two chairs to put at each end so we can all fit. I wear a tank top jumpsuit. It is no-sweater weather, and I place my tan cardigan to the side. The night is still. No breeze.

Summer is my favorite season. It reminds me of the smells of the Jersey Shore—the salt water in the air, barbecues, and citronella candles. It reminds me of swimming in the ocean for so many hours that my fingers pruned. It reminds me of eating sandy peanut butter and jelly sandwiches on a scratchy, wool, army-green blanket. It reminds me of afternoon naps when I'd wake up and notice my mom had draped a light beach towel over me. It reminds me of looking for shark teeth with Kelly. It reminds me of playing gin rummy with Darcy for hours. It reminds me of outside showers, lightning bugs, and the old-fashioned candy store.

We order different types of pizzas for the table, and each takes turns trying the different flavors. We break up into twos, catching up about life, work, relationships, children, and vacations. I pick up the hot, gooey slice of margherita pizza and take a bite off the tip. The cheese, tomato sauce, and spices dance in my mouth. The crust is thin and doughy.

"This is so good," I say.

"Isn't it? I know, their pizza is delicious," Marcie, another beach friend, replies from across the table.

"I'll try a slice," I say to Kelly, pointing to the carbonara pizza at the end of the table. She hands me a piece. The pizza has a sunny-side up egg on it, and my gut tells me that I will not like it, but you never know. The "yes girl" is my natural default. I take a bite, mindfully check in, and decide that it is not for me. I hand it to Maggie, who finishes it for me. I feel stimulated. The night is enchanting. Each day is a brand-new day—a day when I can take on the world.

I matter.

And to be honest, I am downright amazing.

I then grab another slice of margherita and take in the moment.

MEANING

Full recovery is being a proud pet parent.

Mavi, simply put, is my best decision. She brings me tidal waves of joy. My heart expands so much that it nearly bursts like a balloon. I take my role as Mavi's mother very seriously. I am here to protect her and to love her.

Initially, I have an unbendable rule that she is only allowed on the first floor. I place a large white dog gate at the bottom of the stairs. Upstairs is out of the question. I also put one up at the end of the kitchen, separating it from the rest of the house. Mavi transitions without a hitch, and even though she eats through my favorite sweater and pees and poops on each rug that we own, she is precious.

One evening, I sit on my couch, watching a medical drama. I start to hear soft whines from the kitchen. I focus on the doctor putting in the emergency chest tube as her whimpers get louder. Thankfully, she is not a barker! The next night, I remove the kitchen gate and she scampers across the floor so quickly that she skids on the hardwood planks, but she eventually gets her balance. She hops up and plops down directly facing me on my lap. She kisses me for two minutes straight and then wraps her small body around into a sphere and lies down softly. Pure joy.

"Well, she is not going upstairs," I say to Dexter. "Upstairs is our space. Mavi has the downstairs."

"Okay, Mer," he says, grinning.

"I mean it," I reinforce, but this type of inflexibility feels uneasy, and I let go. Instead of controlling the situation, I accept it.

• • •

Dexter is away on business. Having completed his degree, he travels from one hospital to the next on the East Coast, putting together medical machines. One night, I remove the staircase gate. I turn off the TV and the living room lights. I grab a glass of water from the kitchen. I place my phone into the pocket of my terry cloth robe. As soon as I put one foot on the staircase, Mavi's head shoots up from her snooze on the fuzzy blanket. She darts to the stairs, following me diligently to the second floor. She jumps onto my bed and sleeps on the side of my pillow, her body attached to mine.

Obviously, you do not need to be a pet parent to be fully recovered, but for me, it is daily proof that I can love unconditionally. I put her needs before my own. I experience quietude as she cuddles in my arms. I laugh hysterically when she is soaking wet in the bathtub, looking half her size without her curly hair puffing around her. I watch her licking peanut butter, getting zoomies in the backyard, and playing with her bones and toys. I feel the warmth and connection of her body against me as we fall asleep. She is my mindfulness magnet.

Mavi gently taps at the back door, her cue that she wants to go out. I open the back door and let her out to the green backyard with a large oak tree in the center next to the pool. I slide off my walnut-colored Ugg slippers and sit down in a kitchen chair to put on my shoes. I grab the size-eight running sneakers and tie the laces tight. This past year, I realized that my wide bunions do need room to breathe. And I'm okay with that.

LONG HAIR

Full recovery is rocking long hair.

"**S**tand up, dear," my hairdresser says as she gently taps my
shoulder. I nestle into the chair and drop my navy-blue
pocketbook onto the hook underneath the wide mirror.
"What?" I question.

"Your hair is so long that you need to stand up for me to cut it."

"Can you say that again?" I ask. She drops her head back and
chuckles.

Four years earlier, I went to this salon to get my hair done for a
Christmas party. My hair fell right to the top of my shoulders, and
since "doing my hair" meant putting it into a ponytail, I made an
appointment for an updo. About fifteen minutes into it, she asked
if I knew that I had lost a lot of hair. I had noticed that my hair fell
out in clumps during my showers, that my hair had thinned and was
more brittle to the touch, but I was not prepared for what I saw. She
handed me the small vanity mirror and spun me around. I angled
the mirror, and a bald spot the size of a baseball in the middle of the
back of my head stared back at me. She needed to layer my hair so
my scalp was hidden.

"Give me two years," she said. "We can make your hair healthy in two years, but you need to do what I tell you. I am a little more expensive, but I am worth it."

I loved her spunky, confident, and kind demeanor.

"Okay," I answered. "Deal."

After years of recovery, two years is nothing. Every six weeks, I sat in her seat, and within two years, my hair slowly became healthy, robust, and radiant. She has some magical hairdresser powers, and the leave-in conditioner I use is a game changer, but I know that nourishing my body consistently helps. It is a crucial ingredient. It also helps my nails, skin, teeth, digestion, energy level, concentration, mood, and other mental health issues. There seems to be a common denominator here. My eating disorder took away a lot of things during my life, and in full recovery, I get them back one by one.

My heart flutters. I smirk widely. I stand proudly as she snips an inch off my hair and it falls to the ground.

BABY BLUE EYES

Full recovery is living my life in color!

Each day, I pinch myself, literally (in a gentle way). I cannot believe I am living my life without an eating disorder. Sometimes I think that I am playing an imposter, but I am not. Sometimes I think I am stuck in a dream because life, fully recovered, is so different from anything I have ever experienced. I pause in the middle of my day to be grateful. I sense my feelings and express them. I am still polishing my voice, but it's mine and I use it.

Full recovery is painting my black house shutters a bright color, called Baby Blue Eyes, to add a burst of color to my life. Full recovery is keeping the Christmas lights wrapped around my banister all year. Being fully recovered is like waking up in a color TV set. The trees look greener, the flowers and leaves brighter, the sunset more glorious. The sky is Tiffany blue. My life was in black and white and now it is in bright neon colors.

The path of recovery from an eating disorder is different for everyone. So is the path to full recovery. We each have a journey—this was mine. With each slip, fall, relapse, and lapse, I stayed the course. Day after day, month after month, and year after year, I did the work. Each morning, I still look at my vision board that hangs from my kitchen window with Scotch Tape. Pictures of my nephews are front and center because they were the glue that started my journey. A picture of a stack of books is in the corner since I recovered back to reading an entire book in one sitting. A photo of the game Kan Jam is fastened to the paper because I recovered to having the energy and desire to play games with family and friends. There is a cup of coffee because drinking hot coffee with Dexter on the weekends and checking in with one another is my happy place and a way that I attend to our relationship. The colorful paint palette represents me recovering to creativity and new hobbies and because my life is in color. I have a picture of Mavi because being her mom gives me meaning and purpose. A picture of a salad topped with various toppings is attached because I recovered to eating all food and finding pleasure in food once again. I have a red heart affixed to it because I am in love with my life. I am in love with me.

Full recovery for me started as a feeling. I felt this uncontrollable burst of bliss, rapture, and joy. It could not be contained. I felt it buzzing through my entire body. The feelings were sometimes brief and sometimes they lingered, and eventually, they were as natural as taking a breath. Each day, I pause to remind myself that this is my life now—a life without an eating disorder.

In full recovery, I accept my body, attune to my body's hunger and fullness cues, and treat my body with compassion. I am my body's friend and treat it with respect and kindness. I reach out to family and friends for connection and for support. I engage in mindfulness practice to be in the present moment. I find purpose and meaning in my life. I am a great aunt; compassionate friend; loving daughter and sister; strong businesswoman; empathic listener; awesome mother to Mavi; and an honest, loving, and reliable partner to Dexter.

Here is my definition of full recovery:

- I accept and attune to my here-and-now body and treat it

with care, compassion, and respect.

- I experience freedom and joy by connecting to others, feeling my feelings, eating regularly, and living in the present moment.
- I find purpose, meaning, and self-worth unrelated to my body, weight, or shape.
- I become a pet parent (to Maverick, who likes to cuddle in my lap, attacks me with kisses when I walk in the door, and does not shed).

MY GUARDIAN ANGELS

*Full recovery is being completely present with
my four nephews.*

S o, my guardian angels are all grown up. Liam and Noah are
both in college on the West Coast, and Henry and James still
live in California, so, currently, they are all in the same state.
Henry just started middle school and James is in fourth grade.

I plan a long weekend to visit them, even packing the night
before. I walk out of the airport doors and immediately notice the
change in temperature. The sun is bright over the palm trees in
the distance, and the warmth feels good in my bones. I take off my
jean jacket and long-sleeved tee in the Uber, displaying a light-pink
tank top. I roll down the window the entire way so the soft breeze
pushes my hair back and energizes my body. I check into the campus
hotel and then head to the bookstore and stroll around the large,
manicured campus.

I see Liam and Noah walking toward the restaurant entrance
later that night and my grin widens. My heart grows. They both stand
over six feet tall. I raise my chin and give them both hugs, reaching
only to their waists as they arrive at the outside table I reserved.
The smooth night air is flawless. The large heaters send a warm and

delicate wisp of balminess. We sit down to a magnificent meal and catch up, talk, and listen. My face hurts by the end of the night—a smile permanently etched onto my face.

The next day, I go over to see the little ones, Henry and James.

"Here, Mer-Mer, put this on," Henry says as he places a black bulletproof vest in my hands. "Also, these." He hands me indigo-blue safety glasses. I zip up the vest, put my reading glasses down, and slide the safety glasses into place. Next is a tutorial for each of the toy Nerf guns in the lineup. He has already set up three targets on a wrought iron bench on the cement basketball court in the backyard. When I eventually get to the sniper gun, I hit all three targets.

"Rock on!" I scream.

"Awesome, Mer. You got them all!" Henry shouts, throwing his arms into the air.

"Well, you are a great teacher," I say, pulling him into a cuddle.

"I love you, Mer-Mer."

"I love you, pal."

"Babe, chess is starting," Beth yells from the back door. Henry drops the Nerf gun and heads to his bedroom for virtual chess class. Before his door even fully closes, James asks me to play Sorry.

"Absolutely, bud." I softly rake my hand through his thick blond hair. We get the board set up on the kitchen table and Beth joins us. It has been so long since I played this game, I cannot even remember the directions. James, like Henry, is my teacher. As we move our colorful pieces around the board, I sit in the serenity of the moment.

Later, back on campus, Noah and I walk to Liam's apartment a few blocks away. The sun has set, and there is a crisp breeze in the air. I wrap my jean jacket around my body. My flowy, flowered dress falls to my ankles. My long hair drops to the middle of my back. I smirk and my chest drops into relaxation. My arduous journey has led me to this moment. We are going to Rodeo Drive for a fancy dinner. Me and my angels.

ABOUT THE AUTHOR

This is Meredith's first published book. She runs a mental health private practice in Red Bank, New Jersey. She writes a blog at recoveryfromanorexia.com. She is a licensed clinical social worker, a Carolyn Costin Institute certified eating disorder coach, and a certified intuitive eating counselor. She also runs an eating disorder coaching business. She lives in Fair Haven, New Jersey, with her golden doodle, Mavi. She continues to nourish her body and mind and knows that the best is yet to come.

You can connect with Meredith via email at mereditheob@gmail.com, Instagram @ed_recovery_mo/, Facebook @edrecoverymo, Twitter @ed_recovery_mo, Pinterest @meredith_Obrien/, or LinkedIn @meredith-o-brien-31510929.

ACKNOWLEDGMENTS

This book is dedicated to my four nephews. Thank you for bringing joy into my life and giving me a reason to live and to fully recover. You teach me what unconditional love is.

Mom and Dad—thank you for staying supportive during my journey. I know this is not what you envisioned for my life, but you stood by my side.

To my brothers—thank you for bringing laughter into my life and never giving up on me.

To my sisters-in-law—thank you for showing me what a sister really is; you listen to me and validate my experiences.

Tom—thank you for being a beautiful and loving partner. Thank you for accepting all of me. I will never forget the day when we smashed the scale on the driveway.

To Deirdre, my BFF—you are my dearest friend. Thank you for all the memories and making my childhood a happy one.

To Kristen and my "beach crew"—thank you for accepting me into our circle and respecting my changes and growth as a friend.

To John Koehler of Koehler Books—you are an amazing publisher and treated me with respect while also making me laugh out loud.

To the entire Kohler Books team, including Courtney Meunier, Miranda Dillon, Kellie Emery, Hannah Woodlan, and Lauren Sheldon—thank you for bringing my book to life.

To Alice Anderson—thank you for being my first editor and opening my mind to ways that I could expand my story.

To Ethel Baumberg and my entire social media team—thank you for helping me get my story out to others.

To Project Write Now—thank you for giving me a safe and creative space to write.

To Carolyn Costin—thank you for being a caring mentor. Thank you for showing me that full recovery is possible.

To Helen Myers of 3DOTS PR—thank you for helping me to build my brand.

To my private practice team of strong and empathic women—thank you for building a business where we help others and bring some light to this often dark world.

To my clients—you are courageous and strong. Full recovery is possible.

To my treatment teams throughout the years—thank you for listening to me and giving me the skills necessary to fully recover.

To Mavi—you are my best decision.

To every person in any stage of recovery from an eating disorder. You inspire me.

REFERENCES

Chansky, Tamar, E. *Freeing Your Child from Anxiety: Powerful, Practical Solutions to Overcome Your Child's Fears, Worries, and Phobias*. New York: Three Rivers Press, 2004.

Costin, Carolyn, and Gwen S. Grabb. *8 Keys to Recovery from an Eating Disorder: Effective Strategies from Therapeutic Practice and Personal Experience*. New York: W.W. Norton & Company, 2012.

Costin, Carolyn, and Gwen S. Grabb. *8 Keys to Recovery from an Eating Disorder Workbook*. New York: W. W. Norton & Company, 2017.

Gaudiani, Jennifer. *Sick Enough: A Guide to the Medical Complications of Eating Disorders*. New York: Routledge, 2019.

Gay, Roxane. *Hunger: A Memoir of (My) Body*. New York: HarperCollins Publishers, 2017.

Linehan, Marsha, M. *DBT Skills Training Manual*. 2nd ed. New York: The Guilford Press, 2015.

Linehan, Marsha M. *Cognitive-Behavioral Treatment of Borderline Personality Disorder*. 1st ed. New York: The Gilford Press, 1993.

Tribole, Evelyn, and Elyse Resch. *Intuitive Eating: A Revolutionary Anti-Diet Approach*. New York: St. Martin's Essentials, 2020.

Tribole, Evelyn and Elyse Resch. *The Intuitive Eating Workbook: 10 Prinicples for Nourishing a Healthy Relationship with Food*. California: New Harbinger Publications, Inc, 2017.

van Der Kolk, Bessel. *The Body Keeps The Score: Brain, Mind, And Body In The Healing of Trauma.* New York: Penguin Books, 2014.

Waheed, Nayyirah. "Three." Poem

FURTHER READING

Apostolides, Marianne. *Inner Hunger: A Young Woman's Struggle Through Anorexia and Bulimia*. New York: W.W. Norton & Company, 1998.

Bacon, Lindo. *Health at Every Size: The Surprising Truth About Your Weight*. New York: BenBella Books, 2010.

Brown, Brene. *Atlas Of The Heart: Mapping Meaningful Connection and the Language of Human Experience*. New York: Random House, 2021.

Brown, Brene. *Daring Greatly: How the Courage to be Vulnerable Transforms the Way we Live, Love, Parent and Lead*. New York: Avery, 2012.

Burton, Susan. *Empty: A Memoir*. New York: Random House, 2020.

Dooner, Caroline. *The F*ck It Diet: Eating Should be Easy*. New York: HarperCollins, 2019.

Dooner, Caroline. *Tired as F*ck: The Burnout at the Hands of Diet, Self-help, and Hustle Culture*. New York: Harper Collins, 2022.

Goldberg, Robyn. *The Eating Disorder Trap: A Guide for Clinicians and Loved Ones*. Georgia: Booklogix, 2020.

Linehan, Marsha M. *Building a Life Worth Living: A Memoir*. New York: Random House, 2021.

Melton, Glennon Doyle. *Carry On, Warrior: The Power of Embracing your Messy, Beautiful Life*. New York: Scribner, 2013.

Miller, Leslie. *Big Girl: How I Gave Up Dieting And Got A Life*. New York: Grand Central Publishing. 2016.

Reichman, Colleen, and Jennifer Rollin. *The Inside Scoop On Eating Disorder Recovery: Advice from Two Therapists Who Have Been There*. New York: Routledge, 2021.

Scritchfield, Rebecca. *Body Kindness: Transform Your Health From The Inside Out—And Never Say Diet Again*. New York: Workman Publishing, 2016.

Tate, Christie. Group: *How One Therapist and a Circle of Strangers Saved My Life*. New York: Avid Reader Press, 2020.

Taylor, Sonya Renee. *The Body Is Not an Apology: The Power Of Radical Self-Love*. Oakland: Berrett-Koehler Publishers, Inc., 2018.

Waldman, Lucie. *The Jots of Becoming*. 2020.